2021 National Book Award Longlist

2022 Carnegie Medal Nonfiction Longlist

Lukas Book Prize Shortlist

One of Kirkus Reviews' *"Best American History of 2021"* | One of The New York Times' *"11 New Books We Recommend This Week"* | One of Oprah Daily's *"20 of the Best Books to Pick Up This May"* | One of The Oklahoman's *"15 Books to Help You Learn About the Tulsa Race Massacre as the 100-Year Anniversary Approaches"* | A Week's *book of the week*

Praise for *The Ground Breaking*

"A skillful narrative of excavating the truth about the Tulsa race massacre. . . . Candid and self-aware . . . Part of what makes this book so riveting is Ellsworth's skillful narration, his impeccable sense for when to reveal a piece of information and when to hold something back."

—*The New York Times*

"A moving and humane portrait of the massacre . . . *The Ground Breaking* sends a powerful message at this 100th anniversary: that reconciliation is possible only when we directly confront the truth of a painful past and take concrete steps to redress it." —*The Washington Post*

"A stunning narrative." —NPR's *Code Switch*

"*The Ground Breaking* documents Ellsworth's dogged pursuit to excavate the details of what occurred on those days a hundred years ago, since facts about what transpired were intentionally suppressed for decades. . . . By weaving in his personal history and conversations with Tulsa survivors and other natives, Ellsworth combines his gift for storytelling with a historian's dogged persistence to not only track the latest information on the existence and locations of those mass graves but to offer essential insights as to why the Tulsa race massacre is emblematic of why American racial inequality persists and how we need to reckon with it so we can begin to seek true reconciliation. . . . Ellsworth—whose previous book on the massacre, published in 1982, was entitled *Death in a Promised Land*—with his latest masterful work of history, illuminates the hard, never-finished work of unlearning racism and nurturing truth. He also prompts us to question how many other American stories and voices remain buried, waiting for dedicated historians with Ellsworth's persistence and passion to uncover them." —OprahDaily.com

"A thoughtful exploration of the importance of collective memory. It is particularly poignant as 2021 marks the centennial of the massacre. A must-read for all who are interested in how history continues to impact the present." —Rebekah Kati, *Library Journal* (starred review)

"Historian Ellsworth (*Death in a Promised Land*) delivers a riveting investigation into the origins and aftermath of the 1921 Tulsa race massacre. . . . Interviews with survivors and reflections on the debate over reparations and the social, economic, and racial divisions of modern-day Tulsa add depth to Ellsworth's portrait of a community attempting to heal from an unimaginable injustice. This eloquent, deeply moving history isn't to be missed." —*Publishers Weekly* (starred review)

"Immensely readable and thoroughly engaging, *The Ground Breaking* is a remarkable blend of history and memoir that could not be more timely and informative. Taut, tense, and meticulously composed, Scott Ellsworth's elegant narrative is both mesmerizing and enlightening."
—Gilbert King, Pulitzer Prize–winning author of *Devil in the Grove*

"This is a book that fuses history and memory with the unresolved search for justice for the victims of the 1921 Tulsa race massacre. It is also a searing story of Ellsworth's personal journey as he struggles to unearth and come to terms with these events, and the journey of a community as it moves through forgetting, denial, and, finally, some grudging acceptance of what happened. The horrific events of 1921 have been called a riot, a disaster, a pogrom, and, finally, a race massacre. Ellsworth shows how each renaming is a direct result of the persistent efforts of those who would dig up what had been carefully and deliberately hidden. This book should be essential reading for anyone interested in an honest grappling with our racial past and with the task of moving forward."

—Kenneth W. Mack, professor of law, Harvard University

"The persistence, empathy, and painstaking research of *The Ground Breaking* move us much closer to the justice that the victims of Greenwood, and the people of America, deserve. Heartbreaking and inspiring."

—Beto O'Rourke

"In a time marked by raw nativism, gangster capitalism, and white supremacy off its leash, well-funded mobs, winked at from above, committed racially driven mass terror against Black citizens and American democracy. Those who found themselves mystified when America's white power movement stormed the US Capitol in 2021 need to take a good look back at Tulsa, Oklahoma, a century ago. The talking heads chant 'This is not who we are' because they are wholly in the dark about who we have been. Scott Ellsworth not only tells the gripping story of one of America's worst racial atrocities but shows us how we can uncover our past and come to grips with our future. His literally groundbreaking research and engaging prose pull us toward the call of justice today."

—Rev. Dr. William J. Barber II, cochair of the Poor People's Campaign
and author of *The Third Reconstruction*

"America cannot address the crisis in which we find ourselves because we are unwilling to acknowledge the road that brought us here. We are determined to look away, as if hiding the empty cake plate will help us lose weight. What we stand to lose instead is the hope of our democratic heritage. Scott Ellsworth is willing to dig and willing to help us to see who we have been in hopes that we will rise to who we must be. The Tulsa massacre of 1921 is one of the most significant and revealing episodes of American history, and one we must confront in order to find our way. *The Ground Breaking* will rattle you, and it should. It will move you toward a harder wisdom, and it must."

—Tim Tyson, senior research scholar at the Center for Documentary Studies at Duke University, author of *The Blood of Emmett Till*, *Radio Free Dixie: Robert F. Williams and the Roots of Black Power*, and *Blood Done Sign My Name*

"A vital history of a racially motivated mass murder a century ago . . . An essential historical record surrounding heinous events that have yet to be answered with racial justice." —*Kirkus Reviews* (starred review)

"Scott Ellsworth's absolutely riveting book does more than chronicle the Tulsa race massacre of 1921 and its literal exhumation. With a stunning combination of objectivity and empathy, it demonstrates how even in polarized times we can come together in pursuit of truth. Though concerned with past events, it explores every stratum of the American city now—from city hall to dive bars to homeless encampments to the living rooms of the wealthy and the poor, regardless of color or creed. Anyone interested in America's future should read it as a template for the reconciliation that lies ahead."

—Tim Blake Nelson, actor, *Watchmen* and *Just Mercy*; and Tulsa native

"There is no more scholarly or elegant telling of this uniquely American story—the horrible hours a century ago when Tulsa's Black community was obliterated by a white mob; the breathtaking conspiracy of silence that followed; the long coda to the tragedy that is still being written. But this book is also a memoir, and it is Ellsworth's story that has found its way most deeply into my bones. He was the white Tulsa boy changed by an early experience of virulent racism. He was the scholar who dedicated his life to unearthing what happened. He became a truthteller and an example for us all. I believe that the path of true racial reconciliation runs through millions of American whites, whose hearts would be changed if they only knew our history. To those people I would simply say this: Please read this book."

—Tim Madigan, award-winning author of *The Burning: Massacre, Destruction, and the Tulsa Race Riot of 1921*

"This has been the life's work of Tulsa native historian Scott Ellsworth, who has spent nearly fifty years working on uncovering what really happened and then what happened to the bodies of what is the biggest unsolved crime in state history. . . . His book is a must-read for every Tulsan and for those who want a better understanding of what America was like in the years following the first World War."   —Tim Landes

"In this centennial year, which has been marked by racial unrest and uprisings, Ellsworth recounts how survivors, researchers, and historians following the 1982 publication of his seminal book on the massacre served as essential catalysts in breaking long-held silences around an American tragedy with the aim of modeling what racial healing could look like."

—OprahDaily.com, "20 of the Best Books to Pick Up This May"

"Long awaited."   —*Smithsonian Magazine*

"Indispensable . . . impeccable . . . Scott Ellsworth has produced a much-needed book that acts like a mirror. Though documenting a particular place and time, it helps us understand the race-based and sectarian turmoil that is so pervasive today. . . . Fast-paced but nuanced, it's an impeccably researched update of [his] literary debut."   —*The Guardian*

"Ellsworth's book presents a riveting, painful-to-read account of a mass crime that, to our everlasting shame as Americans, has avoided justice. . . . [*The Ground Breaking*] presents us with a clear history of the Tulsa massacre and, with that rendering, a chance for atonement of one of our darkest hours as a nation. Readers of this book will fervently hope we take that opportunity." —Associated Press

"This is the kind of book that, once you start it, makes the hours disappear. It's an emotional one that'll make you skip dinner and lock the door so you can just read. For sure, *The Ground Breaking* will shake you up." —TheTimesWeekly.com

"If one of the public historian's greatest tasks is to make people care, Ellsworth succeeds spectacularly. His character-driven narrative is clear and compelling. . . . The detail with which he recounts Tulsans' lives is rich and effective. . . . What Ellsworth is ultimately making the case for is what some scholars and policymakers have called 'transitional justice'—or a way for societies to redress abuses and atrocities so severe the normal justice system can't handle them. . . . Perhaps one of the greatest achievements of *The Ground Breaking* is that it understands the limitations of the historian's and the media's roles in that project, acknowledging that more political action is needed to sustain a movement that's only just begun." —*Foreign Policy*

"Superb . . . A century after the Tulsa massacre, *The Ground Breaking* is beautifully written, instantly engrossing, and deeply empathetic. It never flinches from a horrifying story, although in places that horror is unbearable, unearthing a cruel secret that America tried for decades to suppress. In the wake of Trump's America and as the United States struggles to come to terms with its living legacy of slavery, brutality, and institutionalized racism, *The Ground Breaking* is an essential read." —Donal O'Keeffe, *Irish Examiner*

THE
GROUND
BREAKING

The Tulsa Race Massacre and
an American City's Search for Justice

SCOTT ELLSWORTH

DUTTON

DUTTON

An imprint of Penguin Random House LLC
penguinrandomhouse.com

Previously published as a Dutton hardcover in May 2021
First Dutton trade paperback edition: May 2022

Photo on page iv from the Leon and Maxine Wiandt collection, courtesy of
the Department of Special Collections, McFarlin Library, The University of Tulsa.

LIBRARY OF CONGRESS CATALOGING-IN-PUBLICATION DATA
has been applied for.

Dutton trade paperback ISBN: 9780593182994

Printed in the United States of America
2 4 6 8 10 9 7 5 3 1

BOOK DESIGN BY LAURA K. CORLESS

For Craig Ryan and Kathy Narramore

Amici veri

CONTENTS

A Note from the Author . . . xv

Prologue . . . 1

BOOK ONE

Chapter 1: *1921* . . . 13

Chapter 2: *After* . . . 41

Chapter 3: *Awakenings* . . . 49

Chapter 4: *Two Summers* . . . 67

Chapter 5: *Death in a Promised Land* . . . 83

BOOK TWO

Chapter 6: *Where Are the Rest?* . . . 101

Chapter 7: *The Lady with a Cane* . . . 121

Chapter 8: *Tulsa Calling* . . . 149

Chapter 9: *Reparations and Reprisals* . . . 167

BOOK THREE

Chapter 10: *The Steps to Nowhere* . . . 185

Chapter 11: *Rolexes and Pickup Trucks* . . . 201

Chapter 12: *Reminding a City of Her Sins* . . . 219

Chapter 13: *Breaking Ground* . . . 235

Chapter 14: *Bodies of Evidence* . . . 247

Chapter 15: *The Dirt Whisperers* . . . 263

Epilogue . . . 273

Acknowledgments . . . 279

Notes . . . 284

Index . . . 308

A NOTE FROM THE AUTHOR

The survivors called it the *riot*.

Sitting at their own kitchen tables, or in front of a television news camera crew, this was the term that they used to describe the horrific events that they endured in Tulsa, Oklahoma, on May 31 and June 1, 1921. Sometimes they would say *race riot*, but most of the time the one-word version would do. "It was pride that fought the riot, it was pride that rebuilt after the riot," was how survivor W. D. Williams put it.

Over the years, however, other names have surfaced as well. Some referred to the tragic happenings as a race war. Others called it a disaster, the Tulsa event, or a pogrom. In an interview with a journalist some twenty years ago, I once likened it to an American Kristallnacht. That wasn't a stretch. Today, the term of choice is *massacre*, as in the Tulsa race massacre.

All of these terms capture something of what took place. But in truth, none of them can describe it completely. For what happened in one American city during the late spring of 1921 defies easy definition.

PROLOGUE

The Canes
Friday
July 19, 2019

N oe saw her first.

We had just dropped down to the lower level, with the railroad tracks behind us and the river in front. Pushing our way past the hickory and ash trees and through the knee-high weeds, we had followed the dirt trail down the embankment to a flat ribbon of earth, maybe one hundred yards long and fifteen yards wide. Sheltered by the high branches of the cottonwoods, the narrow shelf of land had a peaceful, almost cathedral-like feel. Tufts of soft grass carpeted the forest floor, while sparrows and chickadees flitted by overhead. Had it not been for the trash and the overbearing smell of the open-air privy, it might not have seemed like a homeless camp at all.

She had heard us coming. Rising up quickly, she was wearing a white shirt and pink shorts, with newish-looking running shoes and quarter socks. Her reddish-brown hair, in a pixie, had been recently cut, while her complexion was clear and her fingernails were clean. She was maybe in her early twenties. But out on the street, someone's age can be tough to gauge with any degree of accuracy. Later on, I asked Noe, who was an outreach worker with the Mental Health Association of Oklahoma, to create a mini-biography of her, one based both on his experience and on what he'd just observed. He thought carefully before he answered. "She hasn't been out long, but she's likely been homeless before," he said. "Probably not addicted to any drugs. Maybe some mental health issues." Her name was Angel. As we drew near, she lifted the bottom hem of her shirt to show us the handle of the knife stuck into the waistband of her shorts. Above us, you could hear the wind in the treetops.

Angel's campsite consisted of a piece of blue plastic tarp wrapped in a semicircle around a couple of bushes. Within the perimeter was a relatively new bicycle lying on its side, a Coleman lantern, a pair of rolled-up sleeping bags, and a small pile of clothes and personal items. Nearby, scattered throughout the woods and brush, were other tents, some big enough to stand up in, others sun-bleached castoffs from camping trips taken decades earlier. Most looked either abandoned or unoccupied, but it was hard to know for certain.

From her half-circle home, Angel could look out across the slow-moving waters of the Arkansas River toward the oil refineries on the other side. Sometimes fish would rise in the shallows nearest the bank. Other times, wrens and swallows would arc across the river and then disappear into the trees. High above us, maybe fifty yards downstream, the midmorning traffic rumbled along the I-244 bridge, oblivious to the trio of people and the homeless camp on the forgotten patch of riverbank below. We were less than a mile from the heart of downtown Tulsa—population four hundred thousand, with a metropolitan area of nearly one million—in a city that was proud of its beautiful homes and churches, its Art Deco architecture, and its world-class museums and vibrant music scene. Indeed, that very week, Cardi B and Shawn Mendes would each perform in front of thousands of screaming fans at the BOK Center, a glittery, $196 million arena located less than eight blocks away.

"You want some packets?" Noe asked her.

Reaching into the day pack slung over his shoulder, he grabbed a handful of quart-size plastic zip bags. Most of them contained a toothbrush, toothpaste, and travel-size containers of lotion and hand sanitizer. Others held bars of soap, breath mints, mini-deodorants. But each and every packet included a pair of socks. "That's the first thing to go when you're out on the street," Noe had told me back at the outreach center. Angel wouldn't respond at first. Instead she kept looking behind us, her gray-green eyes darting toward the path through the trees that we had come in on. She mumbled something about her partner getting back any minute now. It was obvious that the sudden appearance of two strange men in the nearly deserted homeless camp had made her very nervous. She wouldn't look either of us in the eye.

But Noe kept on talking. He told her about some of the services available to the homeless, about how they could help her find housing and medical care, and he asked if she needed anything. Eventually, Angel relaxed. She took some packets and some bottles of water. And once she had concluded that I wasn't a police officer, she turned toward me.

"Just what are *you* doing here, anyway?"

"Well," I said, "I'm a historian and . . ."

I kept on talking. But to myself I thought, *Really, where to begin?*

Tulsa Police Headquarters
Winter 1973
Around 4:00 A.M.

Inside the break room on the ground floor, a handful of officers unwind after the end of their shifts. Most are recent police academy graduates, young officers who pay their dues by working the fourth shift, which lasts from seven at night until three in the morning. Some have partners, but most work alone, one man to a police cruiser, usually either a Plymouth Fury or an AMC Ambassador, monstrous 1970s machines with V-8 engines capable of topping 130 mph. Two-way radios, mounted on the dash, have two frequencies: one for communication with the dispatcher, the other, the "backside," where officers can talk. But most of the night, you are on your own. It is lonesome work, occasionally dangerous, sometimes stressful, and often boring. Beneath the dash, in a custom-built rack, is a loaded 12-gauge pump shotgun.

The break room, which the officers call the lounge, is a spartan affair. Linoleum floors over concrete slab, cinder block walls painted a shade of municipal beige, fluorescent lights, Formica tables, padded vinyl chairs—"But not very padded," a former officer told me. There is also a wall of vending machines, humming quietly in the background, which sell pop, candy bars, bags of potato chips, and four-ounce paper cups of instant coffee. "Awful stuff," the officer added. On this night, some of the men are smoking cigarettes, others are talking quietly, when Sergeant Wayburn J. Cotton enters the room, carrying a cardboard box.

"If you can keep your mouths shut," he announces, "I've got something to show you."

Fifty-three years old with big hands and bright blue eyes, Cotton was a onetime plasterer's helper and a student custodian at Central High School before he dropped out in the eleventh grade. Married at nineteen, he'd spent eight months in the army before finally joining the Tulsa police force at age thirty-nine in 1959. Revered by some officers, tolerated by others—"a real dinosaur," one ex-cop told me—Cotton knows how to command a room, which he now does by setting the box on the table and opening it.

Inside are dozens of fifty-year-old photographs from the city's notorious race riot of 1921, a much-whispered-about event that, even then, existed in a kind of speculative limbo, one where hard facts were difficult to come by. Some people claimed that before it was all over, machine guns had been set up on the rooftops of buildings downtown, that airplanes had bombed Greenwood, the Black part of town, and that dead bodies could be seen floating down the Arkansas River. If you were to conduct a poll, a majority of Tulsans would profess to know little or nothing about it. But for these young police officers sitting in the break room on this night, that is all about to change. Sergeant Cotton tells the officers that a couple of days after the riot, the police chief ordered his patrolmen to go to every photography studio in town and confiscate any photographs they found of the riot, its victims, and its horrific destruction. And here, Sergeant Cotton adds, is what they found.

The officers are astonished.

Here are photographs of death and devastation unlike any that they have ever seen. Whole sections of the city look like Berlin or Frankfurt at the end of World War II. In one snapshot, the lifeless bodies of an entire African American family—father, mother, son, and daughter— have all been draped over a fence, their arms hanging down toward the ground. In another, the corpse of a Black man is being dragged in the street behind an automobile. In the backgrounds of some of the pictures are office buildings and other local landmarks that the men easily recognize. There is no question that the photos are authentic. Here is a Tulsa that none of them had ever imagined before.

There is one photograph, however, that catches the eye of one of the officers. It shows the burial of victims in a trench. The officer, who had graduated from the police academy two years earlier, studies the photograph for a long time. Finally, he turns to Sergeant Cotton. "Hey," he says, "I think I know where this is." He then describes the location. The older officer, however, is not pleased. Telling the younger policemen never to mention what they have seen, he then takes the photos away. The box of photographs is never to be seen again.

But the young officer does not forget what he has seen, and a few days later he drives down to where he thinks the photograph of the burial was taken, an unoccupied patch of land not far from Crosbie Heights, one of the oldest residential neighborhoods in town. Getting out of his car, he can see the slow-moving water in the river in front of him, and he hears the wind rattling in a bone-dry patch of river cane.

Memorandum

June 14, 2002

To: Dr. Scott Ellsworth
From: Dick Warner
Subject: Interview with Robert Patty, former Tulsa policeman

The photograph that Mr. Patty said would interest us was of a trench with bodies in it. He thought he recognized the area and mentioned it to the Sgt. The Sgt. got very tense and took the photographs away and told the officers never to say that they had seen them. Mr. Patty said the tenseness of the Sgt. was not like him. He was always cool, even under fire, but he got really tense when the location was mentioned.

The photograph was very detailed and taken from not too far a distance. Mr. Patty said that the photograph seemed to have been taken from the east looking west and in the early morning. It was taken from a railroad track. To the north (right) was a slope with a railroad track running along the base. The track made a curve to the right around the sloped hill. At the top of the slope were some trucks containing bodies wrapped in sheets or tarpaulins. Bodies were being carried down the slope. About 100 feet from the

*base of the slope was a trench running east to west. Bodies
were lying in the trench. He estimated there were about
twenty-five bodies on the top level and he thought there was
one or more levels under that one. The bodies were wrapped
in sheets and tarpaulins.*

*A man with a shovel was throwing a white powder over
the bodies which he assumed was lime. An old-style
bulldozer was parked next to the trench. The men in the
photograph were of two kinds. They were all white. Most of
them were in work clothes, but there were several men in
slacks and white shirts who were watching. The man who
seemed to be in charge was in a white shirt and carrying a
shotgun. He had on a black cowboy type hat and a western
tie (not a bolo). Several of the men in white shirts were also
wearing black cowboy style hats and he could see badges on
some of them.*

The photograph had the date, June 3, 1921, written on it.

*The Canes
Friday
July 19, 2019*

"I'm a historian," I said.

Then, "About a hundred years ago, there had once been a terrible
incident here in Tulsa, what some people call the Tulsa race riot or race
massacre. A lot of people got killed. And, well, I'm part of the team of
folks that's looking for the bodies. And we think that some of the people
might have been buried here. So that's why I asked Noe to bring me
down here."

What I didn't add was everything else that people were looking for when it came to the events of 1921. Some wanted reparations, some sought reconciliation, others were looking for justice, and some sought to push it all away. It didn't matter, though. Because the young homeless woman slowly lifted her chin and, for the first time, looked me directly in the eyes.

Then she talked to me like she was talking to a child.

"Well of course," she said, "there's bodies buried here."

I couldn't believe my ears. "How do you know?"

"Because," she said, "I hear their voices at night."

BOOK ONE

Take me back to Tulsa to the scene of the crime.

—Bob Dylan, "Murder Most Foul"

1921

C lose your eyes and you can almost hear them.

It's a Thursday afternoon on a long-ago spring day. In the alleys and on the back porches it is still jacket weather. For even though the dogwoods and redbuds are in bloom, and bursts of sparrows explode out of the trees and bushes, in the shadows there's a lingering coolness in the air. Only they don't care. For today is the maids' day off and they've congregated, in twos and threes and fours, to stop and gossip along the sidewalks and storefronts. Gone are their uniforms, the long white aprons and striped dresses and peaked caps. Gone are the mops and the dust rags, the *yes ma'ams* and the *no sirs*, and the lye soap, starch, and bluing. In their place are smiles and laughter, felt hats and bobbed hair. Today is a day to exhale.

They aren't the only ones out and about. Up and down Greenwood Avenue, a small parade of humanity can be seen. There are ditchdiggers and shop owners, a mother with young children, an old man—born a slave—with ancient eyes and an ash-gray beard. Preachers and hustlers, doctors and dishwashers, a newspaper reporter, a uniformed messenger, and a deputy sheriff can all be found within a five-block radius. Some are getting off work, others are shopping. From a window up above drifts the sound of a Victrola. Maybe it's Mamie Smith, the Harlem singing sensation, belting out "Crazy Blues." Or maybe it's a rag or a Mozart piano sonata. In a second-floor office in the Williams Building, a dentist carefully sets a burr into his drill. Two doors down, an attorney inks one last contract for the day and hands it to his secretary.

Welcome to Greenwood. Spring, 1921.

We are in Tulsa's African American district, home to fourteen churches, two schools, a hospital, a post office substation, four hotels, two newspapers, and at least ten thousand residents, with the number swelling each week. A dozen physicians and surgeons live and work in Greenwood, as do lawyers, insurance agents, real estate salesmen, and pharmacists. In the shops you can buy dresses and three-piece suits, straw hats and bench-made shoes, pipe tobacco and household goods, tools and typewriter ribbon, perfume, eyeglasses, and bottles of patent medicine. There are ten tailors, four shoe repair shops, one filling station, and one feed store. Nor does the district lack opportunities for entertainment. The Dixie Theater seats more than a thousand, while the Dreamland has seating for 750. Both offer motion pictures, musical performances, lectures, and vaudeville acts. Nearby are pool halls and speakeasies.

This is no food desert. There are thirty-eight grocery stores, fruit and vegetable stands, and meat markets. Thirty restaurants serve everything from sandwiches and plate lunches to steaks and chops with all the trimmings. There's the Red Wing Cafe and Kelley's Lunch Counter, the Waffle House and Doc's Beanery, as well as a slew of double-named eateries—Bell & Little, Grace & Warren, Hardy & Hardy, Newman & Howard, White & Black, White & Brown, Wright & Davidson—where ditchdiggers and dentists, chauffeurs and custodians all sidle up to the counter and place their orders. Afterward, diners can pick up some smokes at the Oquawka Cigar Store, or a bag of sweets or some ice cream at Loula Williams's confectionery.

It is said that in Greenwood, a dollar bill will change hands a dozen times before it ever leaves the district. But equally important, its residents need not face the indignities heaped upon them at the white-owned shops downtown—the sighs and furrowed brows of the impatient white clerks, the ones who follow you down the aisles, then won't let you try on clothes beforehand. Here in Deep Greenwood, as the main commercial blocks are called, African American shoppers can purchase clothes at Black-owned stores, drop off their dry cleaning and laundry at Black-owned cleaners, and have their portraits taken in a Black-owned photography studio. Here, there are Black doctors and Black nurses, Black teachers and a Black principal, Black plumbers and Black house carpenters. Whites sneeringly call the district "Little Africa," or worse.

In Greenwood, there are African American men and women who own stores, hotels, and two- and three-story redbrick office buildings. They pay property taxes, conduct business transactions with buyers and jobbers across the country, and live in newly built homes furnished with mahogany sideboards, cut-glass chandeliers, and carports. Their daughters take piano lessons and learn poise and elocution, while their sons dream of glory on the gridiron or baseball diamond. Women entrepreneurs are far from uncommon. Elizabeth Sawyer and Dora Wells operate their own dressmaking establishments. Other women manage real estate and run their own restaurants and shops.

Armed with grit, gumption, business acumen, hard work, and sometimes a bit of luck, the leading Black merchants of Tulsa have flourished. They read the Bible, newspapers, and novels, go to church on Sunday, and dress for dinner. The white bankers downtown know who they are, as do the shipping clerks and freight agents at the railway terminals. And while the overwhelming majority of African Americans a live far more modestly, in rented rooms and shacks without running water, for those who have pulled ahead, Greenwood is a wonder, a living and breathing Black edition of the American Dream.

But Greenwood is far more than just a land of fat wallets and bulging coin purses.

It is also a mindset, a bearing, a way of engaging with the world. In an age when people of color are constantly being told that they are lesser beings, here is a community who knows that they are just as good as anyone. Nationally known African American leaders, such as Dr. W. E. B. Du Bois of the National Association for the Advancement of Colored People, have visited Tulsa to see what all the fuss is about. Jazz bands from Kansas City and Chicago will regularly come to Greenwood to play the latest, genre-busting sounds of a music that is fast capturing the attention of the world. Ideas flourish here as well. In classrooms and living rooms, across shop counters and in columns in the *Tulsa Star* and the *Oklahoma Sun,* they take root and cross-pollinate, are weighed and debated. There are political clubs, reading circles, and missionary societies. Hemmed in by a white world that values only their labor, Greenwood is an outpost of vitality, achievement, and pride.

The evidence is everywhere.

You can see it in the women who drape themselves in pearls and fur for a show at the Dreamland or the Dixie. It's there, as well, in the steely gaze and set jaws of the neighborhood's World War veterans, who gather for reunions on Armistice Day. You can sense it in the comportment of the women and men who run their own businesses. And you can feel it in the presence of independent craftsmen who never, ever have to approach a white man with their hats in their hands. But it is there, as well, in those who take in laundry and scrub floors and wash dishes. For there is a frontier mindset here, an ironclad self-confidence and a can-do spirit. Greenwood isn't a gift from anyone. It is something they have built. It is their own.

By five o'clock, most of the merchants are closing up for the day and locking their doors. The maids are long gone, while the last of the shoppers make their final purchases and start to head home. As the shadows lengthen and wheel across Greenwood Avenue, and the afternoon sun glances off the top floor of the Stradford Hotel, there is once again a slight chill in the air. And while they do not know it yet, the people of Greenwood are on a collision course with the unimaginable.

Memorial Day, Monday, May 30, 1921.

An African American teenager walks along a downtown sidewalk. His name is Dick Rowland. Nineteen years old, a former football player at Booker T. Washington High School, he lives with his mother, Damie, in Greenwood, but works during the day in a white-owned and -patronized shoeshine parlor located downtown on Main Street. When done correctly, a proper shoeshine takes more skill than meets the eye. Seated on a short-legged wooden stool in front of the thronelike chairs where the customers sit, Rowland will use a stiff horsehair brush and a soft rag to remove any caked-on dirt and grime. Then, with a cotton ball stuck on the end of a twisted length of wire, he will daub edge dressing, ink-black and smelling of alcohol, along the outer edges of the sole and heel. As that dries, he will dip a second rag into a tin of shoe paste and expertly apply it to the uppers, paying special attention to the cracks and creases of well-worn brogans and cap-toe oxfords, and to the delicate drilled patterns on the collars and facings of wing tips. Then he will buff and polish each pair to a glimmering shine.

There are no toilet facilities in the shine parlor for Dick Rowland and the other African American bootblacks. So the white owner has arranged for his employees to use the "Colored" restroom on the top floor of the Drexel Building, a block away on Main Street. This is where Rowland is headed now. To get to the washroom, he must ride the elevator located in the back of the building. The elevator is operated by Sarah Page, a white seventeen-year-old who, it is said, is saving her money to attend night school. At the very least, Sarah knows Dick and all the other shoeshiners by sight, as she carries them up to the fourth floor and back down again practically every day.

Only today is not like all the others.

Shortly after Dick enters the Drexel Building, Sarah screams.

And Dick is seen running away.

The police are summoned. Two detectives arrive and speak with Sarah. But they do not appear to be overly concerned. No all-points bulletin is issued, no squads of armed officers are dispatched on a manhunt. For whatever happened or did not happen in the elevator, Sarah Page will not press any charges. A white clerk in Renberg's, a high-quality clothing store located on the ground floor of the Drexel Building, however, is convinced that he knows just as plain as day what occurred between Rowland and Page. And while he did not actually witness anything, he talks to anyone who will listen.

The next morning, police officers arrive at Damie Rowland's home in Greenwood.

They don't stay long.

Dick Rowland is arrested and is taken downtown. He's booked at police headquarters and then, pending arraignment, is locked inside a jail cell located on the top floor of the county courthouse.

By late afternoon, there is lynch talk on the streets of white Tulsa.

But in Greenwood, there is talk of a different kind. At the Dreamland Theatre, an angry veteran jumps up onstage. "We're not going to let this happen," he shouts. "We're going to go downtown and stop this lynching. Close this place down."

Tuesday evening, May 31, around 7:00.

By now, more than three hundred white men, women, and children are gathered outside the Tulsa County Court House, a handsome Greek Revival edifice located at Sixth Street and Boulder Avenue, along the southern edge of downtown. In the soft spring twilight, with the sky slowly turning pink and gold, they pack the nearby sidewalks and have spilled out into the streets. The women are wearing straw hats and light summer dresses, the men in overalls, suits, or dress shirts and ties. Groups of twos and threes and fours are talking and smoking, some sitting on the grass in the front yards of nearby houses. The mood is light and celebratory, with mockingbirds and chickadees chattering in the nearby oaks and elms. But the crowd is also determined, and expecting action.

Only nine months earlier, a large crowd of whites had gathered on these same streets and sidewalks. They had come to demand the release, into their custody, of a white eighteen-year-old former telephone company worker named Roy Belton, who had been charged with the cold-blooded murder of a white Tulsa taxicab driver. Belton had been arrested and was being held in a jail cell on the top floor of the courthouse when the crowd gathered and pressed its demand. At first, the sheriff refused. "Let the law take its course," he said. "The electric chair will get him before long." But it was all a show. When a handful of armed men wearing masks appeared at the courthouse door, the sheriff willingly handed over his prisoner. "We got him, boys! We got him!" the men shouted as they led Belton out of the courthouse. Within a half hour, Roy Belton was lynched a few miles outside town. Tulsa police officers directed traffic.

"It is my honest opinion," the police chief was quoted as saying a couple of days later, "that the lynching of Belton will prove of real benefit to Tulsa." The sheriff agreed, stating that "it shows to the criminal that the men of Tulsa mean business." So did the *Tulsa World,* the city's morning newspaper. "There was not a vestige of the mob spirit in the act of Saturday night," it argued. "It was citizenship, outraged by government inefficiency and a too tender regard for the professional criminal."

Now, one year later, they have come for Dick Rowland.

Only there is a new sheriff in Tulsa County, a veteran lawman named Willard McCullough. Fifty-four years old, with whiskey-colored hair, a piercing gaze, and a prominent mustache, McCullough worked as a ranch hand, farmer, general store owner, and teacher before starting a career in law enforcement. He is also made of sterner stuff than his predecessor. Not only does McCullough refuse to hand Rowland over to the crowd—"Let us have the nigger," they tell him—but he disables the elevators inside the courthouse, blockades the stairwells, and positions six of his deputies, armed with high-powered rifles, on the roof. Despite the fact that the crowd has steadily grown by the hour, McCullough is prepared to defend Rowland. The Tulsa police, meanwhile, are again nowhere to be seen. But a well-known white minister, Reverend Charles Kerr of First Presbyterian Church, arrives on the scene. Mounting the courthouse steps, he exhorts the crowd to go home but is hooted down.

Then, sometime around nine P.M., the crowd suddenly grows quiet. A small caravan of automobiles pulls up in front of the courthouse. From them emerge some two dozen African American men. Many are veterans, and some are wearing their three-year-old army uniforms. The men are armed. Getting out of their cars, they march single file to the courthouse steps, where they are met by McCullough.

We are here to help defend the prisoner, they tell the sheriff.

Get the hell out of here, McCullough replies.

The Black vets pile back into their cars and leave.

But the effect on the white crowd is electric. As bad as the sheriff's refusal is to hand over Dick Rowland, the appearance of armed African Americans at the courthouse causes members of the white mob to see red. Some dash home to get their own guns; others, to spread the word of what just happened. Dozens take off for the National Guard armory, a half mile away, in order to get their hands on the Springfield rifles that are stored there. But when they try to break into the armory, they are held at bay by a group of armed guardsmen, who threaten to open fire if anyone makes a move on the building. Only it doesn't matter. For a dark energy is at work on the streets of Tulsa.

Two hours later, the lynch mob gathered outside the courthouse has swelled to more than two thousand. The mood is now edgier and uglier, and the jokes and the laughter have run dry. Instead, there are questions. *What if she was your daughter or your sister? What are we waiting for?* But Sheriff McCullough still refuses to hand over Dick Rowland, and his deputies are still on the roof, cradling their rifles in the thick night air. As the courthouse crowd teeters on the brink of taking matters into their own hands, rumors explode across Tulsa like heat lightning.

In Greenwood, anxiety has given way to resolve.

Knots of African American men and women cluster outside the offices of the *Tulsa Star*, the city's premier Black newspaper, awaiting news of what's happening downtown. Some of the men are still wearing their old army uniforms. Many are armed. Inside the newspaper office, Barney Cleaver, deputy sheriff, speaks with McCullough on the phone, monitoring the situation at the courthouse. In the residential districts off Lansing and Cincinnati Avenues, in the Addition—an African American residential enclave located along the sides of Standpipe Hill—and out toward Pine Street, nervous parents bring their kids inside and exchange sketchy bits of information with neighbors across the back fence. Not everyone, however, is aware that anything unusual is happening. At a rented hall off of Archer Street, members of the class of 1921 at Booker T. Washington High School are putting up decorations for their prom, to be held later that week. Elsewhere across the district, it is just another late spring evening, with dishes to wash, bedtime stories to read, and lamps to dim.

Then, at around ten P.M., an electrifying piece of news hits Greenwood:

The whites are storming the courthouse.

There is no time to lose. "Come on, boys," A. J. Smitherman announces. "Let's go downtown." In short order, a second caravan is assembled. Only this time it is considerably larger. Now, seventy-five armed African American men have climbed into and onto more than a dozen automobiles, jammed into the seats and riding on the running boards. Some have double-barreled and single-shot shotguns, others hunting rifles, many with pistols. Turning west on Archer, their headlights sweep across the shuttered storefronts as they begin the short drive back downtown, back to the courthouse.

Only the news proves false. The white mob at the courthouse is now bigger and angrier than ever. But, well aware of Sheriff McCullough's men on the roof, it is also hesitant. No one has made a move yet to storm the building. McCullough and his men are still inside, still holding on, still in control. Once again, the Black vets present themselves to the sheriff, and extend their proposal to help defend the jail. It is an astonishing offer. Now outnumbered more than twenty-five to one by the armed whites outside the courthouse, the African American vets are laying their lives on the line for a Black teenager few if any of them actually knew. Once again, the sheriff sends them away.

As they are leaving, an older white man approaches one of the vets.

"Nigger, what are you doing with that pistol?"

"I'm going to use it if I need to," the vet replies.

"No, you give it to me."

"Like hell I will."

There is a brief struggle. Then a shot is fired.

Then another, and another, and another.

George H. Miller, a white doctor who was working late in his office in the nearby Unity Building at Fourth and Main, hears the sharp staccato of gunfire and rushes out into the street, where he comes upon a wounded Black man surrounded by a crowd of whites. He tries to reach the man but cannot. "The crowd was getting more and more belligerent," Dr. Miller will later recall. "The Negro had been shot so many times in the chest, and men from the onlookers were slashing him with knives." The police do nothing to stop it.

Instead, officers start handing out "Special Deputy" badges and ribbons to members of the lynch mob. Nor is that all. Breaking into Dick Bardon's sporting goods store and some nearby pawnshops, white Tulsa policemen begin doling out rifles, pistols, shotguns, and boxes of ammunition to members of the lynch mob who gathered at the courthouse. Laurel G. Buck, a white bricklayer who is sworn in as a "Special Deputy," will later state that a police officer told him to "get a gun and get a nigger."

Nobody is thinking about Dick Rowland anymore.

On the heels of the outbreak of gunfire at the courthouse, the African American vets fight a retreating battle back to Greenwood, slipping into the district well before midnight. The angry whites who were a part of the lynch mob, meanwhile, now have an additional quarry—any African Americans who are seen downtown. Most are janitors, restaurant employees, and others getting off work. Few know anything about the events at the courthouse. One African American woman is gunned down as she runs for safety along Boulder Avenue.

A white civil engineer and Massachusetts Institute of Technology graduate named William Holway is watching a movie inside the Rialto Theatre at Third and Main when someone runs in, shouting about a fight going on outside. "Everyone left that theater on high you know," Holway will later remember. "We went out the door and looked across the street, and there was Younkman's drugstore with those big pillars. Just got there when a Negro ran south of the alley across the street. The minute his head showed outside, somebody shot him." No one helps him. "We stood there for about half an hour watching," Holway will recall. "He wasn't quite dead, but he was about to die."

One block away, in the alley behind the Royal Theatre, a group of white men chase a lone African American man, who bolts through the stage door and rushes inside. "Suddenly he was on the stage in front of the picture screen and blinded by the bright flickering light coming down from the operator's booth in the balcony," a white teenager named Choc Phillips will later recall. "After shielding his eyes for a moment, he regained his vision enough to locate the steps leading from the stage down past the orchestra pit to the aisle just as the pursuing men rushed the stage. One of them saw the Negro and yelled, 'There he is, heading for the aisle.' As he finished the sentence, a roaring blast from a shotgun dropped the Negro by the end of the orchestra pit."

The first fires break out at around midnight. Along the southwesternmost edge of the African American district, a group of angry whites smashes the windows of a pair of businesses, the glass shards spilling out onto the sidewalk along Archer Street. Then they set the businesses ablaze. When a fire truck arrives from Fire Station No. 2, the white rioters prevent the firemen from turning their hoses on the flames. The arrival of the fire officials and the close proximity of white businesses, however, put a damper on this crowd's efforts at further arson, at least for now. Besides, they have other things to do.

A little farther up Archer, an elderly Black couple is kneeling inside their home in prayer when armed whites break down the door, walk into the bedroom, place the muzzles of pistols against the back of their heads, and shoot them to death. Gunshots can now be heard elsewhere across Greenwood as well. Just south of the African American district, armed whites pile into coupes and roadsters, their engines revved and running, and head north. With gun barrels bristling out their windows, the cars roar down residential streets in Greenwood, their occupants shooting into the homes on either side of the street, the bullets smashing into windows, doorways, parlors, and children's bedrooms.

A much larger battle, meanwhile, erupts off Greenwood and Archer, at the foot of Deep Greenwood. From midnight on, armed bands of whites try to sneak across the Frisco and Santa Fe railroad tracks to torch the heart of the African American business district. They rake the Williams Building and the offices of the *Oklahoma Sun* with gunfire, shattering windowpanes, splintering casings and window frames, and peppering brick and mortar with bullets and buckshot. But when they try to cross the tracks, they are met with fusillade after fusillade of shots fired by African American property owners, armed with shotguns and .30-30s, who had positioned themselves on upper floors in Deep Greenwood's flagship buildings. "These brave boys of ours," Mary Parrish will later record, "fought gamely and held back the enemy for hours."

For many in Greenwood, the gunfire proves to be too unnerving, and a quiet exodus from the city begins by starlight, as hundreds of African American families, mostly on foot, begin to make their way toward the countryside north of town. Others decide to ride out the storm, and when the shooting at Greenwood and Archer stops, it appears that they have made the right choice. "Nine p.m. the trouble started," *Tulsa Star* editor A. J. Smitherman will later write. "Two a.m. the thing was done."

Greenwood has survived. Dick Rowland is safe.

It's over.

But across town, a different story is taking shape.

Word of the initial shootout at the courthouse races across the white neighborhoods on the south side of town. But in the telling, passed by word of mouth as there are no commercial radio stations yet—the first in Oklahoma, WKY, wouldn't appear until the next year—this is no longer the tale of a lynching that never happened. Instead it becomes both a warning and an appeal to arms. *What if it was your sister or daughter?* metamorphoses into alarms over a *Negro uprising.* Shadows and stray sounds metamorphose into Negro gunmen waiting to take over Tulsa, just like the demons in *The Birth of a Nation.* Worse, there are reports that a trainload of armed Blacks is on its way from Muskogee. The situation is intolerable, and bound only to worsen, goes the thinking. It is time to act.

In all-night cafés and eateries in white neighborhoods, groups of grim-faced men suddenly appear. Pushing past startled waitresses and busboys, they are looking for recruits to take part in an assault on "Little Africa" the next morning. At the intersection of Fifteenth and Boulder, a man jumps on top of a roadster and tells the crowd gathered there to join another group that's meeting at Second and Lewis. There, by the glow of automobile headlights and kerosene lanterns, perhaps as many as six hundred whites gather to share arms and ammunition and discuss plans for the next day. Again, men jump up onto the hoods of cars and shout out instructions. "We are going in at daylight," one man declares. Another adds, "If any of you have more ammunition than you need, or if what you have doesn't fit your gun, sing out." Then comes a third. "Be ready at daybreak," he tells the crowd, adding, "Nothing can stop us."

Nor is that all. Sometime during the night, a group of unknown individuals slips into the American Legion post at Second and Main. Working together quietly, they remove the machine gun that is on display there, and haul it seven blocks to the grain elevator just across the tracks from the foot of Greenwood Avenue. And in white neighborhoods across the city, others gather over cups of coffee at kitchen tables, counting off the hours on pocket watches. For the night hasn't slowed their ardor or dimmed their determination. Instead, it has given them time to plan.

To this day, nobody knows how many there were. Likely in the thousands.

Before dawn on June 1, they have roughly organized themselves into three main groups, each of them now waiting along the railroad lines that separate Tulsa's white and Black worlds. One group is hunkered down near the Katy tracks off North Main Street. A second is perched near the Frisco freight depot, where some lie crouching behind overturned baggage carts and neat stacks of oil well supplies. The third, perhaps the largest, is encamped near the Frisco and Santa Fe passenger terminal. They are largely men, but there are women as well as boys, some as young as twelve or thirteen, clutching their own single-shot .22s and breech-loading shotguns. Most are seated, talking quietly. Some are smoking. Across the tracks in Greenwood, you can see the glow from their cigarettes.

Just before sunup, a group of white men in a Franklin touring car pulls up alongside the crowd hunkered down near the Frisco station.

"What the hell are you waiting for?" one of the riders asks. "Let's go get 'em." But no one in the crowd moves, and the Franklin heads off alone. Later that day, the bullet-riddled car, and the bodies of the men inside of it, will be seen off Archer.

At a little after five a.m., just after daybreak, a mysterious kind of siren or whistle can be heard echoing across downtown. "A very peculiar whistle," James West, a teacher at Booker T. Washington High School, will later remember. "This seemed to have been a signal for a concerted attack." With it, the whites began to move. At the Frisco station, a lone police inspector, Charles W. Daley, draws his sidearm and threatens to shoot anyone who crosses the tracks, but the crowd ignores him and walks right on by. Gunfire can now be heard again along the edges of the African American district, the pops and cracks of pistol and rifle fire, as well as the deeper roar of shotguns. Only there is a new sound as well. It is the rhythmic blast of the American Legion machine gun, which is now raking the heart of Deep Greenwood from the top floor of the Middle States Milling Company grain elevator.

For Mary Parrish, the time for waiting is over.

Twenty-nine years old, she is a stenographer who earns extra income by teaching evening secretarial classes to young African American women at the Woods Building. Born in Mississippi, she has moved to Tulsa from Rochester, New York, with her husband, a clothes presser and book publisher. While the marriage did not last, Mary has retained full custody of their seven-year-old daughter, Florence Mary, a bright and lively girl who could operate a typewriter all by herself by the time she was three. Mother and daughter live together in a rented room on Greenwood Avenue. Florence Mary, who has her mother's pretty eyes and delicate chin, sleeps on a duofold, a wood-backed sofa.

The night before, Parrish rushed home when she ended her class. "After my pupils were gone I immediately began reading a book which I was very anxious to finish," she would later write, "so did not notice the excitement until a late hour." But her daughter, who was looking out onto Greenwood Avenue from their apartment window, did.

"Mother, look at the cars full of people."

"Baby, do not disturb me, I want to read."

Later that evening, when Florence Mary says that she sees men with guns, Parrish sets down her book. "My little girl and I watched the excited groups from our window until a late hour, when I had her lie down and try to rest while I waited and watched," Parrish will write, adding that later that night she heard gunfire. "When it dawned on me what was really happening, I took my little girl in my arms, read one or two chapters of Psalms of David and prayed that God would give me courage to stand through it all." By three o'clock in the morning, Parrish could see that the Midway Hotel had been set on fire. As the night wore on, there was more gunfire. "Yet, seemingly, I could not leave. I walked as one in a horrible dream. By this time my little girl was up and dressed, but I made her lie down." But when Parrish sees a man get shot and fall, she can wait no longer.

"I took my little girl . . . by the hand and fled out of the west door on Greenwood," she will write. For the first couple of blocks, the avenue is largely empty. "Get out of that street with that child or you both will be killed!" someone yells, while behind them they can hear the steady firing of the machine gun that has been set up in the granary across the railroad tracks. Clutching her daughter by her hand, Parrish is trying to reach a friend's home in the Addition. But as she nears the Addition, her heart sinks into her stomach. "I could see homes on Detroit and Easton burning." There is also a new danger. Machine gun fire is now coming from the west as well, where the local National

Guardsmen have positioned themselves. And above their heads, Parrish and Florence Mary can now hear the steady drone of something else.

Airplanes.

Daylight has changed everything.

With the sun now up on June 1, Greenwood's defenders are no longer facing handfuls of armed whites jacked up on booze, rage, and adrenaline. Instead, looking out from their bedroom and office windows, they witness, for the first time, the nightmare that is about to crash down upon them. A wall of white people is calmly headed their way. Most have guns. Some also carry torchlights and cans of gasoline.

Among the first to go are the businesses off Archer and Cincinnati.

Caver's French Dry Cleaners goes up in a roiling wave of greasy black smoke, along with Brown's Restaurant, T. D. Jackson's barbershop, Leon Williams's billiard parlor, and W. L. Anderson's jewelry store. The Little Pullman Hotel, a two-story brick building, takes longer to ignite. But the whites have brought safety matches and kerosene, and smoke can soon be seen curling up over the roof. Within minutes, Thompson's Drug Store, Frank and Julia Payne's tailor shop, and the offices of P. A. Chappelle, attorney-at-law, will all be engulfed in flame. The scene is so dramatic that a passerby with a camera takes a snapshot from across the street. In time the heat will grow so intense that nearby electric power lines also catch fire, their glass insulators shattering on the streets below.

Four blocks to the east, gunfire echoes along the sidewalks and storefronts on Greenwood Avenue. When it subsides, the white crowd from the railroad freight depot pours into the African American commercial district, breaking into stores and offices, hotels and apartment buildings, theaters and restaurants. Smashing windows and kicking in doors, they bust open cash registers and lockboxes, rifle through desk and dresser drawers, and paw through closets and counter displays, stealing whatever catches their eyes. By the armload they haul away clothes and household goods, millinery and medical supplies, tools and office equipment. Watches disappear into pockets, as do necklaces and fountain pens. One enterprising group manages to crack open a safe. Others search the handful of automobiles still parked along the avenue. When they are finished, out come the matches and the cigarette lighters. As the white looters walk away, you can hear the glass crunching beneath their bootheels.

Despite the odds, Greenwood valiantly fights back.

While hundreds of African Americans are now streaming out of the city, others stand firm. Shootouts erupt across the street from Booker T. Washington High School, at the brickyard, along Lansing Avenue, and at Pine Street near Peoria. At Mount Zion Baptist Church, a furious firefight erupts as neighbors and parishioners hold back the white mob. But the all-white local National Guardsmen then turn their machine gun on the newly built house of worship, raking the walls with heavy fire and shattering the stained-glass rose window. "Pieces of brick started falling, then whole bricks began tumbling from the narrow slits in the cupola," an eyewitness will later write. "Within five or six minutes the openings were large jagged holes." The church is soon a raging inferno, as Bibles and pulpit, choir robes and Communion cups, wooden pews and hymnals go up in thick clouds of smoke. At taxpayer expense, a house of God has been demolished. Only the destruction does not end there. "The men stopped firing the machine gun and almost immediately the houses on the outer rim of the area that had been protected by the snipers," the eyewitness will add, "became victims of the arsonists." A similar fate awaits Vernon AME, Paradise Baptist, Metropolitan Baptist, Seventh-day Adventist, and the Church of God in Christ.

Later that morning, a white woman will come upon First Baptist, on Jackson Avenue. It is still untouched.

"Yonder is a nigger church," she'll say to another rioter. "Why ain't they burning it?"

"It's in a white district."

Only that does not matter. In the end, it too will be torched.

In the sky above the city, becoming more audible over the chaos on the streets below, comes the mechanical drone of airplanes. Single-engine aircraft, usually with open cockpits, they are both private and commercial models, most constructed with canvas sheeting stretched over wooden frames. Some seat only the pilot, others the pilot and one passenger. They can be seen and heard over Greenwood from nearly the start of the invasion. When Maria Morales Gutierrez, a recent immigrant from Mexico, sees an airplane bearing down on two young African American children who are walking alone in the street, she runs out, scoops the youngsters into her arms, and carries them inside her home. "Aeroplanes also began to fly over very low," a teacher will recall. "What they were doing I cannot say."

Other observers will be far more certain. "More than a dozen aeroplanes went up and began to drop turpentine balls upon the Negro residences," one witness will later tell a reporter. "I saw aeroplanes, as they flew very low," another will report. "To my surprise, as they passed over the business district they left the entire block a mass of flame." Mabel Little, who ran a café with her husband on East Cameron Street, will later write that "airplanes dropped incendiary bombs to enhance the burning of Mt. Zion Baptist Church and business buildings." W. I. Brown, a porter on a Katy Railroad train that will arrive in Tulsa that day, will tell a reporter for an Oklahoma City newspaper, "Two airplanes were doing most of the work. They would every few seconds drop something and every time they did there was a loud explosion and the sky would be filled with flying debris." Others will report that the planes "showered load after load of leadened missiles upon them."

Meanwhile, on ground level, the fight is far from finished. And as whites begin pouring into the Black residential areas, a deadly pattern emerges.

First, any African Americans who are still inside their homes are ordered out into the street, where they are led away, at gunpoint, to collection points around town. "Women were being chased from their homes," one eyewitness will later tell a journalist, "with clothes in their hands, and volleys of shots fired at them as they were fleeing; some with babies in their arms." According to an account that will be published ten days later in the *Chicago Defender,* a group of whites "went to the home of an old couple and the old man, 80 years old, was paralyzed and sat in a chair and they told him to march and he told them he was crippled, but he'd go if someone would take him, and they told his wife (old, too) to go, but she didn't want to leave him, and he told her to go on anyway. As she left one of the damn dogs shot the old man."

Second comes the looting. "After they had the homes vacated," one eyewitness will later remember, "one bunch of whites would come in and loot. Even women with shopping bags would come in, open drawers, take every kind of finery from clothing to silverware and jewelry. Men were carrying out the furniture, cursing as they did so, saying 'These d——Negroes have better than lots of white people.'" Nearby, on a hillside, throngs of whites gather to observe. "Women, men and children, even babies, watching and taking snapshots of the proceedings of the mob." In another neighborhood, an African American man named J. P. Hughs hides in a barrel in a small grove of peach trees near his home and watches what happens. "We had two large trunks which they took into the street and burst open, took what they wanted," he will recall. On the wealthier blocks, whites begin to use trucks to haul away sideboards, chests of drawers, iceboxes, pianos, and Victrolas.

Finally, when the looting is done, the homes are set on fire. Block after block, street after street, from Archer to north of Pine, the city's African American district is meticulously destroyed. Tar paper shacks, shanties, and grim rented rooms go up in smoke alongside the residences of merchants, physicians, and hotel owners. "Then the horde of white ruffians went down on Detroit, looting and burning those beautiful homes of everything valuable and then burned them, even breaking the phones from the walls," one resident will later remember. "The machine guns just shattered the walls of the homes. The fire department came out and protected the White homes on the west side of Detroit Street while on the east side of the street men with torches and women with shopping bags continued their looting and burning of Negro homes, while aeroplanes flew over head, some very low."

Up in smoke go the Dreamland and the Dixie theaters, the restaurants and the grocery stores, the dress shops and the doctors' offices, the Stradford and Gurley Hotels, the photography studio and the barbershops and beauty parlors, the apartment buildings and the newspaper offices, the butcher shops and the cleaners. Booker T. Washington School escapes the rioters' torches, but Frissell Memorial Hospital does not. And at 429 E. Archer, the two-story wood frame building that houses the Colored Library Branch proves to be too tempting a target for the white mob. On the streets of Tulsa, they are now burning books.

. . .

There are simply too many whites.

A final shootout erupts on Pine Street, along the northern edge of Greenwood, when a group of African Americans, holed up inside a store, tries to hold off a gang of armed whites. But they are overwhelmed, and the store is torched. And as the morning wears on, more and more white Tulsans head toward Greenwood. A young clerk named Guy Ashby shows up for work at Cooper's Grocery on Fourteenth Street, only to be told to go home. "The boss told me there would be no work that day as he was declaring it 'Nigger Day' and he was going hunting niggers," Ashby will later recall. "He took a rifle and told me to lock up the store." At Central High School, a group of male students bolts from the building when they hear gunshots in the distance, and starts walking north. Along the way, they run into a white man coming the other way. He hands them a rifle and a box of ammunition. "You can have it," he tells them. "I'm going home and going to bed." All across downtown, white office workers are glued to the north- and east-facing windows of the tallest buildings, mesmerized by the thick plumes of black smoke rising up over the north side.

African Americans, meanwhile, are being marched to Convention Hall, the baseball park, the fairgrounds, and other hastily designated internment camps by armed whites. Carrie Kinlaw, who lived on the far north end of Greenwood, will have vivid memories of her captors. "There were boys in the bunch," she will tell a reporter, "from about 10 years upward, all armed with guns." Forced to raise their arms over their heads, African Americans are taunted by their captors, some of whom shoot at their feet for fun. "Sometimes they missed and shot their legs," Harold Parker, a white bookkeeper, will later remember. "It was sheer cruelty." J. C. Latimer, an architect and contractor, is beaten by whites, who then steal his money and make him march more than thirty blocks to the ballpark. But the worst comes as he passes sidewalks lined with smiling white onlookers. "Women and children, and very often men," Latimer will later recall, "would laugh and make merry." Roseatter Moore, a widow, faced the same treatment. "Old and young had to pile on trucks," she will later tell a journalist, "and when we were being driven through town men were seen clapping their hands rejoicing over our condition."

For those Black Tulsans who have fled to the countryside, other dangers await. Mary Parrish is miles north of town, walking along a dirt road with a group of other refugees, when up ahead she sees an African American woman coming toward them. "My lady friend and I went to meet her," Parrish will write. "She advised us to not try to pass through a little adjoining town, for they were treating our people awfully mean as they passed through." Others are not so lucky. Billy Hudson set out from Greenwood that morning by horse and wagon, with his grandchildren at his side. His plan was to head toward Nowata, a country town located some fifty miles from Tulsa. But he is murdered by whites along the way.

The state troops arrive midmorning. Coming by train from the state capital in Oklahoma City, where they were mobilized by the governor, they pull into town shortly before nine thirty, more than four hours after the dawn invasion had begun. Though they are all white, they are also all out-of-towners, with no particular ties to Tulsa. While their officers endeavor to make contact with city officials, the troops prepare and eat breakfast. By now, the fighting has largely stopped. A few whites, however, are not yet done.

In downtown, a group of white men surround a blind African American gentleman who could be seen in front of city hall on most mornings. "He had amputated legs," a white eyewitness, E. W. Maxey, will later recall. "His body was attached at the hips to a small wooden platform with wheels. One leg stub was longer than the other, and hung slightly over the edge of the platform, dragging along the street. He scooted his body around by shoving and pushing with his hands covered with baseball catcher mitts. He supported himself by selling pencils to passersby, or accepting their donations for his singing of songs. He was helpless. He'd carry an old tin cup, sing, and mooched for money."

But he was Black.

So, one of the whites returns with an automobile, a late-model convertible with the top down. "These white thugs had roped this colored man on the longer stump of his one leg, and were dragging him behind the car," Maxey will add. "He was hollering. His head was being bashed in, bouncing on the steel rails and bricks. . . . All in broad daylight on June 1, right through the center of town on Main Street."

At 11:29 A.M. on June 1, martial law is declared.

The state troops fan out across the city, setting up roadblocks and command posts, taking into custody African Americans not already held at one of the internment centers, and disarming and sending white civilians home. Unlike the Tulsa police and local National Guardsmen, the out-of-town military units will win the gratitude of the city's beleaguered Black community. "Everyone with whom I met was loud in praise of the State Troops," Mary Parrish will later write. "They used no partiality in quieting the disorder. It is the general belief that if they had reached the scene sooner, many lives and valuable property would have been saved."

That said, by late afternoon the overwhelming majority of Tulsa's

African American population might as well be in jail. Held under armed guard at the baseball park, Convention Hall, and other locations, they are not allowed to return to the remains of their homes and businesses, and are not told what has become of their loved ones. Most will be held until they can get a white person to vouch for them. Some won't get out for a week or more. A few Black Tulsans, however, have evaded involuntary imprisonment altogether, hiding in the woods outside town or disappearing into the countryside. Just west of the city, on the road to Sand Springs, a white couple named Ruth and Merrill Phelps feed and shelter dozens of African American refugees, who hide in their basement during the day, then travel along the creek beds at night, like runaway slaves three-quarters of a century earlier.

Greenwood is gone.

No longer will there be the click and snap of nitrate film in the projectors at the Dreamland and the Dixie; diners will not sit down in anticipation for the smothered steak with rice and gravy at the Bell & Little Café; and the African American maids and domestics who work in the tree-lined neighborhoods on the south side won't be trading idle gossip on the now cracked and scarred sidewalks anytime soon. Gone are the *Tulsa Star* and the *Oklahoma Sun,* their printing press buried beneath an avalanche of bricks, the lead type melted in pools upon the floor. Dora Wells's dress shop and factory has gone up in smoke, as have Amos Newkirk's photography studio, B. C. Franklin's law offices, and the fifty-room Stradford Hotel. Deep Greenwood is now a ghost town of crumbling ruins, charred timbers, and piles of broken brick. It looks like Richmond at the end of the Civil War.

Out in the residential blocks, soot-blackened trees, their leafless branches reaching into the late afternoon sky, now stand guard over what once were grass-covered backyards. The air is still smoky and acrid, and little fires and hot coals dot the burnt wreckage of what were once wooden bungalows and corner grocery stores. Iron bedsteads, still warm to the touch, rise up like sentinels of dreams broken and deferred, while bits of clothing, shattered knickknacks, wooden spools of thread, and children's toys litter the side streets, discarded by the white crowds as they made their way home with armfuls of stolen property. Gone too are pulpits and pews, psalters and hymnals, collection plates and baptismal registries, now reduced to ashes. Come Sunday, there won't be anywhere for a Black Christian in Tulsa to worship God with a roof over his or her head. Whites have burned down all their churches.

Come nightfall, the streets are quiet.

Police officers and National Guardsmen, working in shifts, guard key intersections and roads leading into and out of the city. Earlier, Sheriff McCullough spirited Dick Rowland out of town, while Sarah Page disappears again into anonymity. Neither will be publicly seen or heard in Tulsa again. At city hall, there are telegrams and long-distance calls to answer, plans to make, directives to be issued. And though the city will remain under martial law for two more days, there are some things, the white authorities decide, that cannot wait.

One begins that evening. O. T. Johnson, commandant of the Tulsa citadel of the Salvation Army, is instructed to bring coffee and sandwiches for four dozen or more to a location near downtown. When he and Ruth Gibbs, a lieutenant in the Salvation Army, arrive, they are met by lawmen. Nearby, illuminated by torches and kerosene lanterns, thirty-seven prisoners from the county jail are busily digging, the sounds of their shovels and leg irons breaking the stillness of the warm June night.

Soon, the first truckloads of bodies arrive.

AFTER

The aftermath followed form.

Meeting in closed quarters downtown, an all-white grand jury was impaneled to investigate the causes of the disturbance. Sworn in with their hands upon a Bible, the jurors interviewed city officials, eyewitnesses, and police officers. Three and a half weeks later, they issued their final report. They blamed African Americans. "We find that the recent race riot was the direct result of an effort on the part of a certain group of colored men who appeared at the courthouse on the night of May 31, 1921," the grand jury found, adding that "there was no mob spirit among the whites, no talk of lynching and no arms." Indictments were issued against a number of Black Tulsans, but no whites ever served prison time for the looting, arson, and murders of May 31 and June 1, 1921. Sarah Page refused to press charges and Dick Rowland was exonerated.

Tulsa's white city fathers, meanwhile, had told the world that they would rebuild Greenwood. Instead, they tried to steal the land where the African American commercial district had stood. "Let the negro settlement be placed farther to the north and east," the mayor declared. The legal device that the city government used was the passage of a new fire ordinance, which would have hampered or outright prevented African American property owners from rebuilding on their own land. Black Tulsans, however, fought back. First off, they started rebuilding anyway, using scrap lumber, wooden crates, anything they could get their hands on, in direct defiance of the new ordinance. A group of African American attorneys then took the city to court, where they won a rare victory when three white judges declared that the fire ordinance was illegal.

Despite the city's efforts, Greenwood rose again.

Slowly at first, but steadily nonetheless. Lots were raked free of ashes, burnt wood, and bits of twisted, heat-deformed metal. Charred bricks and stone lintels were sorted and stacked for future use. Bedrolls and blankets were first laid on bare ground, then on canvas tarps, and eventually on wooden floors. Everything still reeked of smoke, and when the first rains finally came, black water sluiced through the streets. The only lights in Greenwood at night were those of kerosene lanterns and candle lamps, flickering against the sides of Red Cross tents or the patchwork wooden walls of lean-tos and shanties made from cast-off lumber. "We erected a small three-room house on the corner of Marshall Place and Greenwood," riot survivor Mabel Little later recalled. "There was no electricity, water or gas. We had to cook outdoors with wood as fuel." Merchants reopened their shops in tents and in the open air, while congregations gathered in the basements of their demolished churches. Despite all the devastation, week by week and month by month, Greenwood pulled itself back on its feet.

For Black Tulsans, with some exceptions, weren't going anywhere. Instead, they went back to work.

Only something else happened as well. Something incredible.

The massacre disappeared.

Not the event itself, of course, which had been burned into the retinas and memories of those who had experienced it. Those would never go away. And there were still places in town where, if you knew where to look, you could find the physical traces of those horrible hours in the late spring of 1921—a bullet lodged in a downtown doorway, charred bricks in a Greenwood basement. But the public face of the riot, the one that appeared in newspaper stories and documents and was passed around the dinner table, grew fainter and fainter, fading like a snapshot left too long in the sun.

This did not happen merely by chance.

"For a while, picture postcards of the victims in awful poses were sold on the streets," Tulsa oilman Campbell Osborn later remembered, adding that more than a few whites "boasted about how many notches he had on his gun." Others, however, especially the city's white civic and business leaders, realized almost immediately that the riot, with its scenes of death and destruction and martial law, was a public relations nightmare. "I suppose Tulsa will get a lot of unpleasant publicity from this affair," one businessman wrote to his family members back east. Reverend Kerr, of First Presbyterian Church, came to a similar conclusion. "For 22 years I have been boosting Tulsa," he noted, "and we have all been boosters and boasters about our buildings, bank accounts and other assets, but the events of the past week will put a stop to the bragging for a while." In the face of these concerns among the white establishment, a consensus soon developed. The less said about the riot, the better. And that's just what happened. As the oilman Osborn added, "The talk stopped."

So too did references to the massacre in the city's white daily newspapers. By the mid-1920s, both the *Tulsa Tribune* and the *Tulsa World* had quit mentioning the riot in stories and articles, a practice that would last for decades. The *Tribune*, especially, went to great lengths to make certain that the riot disappeared from public view. During the 1930s, the newspaper ran a regular feature on its editorial page titled "Fifteen

Years Ago." Drawing directly from back issues of the paper, the column highlighted local news stories and political gossip from that day's date a decade and a half earlier. In 1936, on the fifteenth anniversary of the riot, the editors of the newspaper should have had a most difficult time trying to figure out what to include in the column, from the mob at the courthouse to the attack on Greenwood to the arrival of the state troops. Instead, this is what the *Tribune* published:

FIFTEEN YEARS AGO

From the *Tribune*, June 1, 1921

Miss Carolyn Skelly was a charming young hostess of the past week, having entertained at a luncheon and theater party for Miss Kathleen Sinclair and her guest, Miss Julia Morley of Saginaw, Mich. Corsage bouquets of Cecil roses and sweet peas were presented to the guests, who were Misses Claudine Miller, Martha Sharpe, Elizabeth Cook, Jane Robinson, Pauline Wood, Marie Constantin, Irene Buel, Thelma Kennedy, Ann Kennedy, Jane Wallace and Edith Smith.

Mrs. O.H.P. Thomas will entertain for her daughter, Elizabeth, who has been attending Randolph Macon school in Lynchburg, Va.

Central high school's crowning social event of the term just closed was the senior prom in the gymnasium with about 200 guests in attendance. The grand march was led by Miss Sara Little and Seth Hughes.

Miss Vera Gwynne will leave next week for Chicago to enter the University of Chicago where she will take a course in kindergarten study.

Mr. and Mrs. E.W. Hance have as their guests Mr. L.G. Kellermeyer of St. Mary's, Ohio.

Mrs. C. B. Hough and her son, Ralph, left last night for a three-months trip through the west and northwest. They will return home via Dallas, Texas, where they will visit Mrs. Hough's homefolk.

A decade later, in 1946, the *Tribune* had added a "Twenty-Five Years Ago" column. Once again, it made no mention of the riot whatsoever. Official records began to disappear as well. The after-action reports of the National Guard troops sent to Tulsa from Oklahoma City vanished from the state archives in Oklahoma City. In Tulsa, police, grand jury, and cemetery documents disappeared. Photographs grew scarce. At the *Tulsa Tribune,* someone removed a front-page article and part of the editorial page from the May 31, 1921, edition in the bound volumes of the newspaper before they were microfilmed by the Works Progress Administration in the 1930s. Oklahoma history textbooks published in the 1920s and 1930s, meanwhile, made no mention of the riot whatsoever. It was as if it hadn't happened.

But there was something else as well.

Simply talking about the riot, especially in well-to-do white neighborhoods on the city's south side, was discouraged. When Nancy Dodson moved from a small town in Kansas to Tulsa with her husband in 1950, she learned firsthand that the riot was a taboo topic. "I was admonished not to mention the riot almost upon our arrival," she remembered. "Because of shame, I thought. But the explanation was 'You don't want to start another.'" Another young white housewife, who had moved to Tulsa from out of state, experienced much the same. "When I would mention the riot to my white friends, few would talk about it," she explained. "And they certainly didn't want to."

Indeed, down at the Tulsa County Court House, a kind of coded language developed, one that got around the sticky issue of mentioning the 1921 massacre, remembered historian John Hope Franklin, who used to attend court with his father in the 1930s. "Whenever there was a case involving the estate of a white person who had 'died on or around June 1st, 1921,'" Franklin said, "you knew it meant someone who died during the race riot."

There was one other twist.

For the curtain of silence about the massacre that descended over the city was not limited to white neighborhoods on Tulsa's south side. And as the years flowed past, and for different reasons, talk of the massacre disappeared in Greenwood as well. Like combat veterans, most survivors filed their painful memories away and got on with the rest of their lives. But doing so ensured that their children and grandchildren were kept uninformed. "All of that was swept under the rug," remembered Brenda Alford, who didn't learn about the massacre until she was an adult, despite the fact that her grandparents had lost their home and family business in 1921. Even the *Oklahoma Eagle,* Tulsa's flagship African American newspaper, avoided the subject for years and years. On the twenty-fifth anniversary of the massacre in 1946, the paper published exactly one sentence about the tragedy: "In 1921 racial bitterness, which had been brooding for several years, culminated in one of the most disastrous race riots in the nation's history."

Newcomers to town were also left in the dark. Maria Brown, a nurse's aide who moved to Tulsa in her early twenties, heard nothing whatsoever of the massacre, despite living in the heart of Greenwood. But as one of the elderly white patients she cared for at a north Tulsa nursing home slipped further into dementia, he started talking about what had happened. "My mother cared for an elderly white man, who on his death bed rambled on about the smoke and the fires and the shooting and the killing," Brown's daughter recalled.

Baffled, Maria Brown turned to the family of her Oklahoma-born husband.

"What is he talking about?" she asked. "What happened in Tulsa?"

Only her in-laws brushed her away.

"Look, we don't talk about that around here," they said. "And don't go asking anybody about it."

How come? Why all the silence?

There were several reasons. "Many survivors of the massacre did not talk about the attack afterwards," Brenda Alford said. "For some, it was too traumatizing. Others remained mum about the massacre because they saw their silence as a way of protecting their future generations from experiencing what they lived through. And still, many were forced into silence by bad actors who threatened their jobs or even their lives." Some survivors grappled with PTSD, sometimes for decades, and naturally shied away from the subject. Others, like Holocaust survivors, purposefully did not want to burden their children with the horrors that they had experienced, so they didn't talk about them at all. But at least one massacre survivor kept a loaded rifle inside his front door for decades, "just in case it happened again." While the physical scars of the riot disappeared, the emotional ones lingered on.

There were, of course, a handful of Black Tulsans who not only vowed to keep the story alive, but brought up the riot regularly in conversations outside the home. Others held on to precious souvenirs of the violence, like a roll of silver dimes that had fused during the fires that swept through Greenwood. And a few families owned copies of Mary Parrish's *Events of the Tulsa Disaster*, the first book ever written about the massacre, which had practically been smuggled into the city after it was privately published in 1922. But for many if not most African American survivors, the horrors of May 31–June 1, 1921, became a topic that was rarely if ever brought up, especially in the presence of the younger generation. Even in Greenwood, the story of the massacre, in all its detail, was in danger of slipping away altogether.

As the years went by, it became clear that the white authorities in Tulsa had been more successful than they might ever have dreamed in sweeping the story underneath the civic rug. Not only had they managed to hastily bury the riot's dead in unmarked graves while their loved ones were held under armed guard, they had also buried the massacre itself.

3

Awakenings

Nancy Goodman had a habit of defying expectations. Raised in the leafy comforts of Highland Park, Illinois, a silver spoon suburb north of Chicago, as a child during the late 1920s and early 1930s she wore tailor-made dresses from New York and was driven to the birthday parties of her classmates at the Faulkner School for Girls by her family's live-in chauffeur. The daughter of a successful mortgage banker and a mother whose family roots stretched back to traders along the Santa Fe Trail, Nancy grew up in a world of catered lunches and outdoor concerts at Ravinia Park, field trips to Marshall Field's and the Art Institute of Chicago, and evening sails on the brilliant blue waters of Lake Michigan. But by the time she hit high school, she had had enough. Ditching the boy-crazy bobby soxer set that made up most of her peers, she had become one of the nation's top female divers. When a broken back ended her dreams of Olympic glory in 1939 at age seventeen, Nancy rechanneled her athletic passion into her studies, where she flourished. By the time she turned twenty-one, she had graduated from Northwestern and had enrolled in the law school at the University of Chicago.

"I was really ignorant," she later recalled, "but I loved it and I really did well." One of only five female law students, with auburn hair and eyes as big as chocolate drops, she not only got plenty of attention from the male students, but she played her coquettish charms to the hilt—especially when asked why she wanted to attend law school, traditionally a nearly all-male institution. "I soon learned that if I said I would like to be a lawyer, that was a very unacceptable answer," she added. "So I'd say, 'There were more boys there than anywhere else and they had the longest vacations of any school.'" When queried how she'd do in the courtroom, she'd shoot back that she planned to "sway the jury with my hips."

One day during her second year in law school, a friend asked Nancy if she would come to a party with a new student, an ex-GI who had enrolled during the summer semester and walked with a cane. Nancy was leery, but agreed to the blind date. Only Raymond Feldman didn't turn out to be like the other law students. "You can cut that coy act with me," he told her bluntly. Instead, she had the night of her life. "They started talking," an acquaintance later wrote, "and never stopped." A year and a half later, following graduation, Nancy Goodman became Nancy Feldman. In 1946, the newlyweds moved to Tulsa, Ray's hometown.

For Nancy, who had grown up in a socially liberal Jewish household in cosmopolitan Chicago, Oklahoma was a shock. Not only was the political and social climate much more conservative than she had been used to, but so were race relations. Riding down by rail from Illinois, when the newlyweds reached the Missouri–Oklahoma border their train suddenly stopped and the previously integrated passenger cars were segregated. Outraged, Nancy moved to one of the "Colored" cars.

Job hunting in Tulsa did not go much better. While Raymond set up his own office, Nancy set out to find work as an attorney at one of the local law firms. After reciting her qualifications, including her degree and her class ranking, the first question she always got was "How fast do you type?" Other lawyers propositioned her. "Well," one said, "we could meet for dinner and we could talk about cases." Frustrated with not being able to find work as an attorney, she finally threw in the towel on a legal career. Instead, she went back to college, this time as a part-time sociology instructor.

Located on a two-hundred-acre plot near the center of town, the University of Tulsa, like its subdued Collegiate Gothic buildings, was a quiet outpost of humanism and moderate liberality in a town dominated by oil money and the church. Campus life revolved around football games, homecoming floats, and formal dances, while the student body, clad in sweater sets and pleated skirts with saddle shoes, or khakis and letter jackets, was almost entirely from Tulsa. And aside from an occasional petroleum engineering student from Asia or the Middle East, the undergraduates were all white.

Nancy Feldman turned out to be a magnificent teacher. Sociology was abuzz in the years after World War II, and despite never having taken a single sociology class in college, she threw herself into the discipline, reading the latest books and articles, and keeping apace of the newest trends and debates. Moreover, she loved stretching the minds of her students, introducing new concepts and getting them to think in ways that they weren't likely to encounter around the dinner table at home or read about in the pages of the *Tulsa World* or the *Tulsa Tribune*. One particular area of interest, dating back to her days as a championship diver, was recreation, particularly for underprivileged youth. Through her contacts in local government and the League of Women Voters, Feldman ended up meeting the sole African American recreation officer for the county health department, a fiftyish-year-old man named Robert Lee Fairchild.

Born in Arkansas but raised in Tulsa, Fairchild was a graduate of the University of Nebraska who also had a master's degree in public health. Friendly and outgoing, with a bright smile and a piercing gaze, he was built like a boxer, with strong arms and a massive chest. Like Feldman, he was a former athlete, and the two became friends. Then one day in about 1948, Fairchild told Feldman about the race riot of 1921, which he had experienced firsthand as a seventeen-year-old. Not only had he known Dick Rowland personally, but he told her about the looting and destruction of Greenwood, and how he and his brothers had survived.

Feldman was stunned. She had known about the bloody Chicago race riot of 1919, which had been set off when whites began throwing stones at a group of African American youngsters, floating on a raft, who had drifted in front of an all-white beach on Lake Michigan. Before the violence ended eight days later, nearly two dozen Blacks and whites had been killed. But what Robert Fairchild described was of a whole other order of magnitude. That evening she called her in-laws and asked if it was true. They told her it was. So, the next day, she decided to tell her students at TU about what she'd learned. "I was teaching a course in social problems and I talked about it," she recalled. "My class just exploded."

I don't believe you, they said.

Me, neither.

Nothing like that ever happened in Tulsa.

"Will you go home and ask your parents?" Nancy said. "They will tell you about it."

They didn't. "The parents denied it," she added.

Only Feldman wasn't finished. She then asked Bob Fairchild to come and speak to her class. That, in itself, was already pushing the envelope as far as race relations went in 1940s Oklahoma. Not only were there no African American students at the University of Tulsa, but practically the only people of color ever seen on campus were cafeteria workers and janitorial staff. Nevertheless, Robert Fairchild came and talked to Nancy's students about the riot. "I was there," he told them. But that was not the end of it. After Fairchild's visit, Nancy was called to the dean's office. If she did anything like this again, she was informed, she would be fired.

"That wasn't the worst of it," Feldman later recalled. "Remember, my students were all white Tulsa kids. They had all grown up here. Yet, before I brought Bob Fairchild into class, not a single one had ever heard about the riot. In less than thirty years, it had been erased from the collective memory. It was as if it had never happened at all." From her toehold at the university, Nancy Feldman had started to poke around the edges of Tulsa's dirty secret. She wouldn't be the last.

Don Ross may not have been the worst student at Booker T. Washington High School, but he was certainly in the running. A low-key cutup and class clown who liked to hang out on Greenwood Avenue with his buddies, he preferred comic books to textbooks and chose his classes on the basis of which ones had the best-looking girls. "I refused to learn. I was obstinate, undisciplined, crude. A near-illiterate trouble maker," Ross recalled, adding, "I wasn't a bad kid. I was just unmotivated." It showed. "I don't think he ever learned where the period went," one of his teachers recalled. A goof-off and mischief-maker, he also became a master at slipping off campus without getting caught by the boys' dean. "I always cut my sixth-hour shop class," Ross remembered, "so I could go to the Big Ten Pool Hall and work on the skills that would earn me big money hustling pool."

And money was something that he almost never had. Born in Tulsa in 1941, the child of Pearline and Isreal Ross, he lived for a few years with his grandmother in Vinita, a big town located about an hour northeast of Tulsa. Here, he got his first lessons in America's racial hierarchy. "There was no playground equipment at our school," Ross later recalled, "while the yard at the white school, in the middle of the Black community, had everything. On evenings and weekends, we played in the white schoolyard, and when police passed they would chase us off. One time they loaded us in squad cars with the red lights blinking and a siren screaming. The cops took us home and reported the crimes to our folks. My grandma told us 'to leave white folks' stuff alone.' Afterward, we took turns watching for the cops." When Ross turned eleven, he moved back to Tulsa with his mother, brother, and a new stepfather, where they lived in a dreary housing project, lorded over by officious welfare caseworkers. Their apartment was so small that Ross and his brother slept in the kitchen, while his wardrobe was a sad parade of well-used hand-me-downs, church bin donations, and two-for-one secondhand shop finds.

But while he found school to be uninspiring, the streets were another matter. For Greenwood in the 1950s was a heady mix of the sacred and the profane. Bootleggers hawked pints of corn whiskey, young toughs eyed hubcaps and unlocked back doors, while the raucous new sounds of Fats Domino, Etta James, Little Richard, LaVern Baker, and Johnny Ace spilled out of jukeboxes and car radios. For a quarter you could see a movie at the Regal or the Rex theaters, or buy a milkshake down in Deep Greenwood. For free you could go to morning services on Sunday at the rebuilt Mount Zion Baptist. And in the back alleys, there were quiet men with suit pockets filled with deadly promises. "There was heroin on one side of the street," was how *Oklahoma Eagle* editor Ed Goodwin Jr. described Greenwood Avenue in those days, "and the Holy Ghost on the other." And Don Ross saw it all. Graduating from high school, however, was another matter. "I ain't got nothing else to do," Ross told Henry Whitlow, a history teacher, near the end of his senior year. "I'll just come back next year."

Only Whitlow had other plans. He leaned on a colleague not to flunk Ross in his class, while classmates pitched in as well. One typed up his entire study book. Another completed an unbegun senior project. It worked, and Don Ross was set to graduate along with the other members of the Booker T. Washington High School class of 1959. But there was another problem: He didn't have any decent clothes to wear to commencement. So, once again, others intervened and phone calls were made. "The principal's wife took him to see several sympathetic white Tulsans and asked for contributions," journalist James Hirsch later wrote. "The money came in, and Don Ross wore a fine sharkskin suit and black shoes for his graduation."

There was one other surprise as well.

"They told me that I had won a scholarship to study at TU," Ross later remembered.

The truth was a bit more complicated. Whitlow and another member of the high school community had reached out to Nancy Feldman, who pulled some strings and not only helped Don Ross get accepted into the university but also found a way to pay for it. "I really thought that I had won something," Ross added, "and I wanted to take advantage of what I had won. Years later I found out that those dear people had paid for me to take those hours." In the end, however, the young Booker T. Washington High School graduate and the University of Tulsa were not a good fit. By Christmas, Ross had enlisted in the United States Air Force. He'd be gone for four years.

Don Ross came back a man.

Strong, fit, and standing six foot two, his physical presence was now matched by a determination to get ahead. He talked his way into getting hired by the local Wonder Bread bakery, becoming the first African American union baker in the state of Oklahoma. Marriage soon beckoned as well, with children to follow. But something else had also happened to him. Having spent four years talking to, working with, and sleeping next to whites, northern Blacks, Hispanics, and Asian Americans every day in the Air Force, he found that both his horizons and his ability to communicate with others had broadened immeasurably. Filled with restless energy, he was determined to make a mark.

There were fifty-four of them this time.

For two months they had talked strategy, filled out membership cards, and made plans. Meeting at Joe Eaton's barbershop at the corner of Pine and Norfolk or in the basement of Vernon AME Church down on Greenwood Avenue, the brand-new Tulsa chapter of CORE, or the Congress of Racial Equality, had been organized in the face of a troublesome reality, namely that as late as January 1964, Tulsa had nothing that resembled an active civil rights movement. Even though Dr. Martin Luther King Jr. had spoken at a packed First Baptist in Greenwood in 1960, thrilling the audience inside the church and releasing a flood of donations, the truth of the matter was that there had been precious little overt civil rights activity in town. While activists in Oklahoma City had staged sit-ins at segregated eateries as early as 1956, getting beat up and arrested in the process, in Tulsa the local NAACP chapter sent two-person teams to white-owned restaurants and had them poll the managers as to whether they would accept African American patrons. Although most restaurant owners said that they would, no direct action was taken against those who would not.

The truth was that nearly a decade after Rosa Parks had refused to give up her seat on a city bus in Montgomery, Alabama, Tulsa had not yet seen its first public protest against segregation. While the eyes of the nation had been riveted by the Little Rock school crisis, the Greensboro sit-ins, the Freedom Rides, and African American schoolchildren going to jail in Birmingham, Greenwood had largely been missing in action in the great moral struggle of the time. "You've got to remember," one activist later told me, "in the fifties and early sixties, there were still plenty of middle-aged folks in Greenwood who had experienced the riot firsthand. There was a fear there that was hard to break through."

On Easter Monday, March 30, 1964, that finally happened.

More than four hundred marchers, carrying flags and signs, walked that morning from downtown to Boulder Park, on the city's near south side, calling for freedom and for the city commission to pass an antidiscrimination ordinance, which it had refused to enact. That afternoon the city's first sit-in took place, at Bordens Cafeteria in the Northland Shopping Center, an outdoor mall on the northern edge of town. Three dozen protesters were arrested, including ten whites. The next day, Tulsa's CORE chapter, which now included Don Ross, assumed leadership of the sit-in campaign. Fifty-four protesters were arrested that night at the Apache Circle Restaurant, while nearly three hundred African American youth jeered the Tulsa police officers who had arrived on the scene. In the weeks that followed, CORE members picketed segregated restaurants and banks and staged further sit-ins at Bordens. Greenwood's young protesters were shaking off the fear that had haunted their parents and grandparents.

The white city government, meanwhile, responded with a muddle of action, inaction, and delay tactics, none of which pleased anyone. At first, the city commission refused to pass an ordinance outlawing discrimination, while in the same breath passing a resolution in favor of integration. A district judge got involved as well, issuing an injunction that put a temporary stop to the sit-ins, while the Community Relations Commission was instructed to record complaints of discriminatory behavior. And then, a couple of months later, it was all over. On June 30, the city commission passed an ordinance outlawing discrimination. CORE protested, saying that the ordinance wasn't strong enough, but it didn't matter. Two days later, at a ceremony in the White House, President Lyndon Baines Johnson signed the Civil Rights Act of 1964, which outlawed discrimination in public places. Tulsa's sit-ins had lasted for less than seven months.

But for Don Ross, the protests had been nothing less than an awakening. Not only had he actively taken part in the sit-ins and begun to find his voice in the CORE meetings, but he also revealed a knack for creativity when it came to actual facts. "One day Billy Rountree, a classmate and previous partner in truancy, and I decided to test Bob's Cafe at Third and Detroit in downtown Tulsa. If refused service we would file a complaint before the Community Relations Commission," Ross later recalled. "Wouldn't you know it. When we got there, Bob's Cafe was locked tight, but Billy and I decided that had Bob actually been there he would not have served us anyway." So Ross filed the complaint anyway. Luckily, a friend on the commission, who knew that the complaint was bogus, tore it up. "He saved me," Ross added, "from a felony conviction."

Even more important, his experiences with the sit-ins had catapulted Ross toward ongoing activism on behalf of the city's Black residents. "We should meet the power structure on any terms that we can," he announced three years later at the founding meeting of Citizens for Progress, a community organization. "But if that doesn't work, I say picket, petition, sit-in, lie-in, drag-in, or die-in." By 1967, Ross was directing a local Urban League program aimed at improving opportunities for minority contractors and union members. He was also speaking in white Tulsa. Meeting with students at Oral Roberts University, which the city's leading televangelist had set up on the far south end of town, Ross told them bluntly that "prejudiced white people" were some of his best friends. "I tell them that they are all right because their prejudice comes from what their mama or the school system told them, but it's the system that is wrong." Standing in front of a lectern or in a church basement or a classroom, Don Ross had found his voice. Soon, it would spread even further.

One afternoon while hanging around the offices of the *Oklahoma*

Eagle, the city's long-standing African American newspaper, Ross felt a tap on his shoulder. "One of the editors had a deadline," he remembered, "and he asked me to get the who, what, where, when, and why." Ross successfully delivered what was needed, and the chance encounter soon led to an invitation to contribute a weekly column. For a young man who not too many years earlier didn't know even the basics of punctuation, it was an astonishing offer. Not only did Ross accept, but he turned out to be a natural, a gifted writer who knew how to tell a story, especially a funny one. He delighted in puncturing inflated egos, derailing the pompous, exposing racism, and lobbing all sorts of verbal firecrackers. *Oklahoma Eagle* readers who didn't know Ross personally soon found themselves turning to his column on page six. A new generation of Black Tulsans had found a new voice.

The column changed Ross as well. The onetime ne'er-do-well who used to spend his time chalking up his cue at the Big Ten Pool Hall suddenly found himself being buttonholed by strangers on Greenwood Avenue asking him his opinion on political matters. No longer a reader of comic books, Don Ross started devouring the *New York Times* and the wire reports coming in on the telex at the offices of the *Oklahoma Eagle.* He read *Ebony* and *Jet, Look* and *Life,* as well as books like Dr. King's *Why We Can't Wait, The Autobiography of Malcolm X,* and *From Slavery to Freedom,* written by Greenwood's own John Hope Franklin, now a renowned history professor at the University of Chicago. As Ross steeped himself in the larger world around him, his columns grew into more than neighborhood observations.

But there was one topic that even the *Eagle* had shied away from.

So Don Ross, naturally, started to poke around.

He had, in fact, *heard* of the Tulsa race riot.

When Ross was a student at Booker T. Washington High School,

eachers, who had survived the violence as a youngster, told
 had happened in class one day. Ross didn't believe it. "I told him
that he was a liar," he recalled, "that nothing like that had ever happened here." Later, he had a private conversation with the teacher, who
told him even more—of the fighting and the fires, the airplanes and the
destruction. To the teenaged Ross, it all seemed more like a nightmare
than a possibility. But he filed it away. No teacher had really spoken to
him like that before.

Now, as a columnist for the *Oklahoma Eagle,* he certainly wasn't
lacking in material to write about, from the showdown in Selma in 1965
and the founding of the Black Panther Party to Tulsa's glacially slow
progress in school desegregation. But Ross hadn't forgotten about the
race riot of 1921, and he'd slowly gotten a number of older Greenwood
residents to open up about what they'd experienced. Finally, in 1968, a
tumultuous year that witnessed the assassinations of Dr. King and Robert F. Kennedy, the violence at the Democratic convention in Chicago,
and the election of Richard Nixon to the presidency, Don Ross began a
series of columns about the race riot. "Tulsans have been trained generally to sacrifice truth and realism, to suppress their history," he wrote
in the opening column, "for the sake of keeping superficial harmony in
race relations." Not here, not now.

Instead, he produced a running tutorial on Greenwood's deepest
secret. Drawing upon two then little-known sources, Mary Parrish's
Events of the Tulsa Disaster and Loren Gill's 1946 University of Tulsa
master's thesis on the history of the riot, Ross laid out a brief history of
pre-1921 Black Tulsa, and introduced readers to Parrish's description of
the southern end of Greenwood Avenue as "the Negro's Wall Street." In
a series of columns that appeared over a period of ten weeks, he discussed the lynching of Roy Belton and the lawlessness in Tulsa, and
dissected the incident in the elevator of the Drexel Building and the
outbreak of violence at the courthouse. Then, on the day after Christmas

in 1968, Ross detailed for his now stunned readers the looting and burning, the use of airplanes, and the total destruction of Greenwood. "This was the first time that the story had hit the public," Ross later boasted. Perhaps.

But what Don Ross had unquestionably done was to pierce the veil of silence about the riot that had hovered over Tulsa's African American community for decades. No longer were the events of 1921 only to be spoken of in whispers, at least in north Tulsa. It was a genuine accomplishment. Yet, while Ross had brought the story out of the shadows, the readership of the *Oklahoma Eagle* did not extend far beyond Greenwood. Across town, in white Tulsa, public discussions of the events of 1921 were still taboo. Only the truth is something that is hard to hide forever. And even on the quiet streets of the city's south side, a new round of digging for answers was about to commence.

Ed Wheeler was as straight an arrow as they came.

A championship marksman and a former US Army intelligence officer who'd spent time in Vietnam, he'd made captain by the time he was twenty-eight. As a college student, he had stumped for the Republican Party when Texas and Oklahoma were still reliably Democratic. Now back home in Tulsa, where he worked as an investment counselor, he was also a history buff who moonlighted as a radio producer. Wheeler had his own weekly program on KVOO, the fifty-thousand-watt Tulsa station that had once been the home of Bob Wills, Leon McAuliffe, and other stars of western swing. For his show, "The Gilcrease Story," named after the city's renowned museum of western and Native American art and airing four nights a week at ten forty-five P.M., Wheeler researched, wrote the scripts, and told tales from American history— complete with sound effects and stirring patriotic music. Married, with a young son at home, and an active-duty officer with the Oklahoma

National Guard, Wheeler was outgoing, opinionated, and energetic, a successful young man in a deeply conservative town.

Only Ed Wheeler had a curious streak as well, one that went back well before his army days. So, during the winter of 1970 to 1971, while the nation at large was still reeling from racial unrest and a bitter divide over the war in Vietnam, he decided to look into Tulsa's mysterious secret. Wheeler figured that, as with his other radio programs, he'd do some archival research, perhaps talk to some old-timers, and then write a story for either the *Tulsa World* or the *Tulsa Tribune*, which they could then run on the fiftieth anniversary of the riot, in late May/early June 1971. As he'd learned while taking courses during his university days and at the US Army War College, the answers could usually be found if you knew where to look.

Wheeler soon discovered, however, that not only were the answers not there, but neither were many of the documents themselves. The after-action reports of the Tulsa units of the National Guard were nowhere to be found, as were records for the state troops sent in from Oklahoma City. "Too many things were missing that should have been there," Wheeler told me years later. "I couldn't help but conclude that the pattern was deliberate." Nor was the pattern confined to military records. At Tulsa police headquarters, he spoke with an older officer who told him that, a few years earlier, he was preparing to move offices when he pushed aside a metal file cabinet that had sat in the corner for years. Underneath was a yellowed typewritten document, some ten pages long, that had been stapled together. "It was a list of names, the officer told me," Wheeler later recalled. "There were some thirty names on each page. It was a list of the riot dead." Wheeler asked the man where the list was now, but the officer didn't know. "He said that he passed it up to one of his superior officers." As far as he knew, that's the last time anyone had seen it.

Wheeler didn't stop there. Finding many elderly whites reluctant to speak to him about the riot, he reached out to the Black community, seeking elderly survivors. And while he got more than his share of polite demurrals, Wheeler soon noticed a pattern with those who agreed to speak with him. "The interviews always took place at night, in a church," Wheeler later told me. "I would show up and sit in an empty sanctuary. After a while, a door would open, and a young man would look out—I guess to make sure that I was alone. Then, a few minutes later, an ancient man or woman would be brought out in a wheelchair. The fear was palpable." Wheeler didn't use a tape recorder, and if he took notes by longhand, they have long since disappeared. But he was starting to get a handle on what had happened.

Only his progress would also come with a price. On two occasions when he was walking to or from his office in downtown, Wheeler was approached by strange men, dressed in overalls, whom he had never seen before. "Don't you go writing that article," they told him. "Don't do it." Anonymous phone calls started to come at home at all hours, threatening violence, and he came home from work late one afternoon to find a dead chicken on his porch. Then one morning as he walked out the front door of his house to go to work, he noticed a note slipped beneath the wiper on the windshield of his car. It read, BEST CHECK UNDER THE HOOD FROM NOW ON. "It was no secret that they were trying to terrorize me," Wheeler recalled. "Remember, I was a US Army intelligence officer. And I had served in Vietnam. But while I wasn't too concerned about my own safety, I was worried enough that I moved my wife and kid to my in-laws'." Then he finished writing the article.

No one would take it.

Not the *Tulsa Tribune*, nor the *Tulsa World*. "It's the best thing I've ever read about that thing," one editor told him. But there was no way that they would print it. Wheeler's investigation into the city's dark secret was about to die stillborn. Then Larry Silvey stepped in. The editor of—of all places—the official magazine of the Tulsa Chamber of

Commerce, Silvey was a quiet but effective presence in the city's business culture. On his own initiative, the thirty-two-year-old had already pushed *Tulsa Magazine,* the boosterish mouthpiece of the chamber, to tackle issues that had more substance than endless puff pieces on local businesses and businessmen. And as soon as he heard about Wheeler's article, and saw some of the photographs that he had managed to pry free from decades-old photo albums, Silvey was all in. On the fiftieth anniversary of the riot, in the late spring of 1971, he'd publish the article in *Tulsa Magazine.*

The gray-haired CEOs and attorneys who sat on the chamber's all-white board of directors thought otherwise. For them, Wheeler's article might as well have been radioactive. Not only was it inflammatory and, to their way of thinking, defamatory to the city that they loved, but for them it brought back an ugly episode that needed to stay buried in the past. And most of them, it should be added, were old enough to have remembered the riot firsthand. In the end, it did not take them long to act. And for the first time in the history of the Tulsa Chamber of Commerce, its board of directors overruled their own editor. They killed the story.

Don Ross would save it.

Now thirty years old, Ross had, along with everything else, become a magazine editor as well. The product of a joint effort by Black leaders and a handful of progressive white businessmen, *Oklahoma Impact* was a glossy community magazine that featured articles focused on Black issues sandwiched between ads for banks, department stores, construction companies, car dealerships, and radio stations. Ross had signed on as editor, and as the fiftieth anniversary of the riot drew near in the spring of 1971, he had been on the lookout for someone to write an article that detailed the history of the riot. He'd even asked a couple of white reporters to take a stab at writing the article, but found their effort to be too "woe is me." But when he caught wind of Wheeler's stalled effort, his ears perked up. No hand-wringing liberal patsy, the Oklahoma National Guard officer and local radio personality had the right kind of credentials in conservative Tulsa to protect the story. And as soon as Ross read Wheeler's article, he was on board. *Oklahoma Impact* would publish it in its June 1971 edition.

"Profile of a Race Riot" proved to be a minor sensation. An initial print run of five thousand copies sold out within twenty-four hours, and a second printing was quickly ordered. While few copies ever made it into white Tulsa, for the African American community, Don Ross had delivered a sledgehammer. For older readers, the magazine was both a revelation and a catalyst for painful memories, while others were stunned by what they saw, particularly the handful of grainy black-and-white photographs that appeared alongside the article. Here were images they had never imagined, much less seen, which gave indisputable evidence of the extent of the devastation. And on warm evenings all that summer, dinner table conversations across Greenwood featured a wide-eyed younger generation listening to their grandparents tell stories they had never heard before. "We broke the race riot story," Ross declared. "Both blacks and whites got on my case for causing trouble. I had violated the conspiracy of silence."

For all the commotion, however, Ed Wheeler's article was, on its own merits, far from inflammatory. While Wheeler allowed for the possibility of a high body count, and duly recorded that some thirty-five blocks of Greenwood had been destroyed, more than a few of his historical conclusions would not hold water. In "Profile of a Race Riot," the violence at the courthouse wasn't the product of an attempted lynching. Instead, it was the result of a confrontation between two mobs, one white and one Black, the latter numbering more than three hundred. Instead of African American vets attempting to stop a lynching, it was

"Armed blacks and whites confronted each other; swore and hooted at one another," Wheeler wrote, "jeered and ridiculed law enforcement officers and harassed bystanders." Instead of Greenwood's citizens banding together, Wheeler wrote of a "Negro civic leader" who had tried to get his fellow African Americans to stop shooting, only to have "a black member of the mob" walk up to him and shoot him "at point blank range." Wheeler blamed Blacks and whites alike for the looting, burning, and killing. It might have made for a compelling story, but "Profile of a Race Riot" was less than solid as a work of history.

Still, in the constricted atmosphere of Tulsa, where the riot had long been hidden from view, what the odd couple of Don Ross and Ed Wheeler had accomplished was not to be denied. They had cracked the door open. While a few had preceded them in their efforts to understand the massacre, more would follow in their wake. And one of them, it turned out, I knew pretty well.

Two Summers

When I was twelve years old, I got my first job.

It was the spring of 1966, and every Saturday, from about eight until twelve, I worked as a stock boy, cleaner-upper, and all-around helper at a lamp store about a mile from downtown Tulsa. Dressed in a collared shirt, blue jeans, and my Jack Purcell Blue Tip sneakers, I would stand on a step stool and fetch tissue-wrapped linen lampshades, opalescent sconces, and cardboard boxes of switches and light sockets. When it wasn't too cold outside, I'd sweep off the entryway and the concrete steps that led to the sidewalk. Other times I would take a feather duster and carefully work my way around brightly colored Italian table lamps with huge barrel shades, sedate desk fixtures with brass fittings, and prim candle lanterns with teardrop-shaped bulbs. Hanging from the ceiling above the showrooms, like the moons of Saturn, were a galaxy of ball-shaped ceiling fixtures. Located at 1637 S. Boston in a 1930s bungalow converted into a cheery, up-to-date boutique, Louise Gillam Interior Lighting was a touch of the Hamptons or Melrose Avenue in buttoned-down Tulsa. "Fourteen

Rooms of Lighting, Fixtures, Lamps and Shades" read an advertisement from the era.

On most Saturdays, there'd be four of us in the shop. Mrs. Gillam, of course, was there, darting from one section of the store to the next. Her husband, a kindly old model train enthusiast who sometimes wore a blue-and-white-striped engineer's cap, sat at the worktable in the back, where he assembled preordered lamps for the wives of local lawyers and oilmen, or built chandeliers out of the parts that he had me bring in from the stockroom. There was also a salesclerk, Connie, I think her name was, pretty and dark haired, probably in her early thirties. Dressed in fashionable tailored outfits from Miss Jackson's, the go-to dress shop for the city's country club set, she wore expensive black leather flats and trailed a heady wake of perfume. But it was Mrs. Gillam, with her salt-and-pepper hair cut short and wearing the kinds of dresses that the old ladies wore who sat way in the back at church, who was clearly in charge. The shop was her pride and domain, and she spent much of her time issuing orders to the three of us and constantly moving from one end of the building to the other. Not many customers came in on Saturdays, but when they did, they were attended to courteously and professionally, either by Connie or Mrs. Gillam, or both.

One Saturday, however, wasn't like the others.

I was walking from the storeroom to the workshop when I heard Mrs. Gillam suddenly suck in a huge lungful of air, as if she had just seen a rattlesnake. Holding her hands out in front of her chest, her fingers wide and shaking, she had fixed her gaze on the walkway that led to the front entrance of the shop. I then looked there too and saw a nicely dressed African American couple, clearly husband and wife, coming up the front steps. He had on a suit, a white shirt, and a striped tie, and wore a hat with a matching band. She was dressed in a shimmery blue mid-calf-length dress, cinched at the waist. She also had on white gloves, and on top of her head she wore a slight, close-fitting white cap, adorned with lace and a dainty silk bow. They looked as if they were on their way to church.

I looked at Mrs. Gillam. She looked like she was ready to explode.

"Niggers," she said. "Those niggers are coming into my shop."

Caught completely off guard and consumed by rage, Mrs. Gillam was also uncertain what to do. The Gillams and my family both lived on the same block, located less than a mile away, and there were no Black families who lived in our neighborhood. No African Americans attended my church, nor were there any students, teachers, or staff of color at Robert E. Lee Elementary School, where I was in the sixth grade. GOLDWATER FOR PRESIDENT signs had been the norm two years earlier on the street where I grew up, while on the Fourth of July and other national holidays, our across-the-street neighbor flew the Confederate battle flag from the wooden flagpole set in her front yard. It wasn't that African Americans didn't exist. It's just that outside of the Black men who hauled away our trash every Friday, they were virtually absent from my world. And none of the businesses along that stretch of South Boston Avenue where the lamp shop was located—not the DX filling station or Mrs. DeHaven's Flower Shop, the soda pop and ice cream store or the dry cleaners—either hired or were patronized by Black customers. It was a perfectly white world. Only it was now about to be turned upside down by a man in a tie and a woman wearing gloves.

Finally, Mrs. Gillam made her decision.

"Connie," she said. "You deal with *them*." The words came out like battery acid.

"Yes, Mrs. Gillam."

When the couple entered the shop, Mrs. Gillam retreated to the back, cursing under her breath. Curious, I lingered off to the side, pretending to dust, close enough to see but not to hear. Connie led the couple through the showrooms, pointing out different fixtures. The husband listened attentively, his hands thrust into the pockets of his suit jacket or clasped behind his back, while the wife carefully assessed each lamp, gently turning over the paper price tags that were tied on by a loop of red thread. The couple discussed a few possibilities, but left the shop empty-handed. A few minutes later, they were gone. I never saw them again.

Mrs. Gillam emerged from the back. She was still fuming.

In her hands she carried a cotton rag and a spray bottle of Lysol. She thrust them both into my hands and directed me to spray and wipe down every single lamp and tabletop that the couple may have touched. "Don't miss a spot!" she said. Afterward, she had me fetch the upright vacuum cleaner from the back room and instructed me to vacuum every single place where the couple had walked. I did as I was told, and carefully moved the vacuum cleaner back and forth across the impressions their feet had left on the plush beige carpet. When I was finished, you couldn't tell that the couple had been there at all.

The same applied to the massacre.

In the Tulsa that I grew up in, the riot was not discussed in the newspapers or on television, there were no books about it that you could check out of the library or purchase at a bookstore, and the ministers and Sunday school teachers at First Presbyterian Church never mentioned it, nor did any of my neighbors or Little League coaches or Boy Scout leaders. Even so, by age twelve I had already caught wind that *something* had happened years earlier. More than once I had heard adults discussing "the riot" when I came into the room, only for them to change the subject. From older kids I had heard the tales of bodies floating down the Arkansas River, which flowed only one block away from my boyhood home at 118 E. 24th Street. There were other stories too, about airplanes and machine guns. But as a child, there was no way for me to know if any of it was really true.

That would begin to change that summer.

It was the last summer that neither I nor my two best friends, Mark Walker and Cliff Cronk, were saddled with full-time jobs or responsibilities, and we sure made the most of it. We'd spend hours down by the railroad tracks, or meandering along the sandbars of the river, looking for muskrats or poking at the carcasses of carp and gar. But on most days we would wander downtown. We'd sneak into the Civic Center or onto construction sites, pool our lawn-cutting money to watch cheesy B movies at the Orpheum or the Rialto, wander past the grim saloons and secondhand shops along First Street or Archer, or slip past the front desk at the YMCA to mess around in the big gym on the second floor, pulling ourselves up onto the parallel bars or trying to do an iron cross on the rings.

But we'd almost always spend some time in the new downtown branch of Tulsa City-County Library, which had opened the year before, a dazzlingly modern edifice with brilliant white travertine walls and a grand staircase and indoor fountain. We'd ride the elevator, mess around in the stacks, listen to phonograph records on headphones, and get into the kind of trouble that would earn frowns and sharp looks from library staff, but not get us booted out the door. It was here, as well, that we laid our own eyes for the first time on something that none of us had ever seen before. It was a microfilm reader. Immediately, we were determined to use it.

And then, something rather remarkable happened. A librarian over at the reference desk saw us fiddling around with the machine, and rather than shoo us away, she taught us how to operate it. Moreover, she also showed us the nearby file cabinet filled with tidy cardboard boxes that each held a microfilmed roll of old issues of the *Tulsa World* and the *Tulsa Tribune*. Somehow, by then, I had learned when the race riot was supposed to have taken place. So the first reel that we fed into the machine was the one that included the June 1921 issues of the *Tulsa*

World. We were flabbergasted. DEAD ESTIMATED AT 100, screamed one headline. NEW BATTLE IN PROGRESS, ran another. In between were stories about machine guns and state troops, a race war and dozens of badly wounded. It was hard for Cliff and Mark and me to figure out what it all meant, but that summer afternoon we had determined one thing, at least for ourselves if for no one else. Something *had* happened. The riot was real.

Three years later, during the ninth grade, the riot was mentioned, ever so briefly, in the textbook that we used for our Oklahoma history class at Orville Wright Junior High, though our teacher didn't bring it up. And during the summer of 1969, when I worked as a busboy at the International House of Pancakes, I learned a little more from an African American cook and some of the dishwashers. But the truth of the matter was that by the time I graduated from Central High School and took off for college in 1972, I knew virtually nothing about the tumultuous events that had taken place in my hometown a mere half century earlier.

William McClendon had other ideas. A Morehouse man, civil rights activist, and intellectual, McClendon had moved to Portland, Oregon, back in 1938, when the city's small but resilient African American population was fighting an uphill battle against racist policing, Jim Crow business practices, and inadequate housing and job opportunities. In short order he founded the *Portland Observer,* a weekly newspaper that soon became one of the leading voices for Black rights on the West Coast. By the time I met McClendon during the winter of 1974 to 1975, he was the director of the Black Studies Department at Reed College, where I was a history major. During their senior years, all Reed students have to research and write a thesis, and by the spring semester of my junior year, I was casting about for a suitable topic when I suddenly remembered the race riot back in Tulsa. One afternoon I mentioned this to McClendon in his office, adding that I was having trouble finding anything written about the riot. He nodded, and we soon went on to discuss other matters.

The very next morning, however, a neatly typed and folded piece of paper appeared in my box at the campus post office. Unsigned, and without any kind of accompanying note, it was a list of a half dozen or so printed sources about the riot. I hadn't run across any of them, and I couldn't imagine how Professor McClendon had found them. But they were just what I needed. I had found my thesis topic. And I was on my way. Or, at least, that's what I thought.

The summer of 1975 unfolded with Gerald Ford in the White House, Steven Spielberg's *Jaws* coming to theaters nationwide, and Bruce Springsteen's "Born to Run" at the top of the rock charts. But for me, it would be the summer that I researched the riot. My parents, following my dad's retirement, had moved to California three years earlier, so not only did I need to find a place to live, but I also had to find a job to pay for rent and groceries, one that would also allow me to research during the day. Through a high school buddy, I ended up getting hired on at Riverside Industries, a fading remnant of west Tulsa's once-vibrant manufacturing sector. Workers at the plant, which was union-free and rarely visited by OSHA, preassembled high-power line towers, using air hammers to bolt together brightly anodized lengths of angle iron, which were then loaded onto railroad flatcars. It was hot, dirty, and dangerous work, as much from one's workmates as from the conditions on the shop floor. One night I saw an ex-con pull a butcher knife on a Vietnam vet in the parking lot. Another time a new guy with a smart mouth ended up going to the hospital with knocked-out teeth and a bloody gash on his back. I worked from five thirty in the afternoon until four in the morning, six days a week. On some mornings I was so tired after my shift that I slept with my work clothes on. But the job gave me what I needed. For a place to live, I found a cheap garage apartment at 14th Place and Carthage Avenue on the edge of downtown. It was time to get to work.

A routine soon emerged. Getting up by at least midmorning, I'd pull on my one pair of J. C. Penney slacks and one of my two halfway decent dress shirts, and try to cram in at least a half day's research before I had to dash back to the garage apartment, lace up my steel-toed work boots, grab my hard hat and gloves, and head across the river to Riverside. I spent days roaming the stacks of the downtown branch of the City-County library, or poking through the subject files at the Tulsa County Historical Society, reading and taking notes on anything that might help me understand what had happened in Tulsa in the late spring of 1921. But the pickings, I soon discovered, were rather meager. The handful of histories of Tulsa that were available treated the riot superficially, minimizing what had happened, praising white leaders, and quickly moving on to more positive events. Equally troubling, when I went to city and county government offices, in search of records that might throw some more light on what had happened, the exasperated looks that desk clerks and receptionists gave me were usually followed by what soon became a common refrain:

We don't have anything like that.

Our records don't go back that far.

I'll need to check with my supervisor first.

My research was going nowhere.

I did, however, have one small breakthrough. On the third floor of the downtown library, in a little-used space named the Oklahoma Room, I discovered a nearly complete collection of Tulsa city directories that ran from about 1905 to the present. The precursors of telephone books, city directories contained listings of every head of household by name, address, and what they did for a living. The directories also had a section in which all the businesses in town were compiled by type of establishment. Finally, there was a section, divided by street names, listing every single street address and what was there. While flipping through a couple of directories one afternoon, I also noticed something else, which followed the names of certain individuals and business establishments. It looked like this: (c). At first, I wasn't sure what to make of it. And then it hit me. The *c* meant *colored*. In other words, any person marked with a (c) was African American. The same applied to businesses as well.

This gave me an idea.

Since one of the things that I wanted to do was to get a better idea of what Tulsa's African American district looked like before it was destroyed, I decided that the city directories might be a way to do so. But first, I headed over to the city engineer's office in city hall, where a bemused if amenable employee ran off large-size copies for me of old plat maps that showed the streets in Greenwood. Then it was back to the library, where I started writing down all the addresses and business names on streets or portions of streets that were marked with (c). When I got back to my garage apartment, I taped the maps together and, using a ballpoint pen, started writing in the names of each business or individual on the map. It took more than one session to fill in the map, but by the time it was finished, I had a good idea what pre-riot Greenwood looked like. I knew that H. O. Abbot's print shop, at 121½ N. Greenwood, was sandwiched between A. S. Newkirk's photography studio at 119, and the Union Grocery at 123. Right across the street was the Dixie Theater at 120 and Samuel Stokenberry's shoeshine parlor at 120½.

Only something else happened as well. For as I slowly wrote out all the names of the businesses that had been destroyed, the human dimensions of the loss slowly took root inside me. No longer was it thirty-five square blocks or eleven hundred homes and businesses that had been looted and burned. Now the losses had a name. They were Mary Hoard's hair salon, Arthur and Annie Scarbough's tailor shop, and Dr. Travis's dental office. And with the physical destruction came other losses as well, from dreams of sending a child to college to a nest egg to pass along to the next generation. The city directories weren't some soulless, bureaucratic volumes filled with names and numbers. They were a ticket to help me resurrect a lost world.

As June melted into July, I plodded on.

I read everything that I could lay my hands on about the early history of Tulsa. I got a handle on how a single oil well transformed a sleepy Creek village into a vibrant city in less than a decade and a half. I read up on local crime and policing, and what little I could find out about the Ku Klux Klan. And I dove into the domestic history of the United States in the years during and right after World War I, a bitter era marked not only by lynchings but also by a series of events that were known in those days as race riots. Set off by often relatively small incidents, they involved gangs of whites attacking African Americans and invading Black neighborhoods with murder, assault, looting, and arson on their minds. No longer a single, isolated incident, the Tulsa riot was starting to fit within a larger pattern of American race relations at the time.

I did, however, have a problem. And it was a big one.

I couldn't figure out *why* the riot had happened. Or, for that matter, *how*.

For certain, I had read enough to know about all the contributing factors, and the tenor of the times, to help explain what had fueled the violence in Tulsa in 1921. The rebirth of the Ku Klux Klan in 1915, the up-front racism of D. W. Griffith's smash motion picture *The Birth of a Nation,* the increasing violence against African Americans in cities nationwide—it was easy to see how these factors helped to create an atmosphere where the riot could take place. Equally important was the mindset of many African Americans, especially veterans, in the years following the war, as well as the deep desire of Black Oklahomans to fight Jim Crow in what was, for many, their new home. And then there was Tulsa itself, which despite all its modern office buildings, soaring church steeples, and brand-new brick mansions, was still in many ways a lawless boomtown. Moreover, it made sense that some whites might have been jealous of the Black wealth that existed in Greenwood. I got all that. But something still wasn't adding up for me. Something was missing.

It hit me almost by happenstance. As late as the mid-1970s, photographs of the riot were still extremely difficult to find. Buried in attics, hidden from view, they almost never appeared in books or on display. A handful of grainy photos had accompanied Ed Wheeler's "Profile of a Race Riot" article, and a few others had appeared in a recent photographic history of Tulsa. But these were by far the exceptions. One afternoon, however, as I was looking at an article about the riot in a now defunct 1920s newsmagazine on the second floor of the City-County Library, I came upon a photograph that I had never seen before. It was a panoramic shot of Greenwood after the riot. And it was shocking. Here were block after block of ashes and metal bed frames, the brick rubble of destroyed buildings, and the bare limbs of leafless trees. The first thing that I thought when I saw the photograph was, *It looks like Hiroshima.*

And therein lay the problem.

How did an incident involving only two people in an elevator suddenly turn into a roar of gunshots and a wall of fire, one that destroyed more than a thousand homes and businesses, killed an unknown number of individuals, and left more than ten thousand people homeless? A historian at TU had alerted me to a 1946 master's thesis about the riot, and it had helped. But the basic question remained unanswered. How did Tulsa go from zero to nightmare in a matter of hours? None of the perfunctory descriptions of the riot in the history books could explain this. And as I dug deeper into old issues of the *Tulsa Tribune* and the *Tulsa World*, there was something missing there as well. Despite all my hard work and good intentions, I still couldn't explain to myself, much less to anyone else, exactly how this madness had happened. I was stuck.

Enter Ruth Avery.

Her life had been changed forever at age seven when a truck carrying the bodies of riot victims passed in front of the house that she lived in with her widowed mother on East 8th Street, heading west. A native Tulsan and former Girl Scout, she worked as a nurse and as a secretary in an oil company before she married and started a family. Now age sixty, with intense eyes and a soft round face, she had spent quiet decades, on her own, trying to understand and preserve what had happened during the riot. Ruth was honest and hardworking and talkative, and despite the fact that she would never finish her magnum opus about the riot, *The Fifth Horseman,* her efforts came from the heart. She also knew my mom's best friend, which is how Ruth and I became acquainted. And one afternoon that August, just as my time in Tulsa was about to run out and I would be headed back to Oregon, I ran into Ruth on a downtown sidewalk. She asked me how my work was going.

"Well, to tell you the truth," I said, "I've kind of run into a brick wall. You see, I can't quite figure out how the riot got started. I'm not sure how things went from Dick and Sarah in the elevator to this massive race war."

Uncharacteristically, Ruth was quiet for a moment.

Then she said, "You ought to talk with Mr. Williams."

"Who's that?"

"He's this retired teacher from Booker T. Washington. They say he knows a lot about the riot." She dug into her purse and pulled out a small notebook. "He lives on North Boston. You can find his number in the phone book.

"Good luck," she added.

. . .

W. D. Williams had been waiting all his life to tell his story.

He'd waited for a phone call from a journalist from a national news-magazine, a network television producer, or even a local TV camera crew. Or perhaps it would be a university professor. But no letters arrived in his mailbox, and no knocks came upon his door. He knew that what he had to say had power, and he had told bits and pieces of what he knew to both those who asked and those who didn't, including generations of often shocked students at Booker T. And during the spring of 1971, Williams had organized a small public gathering of riot survivors in Greenwood, to talk openly of what had happened to them in those dark days in 1921. Now, fifty-four years later, he was still waiting.

Only he sure as hell wasn't waiting for me.

A twenty-one-year-old who didn't own a tape recorder, much less a television camera, I hadn't published a book, written a single article, or helped to make any kind of documentary. Even worse, I had grown up on the same side of town that, fifty-four years earlier, the people who had tried to murder him, his mother, and his father had come from. Nevertheless, when I called him on the telephone, he agreed to meet with me at his house a couple of days later. If he had any second thoughts, he kept them to himself.

"So, here you are," Mr. Williams stiffly greeted me at the door. His home was an immaculate brick residence, with a carefully manicured lawn, an elegant living room, and, unlike my ratty garage apartment, fully functioning air-conditioning. We sat down at his kitchen table, and I pulled a yellow pad and pen out of my pack. "Tell me again what this is all about," he said.

I did the best that I could—"I'm a student at Reed College, and . . ."—but Mr. Williams just sat there silent and impassive. I mentioned some of what I felt were the basic facts of the riot, and talked about some of the books and articles I had read and why I thought that some of them were problematic, and I tried to convey the message that *I* certainly wasn't prejudiced. But all I got back was an occasional "Hmm." It was obvious that I wasn't getting anywhere, and even though this was my first-ever oral history interview, it seemed clear that I wasn't going to learn much of anything. I decided that it had been a mistake to come here, and I started to think of how I could politely wrap things up and leave as soon as possible.

It was then that I remembered my map.

I pulled it out of my pack and unfolded it, all the while explaining what it was and how I had made it, using old city directories and plat maps from the city engineer's office. I'm not sure if Mr. Williams heard anything that I said. Instead, he bent over the map, smoothed it out over the top of the kitchen table, and began tracing a finger over each building and each block of North Greenwood Avenue, stopping to read each notation that I had written down. It was then that I realized that my map wasn't just a record of a lost world, it was also a guidebook, and an almanac to Mr. Williams's youth. And as he looked at all the names of the businesses that had once lined both sides of the avenue, and the people and families who lived there, some of whom he hadn't thought about in years, the atmosphere in the kitchen changed completely. A slow grin blossomed on his face, while his head shook back and forth in quiet wonder. I didn't know it yet, but I had just passed a test, and with flying colors.

Then he stopped and looked me in the eye.

"Now, tell me again," Williams said, "exactly what you want to know."

My first question came out of a recent discovery I'd made. In the microfilm copies of the *New York Times* that were kept at the downtown library, I had read a story about how handbills had been tacked on trees and telephone poles in Greenwood two days before the riot, warning African Americans to leave town. *Aha,* I'd thought. *So the attack on Greenwood had been preplanned after all.* The riot was now starting to make sense. I asked Mr. Williams about the notices.

He looked at me like I was crazy.

"What handbills?" he said. "There weren't any handbills."

Sometime later, I figured out that the news desk at the *Times* had conflated wire reports about notices appearing in another Oklahoma town that warned African Americans to leave town with the events that had happened in Tulsa. And while neither of us knew it at the time, and perhaps he never would, with his answer about the handbills, Mr. Williams had passed a test as well. It soon became abundantly clear to me that he was only interested in the truth. And for the next few hours, I was spellbound by what he had to say.

Instead of phantom notices, he told me about the complete contents of the May 31, 1921, edition of the *Tulsa Tribune*, the one that had the articles cut out or torn away. Along with the front-page article that claimed Dick Rowland had sexually assaulted Sarah Page in the elevator of the Drexel Building, there had been an editorial titled "To Lynch Negro Tonight." Williams knew about it because he had read it. Now the reason why the lynch mob had materialized so quickly in front of the courthouse that afternoon was suddenly becoming clear. The *Tribune* had planted the seeds.

There was more. Williams, who was a sixteen-year-old high school student in the spring of 1921, had been down on Greenwood Avenue when word first hit the African American community that whites were gathering to lynch the accused nineteen-year-old shoeshiner. He had been inside the Dreamland Theatre, which his family owned, a couple of hours later when a Black veteran suddenly leaped up onstage and demanded that the theater be shut down. And he was out on the street, and looking out the window from his family's apartment on the corner of Greenwood and Archer, when both caravans of African American men left to go and help defend Rowland.

Mr. Williams told me as well about how, after the shooting had begun, he had helped load the .30-30 rifle and the repeating shotgun that his father used so they could keep whites from crossing the tracks during the long night of May 31 into June 1. And he told me how, after dawn broke and the wave of white invaders came, he had slipped away to safety before he was met by three armed whites, who ordered him to "Hold up your hands, nigger."

When what I had thought would be at most a sixty-minute interview stretched into two and then three hours, my world and what I knew of it had irretrievably shifted. Sitting there across from Mr. Williams at his kitchen table, with my rumpled map of pre-riot Greenwood lying between us, I now had begun to understand how Tulsa had gone from a seemingly innocent and accidental incident in an elevator on May 30 to the murder and looting and arson that had enveloped the city less than thirty-six hours later. The pieces finally fit together. Mr. Williams had shared more than I ever could have expected or even dreamed. We sat together quietly for a couple of minutes, while the enormity of it all started to sink in.

Then I glanced at my watch. *Dang it,* I realized, *I'm late for work.*

Only it didn't matter. For that afternoon, I had been given a precious gift—of knowledge, of perspective, and perhaps more than anything, of trust—and I knew it. It was a day that I would never forget, the kind of day that a writer and historian lives for, the type that almost never happens. I thanked Mr. Williams and told him that I would be back in touch. Then I got into my car and headed out for the other side of the river.

DEATH IN A PROMISED LAND

Two and a half years later.

At a kitchen table in North Carolina, beneath a lazy blue cloud of cigarette smoke, history is on trial. After months of prodding, my graduate adviser at Duke, a brilliant and ornery former Texas journalist and civil rights activist named Larry Goodwyn, has finally agreed to read my Reed thesis on the riot, which he is now doing. He absentmindedly drops ashes everywhere, while his can of Budweiser leaves wet rings on the pages. But he is clearly lost in the story. "Well, I'll be damned," he finally says. "There's a book in here." Even though I'm supposed to start researching my dissertation that summer, a new plan quickly emerges. A small bit of funding was conjured up, and as June 1978 opened to a nation that was sleepwalking through the relative calm of the first half of the Carter administration, I was headed westbound on I-40 for another summer back in Tulsa. I had three months to finish my research on the riot and to begin writing my book.

As soon as I hit town, I caught a break. A friendly professor at the University of Tulsa arranged for me to have a free dorm room on campus all summer. There would be no return to Riverside Industries, no sweating out the long summer nights in the garage apartment. Armed with a Smith-Corona portable manual typewriter, a nineteen-dollar Radio Shack cassette recorder, a stack of notepads, and a box of blue Bic ballpoint pens, I got back to work.

The first big revelation was Mary Parrish's *Events of the Tulsa Disaster.* An exceedingly rare volume—it was said that fewer than fifty copies had been printed—it was her eyewitness account of what had happened to her during and after the riot, the accounts of others, and a fact-filled treatise on the economic devastation that had befallen Tulsa's African American community. I discovered a copy in the Special Collections Department at the TU library and was enthralled by Parrish's remarkable book. It was easily the single most important source on the history of the riot. But it was only a beginning.

I spent hours going through old issues of the *Tulsa World,* the *Tulsa Tribune,* and the *Tulsa Democrat,* as well the city's first African American newspaper, the *Tulsa Star,* and I combed through court records, legal documents, Chamber of Commerce proceedings—anything, really, that might shed some light on the riot and its aftermath. And while nearly all of the new crop of clerks, archivists, and librarians I ran into treated my requests to see old records with a kind of begrudging indifference, a new problem soon arose. Official documents were missing. Lots of them. At the state archives in Oklahoma City, most of the records for the National Guard units that were involved with the riot weren't where they should have been. At Tulsa police headquarters, I was told that the department had no records relating to the riot whatsoever. When I asked an officer named Bill Wilbanks about the list of riot casualties that he had discovered beneath a file cabinet at the police academy years earlier, he said he had no idea where that was now. "I passed it up to the chief's office," he said.

Another mystery lingered as well.

When the first, or "bulldog," edition of the *Tulsa Tribune* hit the streets a little after three o'clock on Tuesday afternoon, May 31, 1921, the newspaper featured both an incendiary write-up of the alleged elevator incident on the front page as well as the "To Lynch Negro Tonight" editorial that W. D. Williams had told me about. But when the old issues of the *Tribune* were microfilmed by the WPA in the 1930s, both articles had already been cut or torn out of the newspaper. The text of the front-page article, "Nab Negro for Attacking Girl in an Elevator," eventually turned up in the "state edition" of the *Tribune*, but the editorial was still missing. I talked Jenkin Lloyd Jones, the stalwartly conservative publisher of the *Tribune*, into allowing me to look at the actual bound volumes of the newspaper that were tucked away in a westside warehouse, but, again, nearly a third of the editorial page of the May 31 edition had been torn out. I didn't doubt that the editorial existed. A survivor in Parrish's book, identified by the initials "A.H.," had written that the May 31 *Tribune* said "that a mob of Whites were forming in order to lynch the Negro," something that was notably missing from the front-page article, a fact that was also echoed by a local pharmacist. But it was frustrating not to be able to read what the editorial actually said.

There was another hole in the evidence as well. As a general rule, older white Tulsans would simply not talk to me about the riot, at least during the 1970s. Time after time, upper-middle-class whites would proudly relate to me stories of how their parents and grandparents had heroically protected their African American domestic employees in the quarters behind their homes. And even at First Presbyterian Church, where I had been baptized, confirmed, and even given a college scholarship, the official church history noted how African Americans had been sheltered in the sanctuary during the riot. What went unmentioned was the advertisement that the church had run in the papers a couple of days later, letting members know that the church had now been "well fumigated." But nobody would admit, at least to me, that anyone in their family had taken part in the shootings and lootings. After all, there was no statute of limitations on murder. And by 1978, all the city officials who were in office in the early 1920s were deceased. Then I hit upon what I thought might be a worthwhile angle to pursue.

After writing down all the names of patrolmen and officers in the Tulsa Police Department in 1921, and then looking up those names in the then-current 1978 Tulsa telephone directory, I realized that two of the officers on the force during the riot, both of whom were white, were still alive. If they would open up to me about what had happened, the information could be invaluable. But when I called the first officer and explained that I was a graduate student at Duke who was writing a history of the riot, he hung up on me. I now had only one chance left. So, for the second officer, I tried a different approach.

"Hello," I said into the receiver. "My name is Scott Ellsworth, and I'm writing a book about the early history of the Tulsa Police Department. And I was wondering whether I might be able to come and interview you about your years on the force."

"You bet!" he replied. "When would you like to come over?"

We met the next day at his home, an older wooden bungalow on the east side. He enthusiastically told me how he'd joined the force, and all the techniques that he'd used to apprehend criminals. I asked him about the riot, but he wouldn't say much, and quickly started talking instead about Ma Barker, Alvin Karpis, and how, in the 1930s, all the officers in town had known where Pretty Boy Floyd was hiding out. He also brought out a photo album filled with old black-and-white photographs. Most were of him in uniform, but to my surprise, there were also some riot photographs. Earlier that year, for a photography class at Duke, I had borrowed my brother's 35-millimeter Nikon F camera, which I had brought with me. I asked the officer if it was OK if I photographed some of his old pictures of him in uniform. He said sure, and I started maneuvering the images on the living room carpet, propping them up one way or another to get the best light without any glare. He appeared to be satisfied, but when I tried to take a shot of one of his riot photographs, he quickly snatched it and all the others away. "Not those," he said.

This was a recurring problem. Even in 1978, it was almost impossible to get access to more than a handful of riot photographs. What was then called the Tulsa County Historical Society didn't have any, though I learned that the president of the society, a man named Beryl Ford, might have some in his private collection. An energetic Tulsa booster and an amateur local historian, Ford had a knack for acquiring every item he could find that was connected to the city's past, especially those he could get for free. He'd rescue doors, windows, and architectural elements from old buildings that were being torn down, and rifle through dumpsters for old photographs. I tracked him down by phone, and he agreed to meet me at one of his storage sites.

The meeting did not begin auspiciously. Ford was dressed in a shirt and tie, with his hair slicked back in a 1950s pompadour, and I could feel his sneer from the moment he laid eyes upon my longish hair, mustache, and thrift shop cowboy shirt. Forging on, I told him who I was, adding that we were both Central High School graduates, and said that I was writing a book about the race riot, and that I was hoping to be able to see some of his riot photographs.

"What for?" he snapped.

This wasn't a question that I had been expecting, and I tried to come up with an answer that wouldn't rile him up even further. "Well," I said, "one thing that I would like to do is to look at how the white rioters were dressed. I want to see if that might tell me something about what social classes were represented."

"There weren't any white rioters," he declared.

I couldn't believe my ears.

"They were all Mexicans and Indians," he added.

Of all the lies, obfuscations, and attempts to absolve everyday white Tulsans from any responsibility for the violence and destruction in 1921, this surely took the cake.

Then Beryl Ford shooed me away. I damn sure wasn't going to be seeing anything of his, at least not while he walked upon this earth. And I never did.

Better tidings awaited me across town. W. D. Williams welcomed me back to his home on North Boston Place, and we did another interview together, this time with my tape recorder rolling. Throughout the summer, we'd talk on the phone from time to time, with me asking him question after question about one detail of his story or another. He also let me copy a photograph of him and his parents in their 1911 Norwalk roadster, likely the first automobile owned by African Americans in Tulsa, as well as a shot of the Dreamland Theatre before it was burned down. But more important, he agreed to help try and find other elderly riot survivors whom I could interview.

This was a matter of some delicacy. Not only was I for all intents and purposes an outsider, but I was also white. And even though on my own I likely could have come up with a list of names and phone numbers of elderly African Americans who had been business owners in Greenwood in 1921 and still lived in Tulsa in 1978, the chances of me cold-calling them at their homes and getting them to agree to an interview were slim. In fact, I had tried this a couple of times and gotten nowhere. I needed an intermediary, someone from the community who could vouch for me and help make an introduction. And Mr. Williams, to my everlasting gratitude, took on that role.

Phone calls were made, meetings were arranged, and one by one, interview by interview, the old stories began to emerge. Robert Fairchild had known Dick Rowland, and he spoke of how Rowland would never, ever have laid a hand on Sarah Page. Seymour Williams had fought in France during the First World War. When the riot broke out, he grabbed a gun and fought to defend Greenwood. Nathaniel Duckery, Victor Hodge, B. E. Caruthers, and N. C. Williams, all of whom were adults in 1921, shared their memories, in some cases speaking openly about the riot for the very first time. Many of these elderly Greenwood pioneers had never had their voices recorded before, and never would again. Unknowingly, I had become their witness. Interviews with slightly younger members of the community were arranged as well, including Greenwood historian Henry Clay Whitlow and *Oklahoma Eagle* publisher Edward L. Goodwin Sr., who were twelve and eighteen, respectively, at the time of the riot.

Not everyone, however, would agree to talk with me. Despite repeated efforts, I could never get Mabel Little to agree to an interview. Long a stalwart member of the Greenwood community, she and her husband, Pressly, had co-owned and operated the Bell & Little Café at 525 E. Cameron. Not only did whites torch their café, but they burned down their home as well. Brilliant, outspoken, and still angry about what she had suffered, hers was a voice that I wanted badly, but got nowhere in pursuing. "I'm not speaking with *you*," she told me pointedly one day, "after what *your* people did."

But even without Mabel Little's participation, the interviews were transformative. Almost single-handedly, they refuted and rebuked the watered-down versions of the riot that had appeared in my ninth-grade

Oklahoma history textbook and in boosterish histories of the city. But they also brought to life the human drama of Greenwood itself, by the generation that had built it.

Meanwhile, as the summer waned, an unexpected ally suddenly appeared.

Mozella Denslow Franklin Jones was the matriarch of one of Greenwood's most distinguished families. The descendant of runaway slaves and a Native American grandmother who, as it was said, "could sit on her hair," Mozella was named after her mother's Latin teacher. Her father, B. C. Franklin, was an attorney who not only survived the riot, but led the successful legal effort that kept the City of Tulsa from stealing the land where the African American business district had stood. After attending boarding school in Tennessee, Mozella graduated from college in West Virginia, then returned home to Tulsa, where she taught school for more than three decades. She also married Waldo Emerson Jones Sr., who soon became one of Tulsa's most highly regarded African American attorneys.

But it was Mozella's baby brother, John Hope Franklin, who would rise to both national and international prominence. Fondly nicknamed Double Head by some of his Booker T. Washington High School classmates in the early 1930s for his dazzling intellectual gifts, Franklin became a Fisk- and Harvard-trained historian whose classic textbook, *From Slavery to Freedom*, first published in 1947, literally changed the way that Blacks and whites alike understood the African American past. Later the chair of the History Department at the University of Chicago, he would eventually become the president of numerous major American historical associations and be a recipient of the Presidential Medal of Freedom.

I'm not sure why Mozella wanted to help me, but there was no question that I benefited from her guidance and support. Proud and fiercely independent, she had arranged the first historical exhibit focusing on the history of Greenwood—ever—to appear at the Tulsa County Historical Society during an era when white deniers like Beryl Ford were still tossing their weight around, and she had handily dealt with condescending Tulsa school board officials for decades. For my part, I loved spending time with Mozella, and listening to her take on our mutual hometown. She also knew how to make an entrance. Once, as a thank-you, I took her to lunch at a restaurant frequented by white attorneys, city managers, and office workers a block from the Civic Center, on the edge of downtown. As she walked into the restaurant, dressed in an electric-colored pantsuit with a brilliant purple fedora and matching shoes, purse, and belt, you could have heard a pin drop. And when the white maître d' failed to dispatch a waitress to our table in what Mozella decided was a timely fashion, she fixed him with a stern look and a wag of her finger. She was a force of nature, and I was lucky to have her on my side.

Mozella also wanted me to meet her famous brother, who would always make a yearly visit to Tulsa. John Hope Franklin had first come to my attention during my junior year at Reed, when I discovered to my utter amazement that the author of *From Slavery to Freedom* was from Tulsa. Mozella was insistent that we meet, and when the appointed day arrived, I drove over to her and Waldo's house for an early supper. After greeting them both at the door, I was pointed to a sunroom off the living room. "He's in there," she told me.

Indeed he was. Sitting on a couch, staring intently at a TV set that was airing the nightly national news, John Hope Franklin was anything but happy. There was a story on having to do with the ramifications of the successful anti–affirmative action lawsuit filed by Allan Bakke, a white applicant to the medical school at the University of California, Davis, who claimed that he had been denied admission because of his race. For several minutes, Franklin paid no attention to me whatsoever, and once he noticed that I was in the room, he tersely grilled me on my work. He then made some comment about the riot. I can't remember what it was, but it was wrong. And rather than let it go, I opened my big fat mouth.

"No," I said, "that actually isn't true."

Mozella and Waldo had by then joined us in the sunroom, and after I laid out my case beneath her brother's withering gaze, Mozella's eyes grew as wide as saucers. She quickly changed the subject, and we all moved into the dining room for dinner, which proceeded without incident. The evening ended pleasantly. But I had undoubtedly crossed a line. I, a twenty-four-year-old nobody, had just challenged the world's leading authority on African American history on his own turf. And while Mozella and I were fine, I didn't expect to see John Hope Franklin ever again. He left town the next day.

Not long thereafter, I had another encounter. I was standing in the middle of Greenwood Avenue late one morning, just off Archer, taking some photographs of and writing some notes about the post-1921 commercial buildings that had replaced the ones that had been destroyed during the riot. A number were vacant, some boarded up. It might have been a Saturday, because there wasn't any traffic. Regardless, suddenly, out of the corner of my eye, I noticed that the outer door to the offices of the *Oklahoma Eagle* had popped open, and a sharply dressed man in his late thirties was making a beeline for me.

"Hey!" he said. "Who are you? And what are you doing?"

It was Don Ross. We talked a bit about the various buildings, and I told him about some of the survivors who had spoken with me. He asked whether I knew Ed Wheeler, and it was then that I remembered why Ross's name seemed familiar. He had written a couple of articles about Greenwood that I had used for my Reed thesis. Ross had just moved back to Tulsa after living and working for five years in Gary, Indiana. I told him that once my book came out, I'd send him a copy. "You do that," he added. Then he walked back to the *Eagle*.

A couple of weeks later, with the summer gone, I left as well. Along with my typewriter and tape recorder, my brother's camera, and my notes, I now had something else. It was a rough draft.

It took another two years to turn that pile of pages into something resembling a book manuscript. Larry Goodwyn, my adviser back at Duke, was a ruthless editor, and he slashed his way through it with "Too vague" and "Say what you mean!" and "Why is this important? Please explain" scribbled across page after page. More research, writing, and rewriting followed. I was living in Washington, D.C., when I finally finished, working as a writer and editor for a think tank off Dupont Circle. One big benefit of my job was that I now had access to an IBM Selectric typewriter, and I'd stay at my desk after hours, rewriting the manuscript at night. By the late summer of 1979, with disco music dominating the airwaves and a revolution brewing in Iran, it was time to find a publisher.

As it turned out, I already had one nibble. The 1978 convention of the American Historical Association had been held in San Francisco when I was out visiting family members over the Christmas holidays. I had walked up to the Louisiana State University Press booth in the exhibit hall, where I introduced myself to an editor there named Beverly Jarrett. LSU Press had been publishing some groundbreaking books about race relations and racial violence, and I thought that the book might be a good fit. Jarrett, who was both welcoming and down-to-earth, said that she'd love to see the manuscript when it was ready.

Goodwyn, meanwhile, thought that I ought to try for a New York publisher, but I was hesitant. For one thing, despite the fact that I had not written the book for scholars, I believed that because of all the years of downplaying the significance of the riot, it was important that the book be fully footnoted and sourced. Moreover, I was also a little worried about how a book from liberal New York might be viewed in conservative Tulsa. And, anyway, I already had my top choice of publisher in mind. Not only had the University of Oklahoma Press put out scores of well-regarded books on the history of the Old West and Native American life, but they were *the* publisher when it came to books about Oklahoma. Having OU Press publish my book would be a clear statement that the riot had, in fact, happened. So, once I had made my final revisions to the manuscript, I sent off a query letter.

This is what I got back in return:

> University of Oklahoma Press
> 1005 Asp Avenue
> Norman, Oklahoma 73019
> August 7, 1979
>
> Dear Mr. Ellsworth,
>
> Thank you very much for your letter of July 23, 1979, regarding your manuscript on the Tulsa race riot of 1921. While we read your letter with a good deal of interest, we do not feel that we are the appropriate publisher for your work.
>
> We do appreciate your thinking of us in connection with your publishing plans, and we would like to wish you success elsewhere.
>
> Sincerely,
> Luther Wilson
> Editor-in-Chief and Assistant Director

That was that. They wouldn't even look at my manuscript.

I was all in with LSU Press now, and things went smoothly. Readers' comments were responded to, and edits were either accepted or successfully fought. One afternoon a few months before publication day, Beverly Jarrett called to tell me that she was putting a set of galleys in the mail. "There's also a little surprise for you," she added. But she wouldn't tell me what it was. A couple of days later, a thick envelope arrived in the mail from Baton Rouge.

Seeing one's name typeset for the first time is a thrill that no writer ever forgets. I had never taken a writing class in college or graduate school, and had never sat in on a writers' workshop. Nor had I published a single newspaper or magazine article. But I was about to become an author. Beverly Jarrett's surprise lay a little further in the galleys. It was a foreword written by John Hope Franklin. "We all have our personal versions of the riot," he wrote, "but Ellsworth has written an account of the events that comes as close to being *the* definitive history of the Tulsa riot as I have seen. In so doing he has written a version for all of us, meanwhile warning us to be careful in the way we use our own version. On his behalf I invite the reader to take most seriously his account, which has both integrity and authenticity."

Holy moly.

Death in a Promised Land: The Tulsa Race Riot of 1921 was published in February 1982. The *Oklahoma Eagle* ran a positive review, but as far as white Tulsa went, the book didn't make much of a ripple in the media of the day. Mozella Jones and W. D. Williams, however, insisted on throwing me a book signing. Hosted by the Friends of the Rudisill Library, the city's African American branch library, the event took place in a room packed with elderly Black Tulsans. I suppose that I said some words, though I can't now recall what they were. But what I do remember quite vividly was the long line of gray-haired African American women and men, some holding on to canes, others to each other, who queued up to have their copies of *Death in a Promised Land* signed. All of them, it seemed, were old enough to be riot survivors, and I was both honored and humbled to be in their presence. And then, to my utter surprise, the fifth or sixth person in line was none other than Mabel Little, her lips pursed and her dark eyes drilling holes through her eyeglasses.

"I want you to write," she said, handing me her copy of the book turned to the title page, "how you are sorry that you didn't interview *me*."

I looked at her in disbelief.

"You write that," she said, nudging the book closer.

I didn't know what to do. I didn't want to lie, but I didn't want to be unfeeling toward someone who had lost everything in the riot. So I trod a path between the two, and wrote something like "For Mrs. Mabel Little, whom I wished that I could have spoken with." I turned the book around so she could read what I had written, and asked her if it was OK. She bent over and read what I'd written. Then she nodded her approval and walked away, holding the book close to her chest.

Back in Washington, friends hosted a signing at a bookshop off Dupont Circle. But one of my best friends, Jane Vessels—daughter of Billy Dale Vessels, the 1952 Heisman Trophy winner at the University of Oklahoma—went even further. She got a copy of *Death in a Promised Land* into the hands of Pete Earley, a national staff reporter for the *Washington Post* who had once lived in Tulsa. Not only did he like the book, but he wrote a lengthy op-ed piece for the *Post* titled "The Untold Story of One of America's Worst Race Riots." Earley also broke through another barrier. His op-ed was the first *national* story about the Tulsa race riot since 1921.

Back in Tulsa, I heard stories about how copies of *Death in a Promised Land* were quietly passed back and forth among reporters at the *Tribune* and the *World,* and how a city councilor had purchased copies for every member of the city council. For a number of years, *Death in a Promised Land* became the second-most stolen book in the Tulsa City-County Library system, disappearing from branch libraries just as regularly as from the central library downtown. Once a year, I would send them a box of books.

What I didn't know was that once they are published, books have lives of their own. And as I went about trying to chart some kind of a career, *Death in a Promised Land* was quietly having an impact of its own. "My life was changed by reading it in law school," Ken Levit, later the executive director of the George Kaiser Family Foundation, Tulsa's largest philanthropic entity, once told me. Others found the book to be disturbing, maddening, affirming, enlightening. I ran into Beryl Ford once after the book came out, and he launched at me for including his ludicrous line about "Mexicans and Indians" in the book's concluding chapter, even though I didn't identify him as its source. Some people claimed that I was really a New Yorker, or Black, or both. Nonetheless, slowly and surely, *Death in a Promised Land* began to do its part to help lift the riot out of the dark, at least in Tulsa. "Nobody really started talking about the riot," reporter Randy Krehbiel later said in the *Tulsa World*, "until Scott Ellsworth's book came out."

Of course, not everyone was on board with that.

On May 5, 1981, ten months before *Death in a Promised Land* was to be published, I wrote a letter to Jenkin Lloyd Jones, the editor and publisher of the *Tulsa Tribune*. After mentioning that my book on the riot would come out early the next year, I suggested that the newspaper publish something about the riot on its upcoming sixtieth anniversary, to take place later that month. "It is my hope that the Tribune will commemorate the riot on or near its upcoming anniversary. I have absolutely no doubt that the Tribune's readership will find the story of the riot fascinating," I wrote, adding that I would be more than happy to connect the newspaper's reporters with elderly Tulsans who had experienced the riot firsthand, and to share with him my manuscript and its attendant photographs.

Three days later, Jones wrote back. After mentioning that the *Tribune* would be publishing a review of a book "written by a black historian" about the history "of blacks in Oklahoma," he turned to the issue of the riot and whether it had any place in the pages of the *Tulsa Tribune*. "I'm not sure I want to stir up any more animals," Jones wrote. "Rehashing race warfare tends to bring out the irresponsible of both sides." Sixty years after it helped launch the attack on Greenwood, the *Tribune* would again be mum. The curtain of silence still held. But what neither Jenk Jones nor I knew was that, in time, the story of the riot would be buffeted by winds far more powerful than mere words.

BOOK TWO

6

WHERE ARE THE REST?

According to eyewitness accounts and security camera photographs, the yellow Ford F-700 truck pulled onto N.W. 5th
Street at nine o'clock in the morning, heading east. Just past
North Harvey Avenue, the driver eased the truck in front of the drop-
off zone for the day care center, and turned off the engine. He then exited the cab and took off on foot, zigzagging in a northeasterly direction
in the warm spring sunshine. Two minutes later, the truck, which was
packed with more than two and a half tons of ammonium nitrate fertil-
izer and nitromethane, exploded into a ferocious fireball, atomizing the
north face of the Alfred P. Murrah Federal Building and shattering windows throughout central Oklahoma City. One hundred and sixty-eight
people were killed in the blast, including three pregnant women, fifteen
children in the America's Kids day care center, eight federal law enforcement officers, and six active-duty military personnel. Though it
would later be eclipsed by the September 11, 2001, attacks, which top-
pled the twin towers of the World Trade Center in New York City, the
April 19, 1995, bombing in Oklahoma City was then widely considered

the most devastating incident of terrorism to ever occur on American soil.

People of Middle Eastern descent, possibly trained Arab jihadists, were immediately suspected of causing the attack. But the guilty party instead turned out to be a pair of homegrown white American males. Twenty-six-year-old Timothy McVeigh was an awkward computer nerd and college dropout who had served in the US Army during the Gulf War. Unable to join the Special Forces, he quit the military and languished in a series of low-paying civilian jobs, gambling away his paychecks, before he adopted an anti-government political philosophy. Convinced that the federal government was the source of all his problems, he increasingly turned to violent, conspiracy-laden, white supremacist writings. "Do we have to shed blood to reform the current system?" McVeigh wrote in a letter to the editor of his hometown newspaper in Lockport, New York. "I hope it doesn't come to that. But it might." His primary accomplice in the bombing, a former Michigan farm kid named Terry Nichols, had a similar résumé. Neither expressed remorse for their actions. Of his victims, McVeigh said, "Think about the people as if they were storm troopers in *Star Wars*. They may be individually innocent, but they are guilty because they work for the Evil Empire."

The bombing itself, meanwhile, had become *the* news story of the day. While a team of two dozen forensic experts used dental records, skeletal analysis, and DNA testing to try and identify the human remains that were found inside the wreckage of the Murrah Building, television news producers, camera crews, and newspaper reporters flooded into Oklahoma City, bringing in satellite link-up trucks and emptying out the rental car counters at Will Rogers Airport. Reflecting the magnitude of the story, NBC's *Today* show dispatched its on-air team to broadcast live from Oklahoma City for a week, including Bryant Gumbel, the first African American host of a network news program in the United States.

One day on the set, Gumbel was approached by a state legislator, a member of the state House of Representatives who represented north Tulsa.

It was Don Ross.

"You know," Ross told Gumbel, "as horrible as this tragedy is, there was another tragedy, even worse, that happened in Tulsa. And no news organization has ever given it the attention that it deserves."

Then Ross handed Gumbel a copy of *Death in a Promised Land*.

Don Ross's drift into electoral politics had followed a natural progression. He followed up his activist experiences during the civil rights movement by serving as the labor affairs director for the Tulsa chapter of the Urban League. And his weekly column for the *Oklahoma Eagle* had brought him into direct contact with Greenwood's movers and shakers. But it was the five years in the early to mid-1970s that he spent in Gary, Indiana, that drove Ross into the political arena—especially his contact with its tradition-shattering mayor, Richard Hatcher.

Though he is a largely forgotten figure today, Hatcher set off a political earthquake in the fall of 1967 when, against the wishes of both the white-dominated Lake County Democratic machine and the local Republican Party, he was elected as the chief executive of Indiana's second-largest city. An impassioned orator and defender of civil rights and the urban poor, Hatcher had run, he said, to make the city a better place for his "brothers and sisters." But as the first well-known Black mayor of an American city—a list that would eventually grow to include Detroit, Cleveland, Newark, Dayton, and Atlanta—Hatcher soon rose to national prominence. He campaigned alongside Robert F. Kennedy, delivered speeches with the Reverend Martin Luther King Jr., and even caught the ear of President Johnson. And in 1972, he persuaded the National Black Political Convention to hold its meetings in Gary.

That same year, when Don Ross was offered a position as an assistant managing editor at the *Gary Post-Tribune,* he leapt at the chance to observe a new kind of Black politics, in a majority Black city with a Black chief executive. He would not be disappointed.

Despite his best efforts, however, Hatcher took over the reins of Gary just as the city was pitching headfirst into an era of serious decline. Once described as "the most industrialized place on earth," Gary and its steel mills, blast furnaces, and dozens of factories had been a key component in the Arsenal of Democracy during the Second World War. But by the dawn of the 1970s, foreign competition and the rise of manufacturing in the union-free Sunbelt had shuttered most of the local industrial plants, wiping away the tax base and sending the city into a downward spiral of unemployment and poverty. No longer the namesake of a beloved song from a Broadway musical, Gary, Indiana, became synonymous with crime, poverty, and hopelessness.

For Ross, the city was an eye-opener. "I had never lived in a predominantly Black community, with a Black mayor," he later said. "At the time, Gary was the headquarters of the drug culture. It was a tough place." But Gary also served Ross as a kind of graduate school. Not only did it help reveal how both cities and states actually operated, but it provided him with a potential pathway to the future. "As a journalist, I was covering that scene, watching the power work," Ross added. "I was able to draw my own conclusions about what should be done." In 1977, Don Ross came back home to Tulsa. Five years later, he successfully ran for political office, representing District 73 in the Oklahoma House of Representatives. He was forty-one.

Don Ross became a superb politician.

It didn't happen overnight, and in a deeply conservative state with only a handful of other African American state representatives, almost every battle was an uphill fight. But Ross paid his dues and, more important, he paid attention, especially to those who wielded the most power. Funny, gregarious, and armed with an endless supply of good stories, he could sweep up on a group of state legislators nursing 7 and 7s at a watering hole near the state capitol and, within minutes, have them howling with laughter. A student of human nature, he could glad-hand and cajole when necessary. And when it wasn't, Ross could deliver waves of sonorous oratory, calling upon the better angels of his fellow legislators. Focusing on civil rights, affirmative health care, social services, and other issues that were important to his constituents back home in Greenwood, he also became an advocate for economic development, education, and the arts.

And in time, Don Ross began to deliver. In 1989, through his leadership, Oklahoma became the first state in the union to remove the Confederate flag from the grounds of the state capitol. He helped to craft the legislation that recognized Dr. King's birthday as a state holiday, and steered tens of millions of state dollars toward development projects in north Tulsa. Whenever an opportunity had presented itself to advance the interests of his constituents, Ross had acted. And when it came to the upcoming seventy-fifth anniversary of the massacre, he would not act alone.

Ken Levit was a local boy made good. The son of a noted cardiologist and a graduate of Holland Hall, Tulsa's prestigious private school, he had headed east to study public policy and Russian history at Brown, then went on to law school at Yale, graduating in 1994 as senior editor of the *Yale Law Journal*. Before he left New Haven, he had read *Death in a Promised Land*, and had been deeply disturbed by what he'd learned. Returning to Tulsa the next year, Levit was determined that something needed to be done, perhaps a memorial erected, in time for the seventy-fifth anniversary. Bright and resourceful, he found his interest also fit well with the heritage of Tulsa's small but influential Jewish community.

To say that Jewish life in Tulsa could at times seem schizophrenic was an understatement. Despite the fact that the community had always been small, Jewish families played an outsize role in the city's commercial, artistic, and philanthropic life. A number of Jewish wildcatters had struck pay dirt in the oil fields, while some of the city's most successful business ventures, from clothing and department stores to oil-well supply companies, had been the creations of Jewish entrepreneurs. As Tulsa had boomed in the early decades of the twentieth century, the city's close-knit Jewish community had reaped some of the benefits.

But they had not always been allowed to sit at the table.

Jews were routinely banned from membership in country clubs, bank boards, and leadership positions at the chamber of commerce, while both the school system and a number of oil companies had unwritten rules barring the hiring of Jewish job applicants. There was more. As the membership of the Ku Klux Klan exploded in Tulsa in the 1920s, Jews were among its targets. Max and Harry Madansky, two Russian-born brothers who opened a men's clothing store downtown in 1908, changed their store's name to May Brothers in an effort to thwart unwanted attention from the Klan. That didn't help Nathan Hantaman, who was kidnapped by Klansmen in 1923 and whipped nearly to death. Tulsa Jews prevented the Silver Shirts, a pro-Nazi organization, from opening an office in the city in 1934, but five years later a swastika was painted across the front of a local synagogue. Even in my own youth in the 1960s, I remember when one of my teachers at Robert E. Lee Elementary smirked in triumph after she had given the word *God* to an Orthodox Jewish classmate during the late rounds of our fifth-grade class spelling bee. When he spelled the word "g, dash, d," she immediately disqualified him.

A number of Tulsa's Jewish families tilted more liberal politically than their Protestant next-door neighbors, especially on matters of race. Before Pearl Harbor, Rabbi Abraham Shusterman had even invited a local African American minister to preach from the pulpit at Temple Israel, decades before any of the city's white churches would entertain such a notion. Given this heritage, Ken Levit's decision to help commemorate the losses that the Greenwood community had suffered in 1921 was well in line with local Jewish values. Soon, he connected with Don Ross and, together, the two of them got to work.

The segment for the *Today* show came together quickly. Don Ross and I were interviewed, as was a survivor named George Monroe. While a documentary about Greenwood had appeared on some PBS affiliates a few years earlier, never had the riot been featured on network television nationwide. This also gave me an idea. Leveraging the fact that the *Today* show would be airing a segment on the riot, I parked myself in an empty office at the Greenwood Cultural Center and started making phone calls. Over the course of two or three days, the *New York Times,* the *Washington Post,* and the Associated Press had all agreed to do stories about the riot. Wade Goodwyn, the son of my adviser at Duke, was now a reporter for National Public Radio, and he flew up from Texas to report on the anniversary. For the first time since the 1920s, the nation's press was taking an interest in what had happened in Tulsa in 1921. We were catching a moment. The *Today* show had opened the door.

Don Ross, Ken Levit, and their associates, meanwhile, had given the media something to look at. A stunning black marble monument, reminiscent of the monolith in Stanley Kubrick's *2001: A Space Odyssey,* was erected outside the Greenwood Cultural Center. With 1921 BLACK WALL STREET chiseled in stone near the top, the monument clearly reflected the mind of Don Ross, who had written a statement that had been laser-cut into the dark marble. But it was the *back* of the monument that would cause visitors to still their voices and look up in awestruck wonder. For here, in six long columns, were the names of nearly three hundred businesses, businessmen, and businesswomen who had lost their livelihoods during the riot.

The seventy-fifth anniversary of the massacre took place on May 31 and June 1, 1996, a Friday and a Saturday, traditionally slow days for news. The events of 1921 nonetheless captured their share of the spotlight. The riot made the front page of the *Washington Post,* complete with a photograph of Robert Fairchild and George Monroe. The *New York Times* also ran a substantial article, while newspapers around the country picked up on the wire service stories. And then, like that, the spotlight moved elsewhere. The Chicago Bulls captured their fourth NBA title, nineteen American servicemen were killed by a truck bomb in Saudi Arabia, a panel of federal judges in Philadelphia blocked an effort to ban internet pornography. The news cycle moved on.

Don Ross, however, had a longer game in mind.

"What are reparations?"

That, according to the account that journalist James Hirsch wrote about in his 2002 book, *Riot and Remembrance,* is the question that Don Ross had posed to John Hope Franklin one day back in the 1960s. Whether it is 100 percent true or not is debatable. Despite his talent as a politician, Ross knows the value of a good story—never mind if some of the details get shifted along the way. Regardless, following the seventy-fifth anniversary activities, he was determined to try and win reparations for massacre survivors. He also knew the ground on which he stood. And it is a testament to Ross's skill as a legislator that he launched this effort the way he did. Instead of making an impassioned plea for reparations on the floor of the state capitol, he asked for a report.

It went like this.

Taking with him all the press that had been kicked up during the seventy-fifth anniversary, Ross then went to both the governor, Republican Frank Keating, and to his colleagues in the state legislature, with a proposal. He argued that despite all the recent attention to the riot, there had never, *ever* been an official study made of what was clearly one of the most devastating events in the history of the state. Not only should a report be made to the governor and the state legislature, but a commission should be created to issue findings and make recommendations on any follow-up actions that should be pursued by the state government. Ross's proposal was, at least on the surface, an easy pill for the leadership in the governor's mansion and the legislature to swallow. It also worked. The next year, a small amount of funding was earmarked for the study, while the Oklahoma Commission to Study the Tulsa Race Riot of 1921 was established. The commission's members would be selected by the governor, the state legislature, and the mayor of Tulsa.

But Don Ross knew how to count votes. Especially when it came to reparations.

And by the time what became popularly known as the Tulsa Race Riot Commission was formally launched in late 1997, he had what he needed, and a great experiment was about to begin.

The green screen on the local Tulsa evening news said it all. Looming up behind the announcer in big, bold letters were the words RIOT COMMISSION. But the giveaway was what was fluttering by in the background, namely pixelated versions of dollar bills. Rather than

any kind of reckoning with the city's deeply tragic past, or
bridge to reconciliation between Tulsa's racially divided
citizenry, or even as a worthy governmental exercise, the not-so-subtle
implication was that the Tulsa Race Riot Commission was really all
about money. And not just anybody's money, but the taxpayers' money
that, it was implied, might be going to *Black* people.

There was, of course, a huge grain of truth to that. Don Ross may
have been able to work his magic in helping to select a set of commissioners, which he scribbled down for me on the back of an envelope in
a Tulsa restaurant one evening, who might look favorably upon the idea
that riot survivors were deserving of reparations for what had been
done to them and their families in 1921. But he had not been the only
one to figure that out. And as the Riot Commission got to work, there
was no question that if one was searching for a lightning rod issue,
reparations would more than fill the bill.

"Now, where are the *rest* of the documents?"

The voice belonged to Don Ross. The setting was the Oklahoma
Historical Society building in Oklahoma City, an aging marble structure that housed a well-used reading room, an archive, and a museum
whose exhibit space featured far more images of Confederates than African Americans. I had been brought on board as the historian for the
riot commission, a consultant whose job was to do research on its behalf. Ross and I had come to the society to see what kinds of records
they might have. A museum employee had been dispatched beforehand
to find every document he could relating to the race riot in their collections. He had no doubt taken his job seriously, and had proudly come
up with a skinny manila file folder filled with twenty-five or so photo-
copied pages. But when Ross made his comment, the researcher's

expression quickly went from disappointment to resentment. It was clear to us both that finding some forgotten cache of riot documents in the marble museum was a lost cause.

Ross, for his part, had a point. It was also one shared by almost all the African American members of the commission, as well as by most Black Tulsans. In essence, there was a deep belief in Greenwood that most of the records pertaining to the riot had never seen the light of day. Moreover, there was a belief that "they"—which usually meant some variant of rich and politically powerful whites—were holding on to these materials still. Given that the riot had been either sugarcoated or actively suppressed for decades, it was a reasonable assumption.

For the most part, however, it struck me as being largely incorrect. While researching both my undergraduate thesis and *Death in a Promised Land,* I had scoured every archive, library, and record repository in the state that I could think of that might house any records, particularly official ones, relating to the massacre or its aftermath. While there had surely been more records back in the early 1920s, I was confident that we weren't going to find them, because they had long since been destroyed.

In the meantime, however, I needed to figure out what to do. I was determined to make some kind of new contribution to our understanding of the riot. What, I asked myself, were the big research holes that needed to be filled? And what were the big issues about the riot that were still unresolved? The second question was easier to answer. Put simply, it was two other questions: How many people died in the riot? And where were they buried?

And that's what I decided to try and find out.

But first, there were some calls to make.

. . .

George Monroe lived alone in a one-story ranch home on East Young Place, a good mile and a half north of Archer. Back in the 1950s, after Greenwood had been rebuilt, this was a neighborhood filled with families, children on bikes, and a community that was knit together by the church, the schools, and the ever-present voice of the *Oklahoma Eagle*. But in the decades that followed, the neighborhood had withstood one assault after another, from urban renewal to drugs. Empty lots were now more common than dwellings, and those that remained were sometimes occupied by less than ideal neighbors. "See those crackheads over there?" George told me one day, motioning toward a small cluster of adults sitting on the steps of a sagging bungalow behind his house. "They're always watching me. Well, I'm watching them too." For both George and for Amley Floyd, a US Army veteran who, along with his wife Patricia, kept an eye out for their elderly neighbor, the tearing down of nearby houses and depopulation of the neighborhood had happened for one reason and one reason alone. "The white folk want this land," Amley said. "They always have."

Despite that, George had led a remarkable life. During the depths of the Great Depression, he paid his way through Wiley College, down in Marshall, Texas, by playing drums in a jazz band. When the war came, he was shipped out first to England, as part of an all-Black regiment, and then after D-Day into France as part of Patton's Third Army. Supplying fuel to tanks, George's unit got so far into enemy territory that they regularly came under German fire.

Returning home to Tulsa, where he became a husband, and a father to four sons, he opened his own restaurant, George's Sandwich Shop, serving up chicken salad and BLTs, chicken fried steak, hot dogs, and hamburgers. SOMETHING NEW IN SANDWICHES—AIR-COOLED, read an advertisement in the *Oklahoma Eagle*. He hustled extra work on weekends by waiting tables and tending bar at Southern Hills, the fancy all-white country club on the south side. He also became the first uniformed African American Coca-Cola salesman and truck driver in Oklahoma, and later worked for the Tulsa County Health Department. Whip smart, well liked, and good with the public, George Monroe was willing to try just about any job.

Only George had known plenty of heartache as well. One son was in prison for selling drugs; another lived for free in another house that George owned, refusing to work. A third son had died while working for the sheriff's department. And a fourth had been killed, in Chicago, when a stray bullet smashed through the window of a restaurant where he was eating dinner. George's wife of forty-seven years, Martha, had passed away in 1996. By the end of the 1990s, he was an old man, living alone in a neighborhood that "urban renewal" had torn the heart out of. But he was also far from finished.

Beginning with the seventy-fifth anniversary of the riot, George quickly became a media favorite. He was tall, slim, and graced with movie star looks, his bright eyes and devilish smile matched by an immaculate wardrobe of light-colored suits with coordinating ties and pocket squares. Careful and precise with his language, he also had a harrowing story to tell. Five years old in 1921, he lived with his mother, father, and his brothers and sisters in a wooden bungalow on Easton Street. His folks, Osborne and Olive Monroe, owned what was easily one of the happiest places in all of Greenwood, a roller-skating rink. Here, teenagers and courting couples, all under the watchful eyes of adults, could rent skates, the kind that you tightened with a metal key, and take spin after spin around the wooden track. But like everything else in Greenwood on the morning of June 1, 1921, its fate hung in the hands of others.

"You go on now," Olive told her husband in the front yard of their home. "They won't hurt me and the kids. But they might kill you."

Osborne agreed and took off. It wasn't much longer until the first wave of white rioters arrived. Olive pleaded with them to spare their home. Instead, they led her away at gunpoint. In the commotion that followed, George and an older sister ran back inside the house, and crawled under their parents' bed.

"I could see the shoes of the men when they walked into the bedroom," George would later tell millions of television listeners and newspaper readers. "One of them stepped on my fingers. I started to cry out, but my sister threw her hand over my mouth to keep me from crying.

"We could then hear the men going through my folks' dresser.

"Then they set fire to the curtains."

The white men left. Luckily, George and his sister got out before the house itself burst into flames. The family survived.

Anyone hearing George tell that story, either in person or on television, was spellbound by what they heard. As a result, he had become not only the most prominent riot survivor but also the unofficial representative of the survivor community. It was in this regard that I sought him out at his home on a spring afternoon in 1998. We had already become friends, and once the riot commission got going, we'd get together whenever I was in town. Even though there was a chill in the air, George was out on the porch when I pulled up into the gravel drive. He smiled a hello, then we retreated to the den with the TV, what he and Amley had rechristened the Spin Room.

"George," I began, "I've got a question for you."

"OK. Shoot."

"So, you know that I'm doing some work for this riot commission. And, well, one of the things that I wanted to research is exactly how many people got killed in the riot. But, you know, there's also been a lot of talk over the years about the bodies of riot victims being buried in unmarked graves. I'd like to see if I can find out where these people were buried. What do you think of that? Would this be a good thing to do?"

George shot a long and wistful look at me. Then he spoke.

"I can't imagine anything that would mean more to the families that lost someone. Yes, go and find out where they buried those bodies."

I then spoke to a handful of other survivors, and posed the same question to them. Every one of them, women and men alike, urged me to do this. Then I asked Don Ross. "I don't know a Black person in Tulsa who would not want to know," he told me. After that, I went to the commission and asked for their permission to start the search. Yes, yes, came their reply, go ahead.

Officially, at least, the search for the riot dead had begun.

Only I wasn't sure exactly how to begin. On the one hand, I hoped, the fact that the Tulsa Race Riot Commission was a creation of the State of Oklahoma might open some doors that had remained closed in the past. Would a coroner have been involved? If there were truly no records related to the riot in the Tulsa Police Department, would other government agencies have materials that might throw some light on how many people were killed in the riot, and what happened to their bodies? But I wasn't clear on what kinds of documents might exist, or where to find them. I did know someone who might be able to help.

Mike Wilkerson was a former Oklahoma State Bureau of Investigation officer who had worked on one of the most notorious murder cases in the history of the state. On a stormy Saturday night in June 1977, three Girl Scouts, aged eight, nine, and ten, were raped and murdered at Camp Scott in rural Mayes County, about an hour east of Tulsa. Suspicion quickly centered on Gene Leroy Hart, a convicted rapist and escaped convict. Of Cherokee descent, Hart had also grown up near the camp. Unable to get a lead on their suspect, Wilkerson and the other OSBI agents ended up turning to a local Cherokee shaman, who helped them track Hart, whom they arrested in a hideout in some nearby woods. Hart also liked to wear women's eyeglasses, a pair of which was found near the scene of the crime. The agents had, they were confident, got their man.

Only the trial turned into high political theater. Activists claimed that Hart had been railroaded because of his race, and was just another victim of racist white policing. The jury apparently agreed and Hart was acquitted of the murders—though he would remain behind bars for his earlier escape. Distraught, Wilkerson and the other agents brought the news of the verdict directly to the shaman. "Don't worry about it," he told them. "God has ways of taking care of things." Three months later, in a prison exercise yard, Hart died of a massive heart attack.

But for Wilkerson, his sense of injustice didn't go away, and he left the OSBI to write about the case, and then to make a documentary about it. His film, *Someone Cry for the Children,* was a powerhouse. Narrated by Johnny Cash and aired on the Discovery Channel, it also launched Wilkerson's career as a filmmaker, both for the cable networks and for the then-booming home video market. Along the way, he had decided to make a documentary about the Tulsa race riot, which is how we had first come in contact. I went to see him at his Tulsa studio, located on the second floor of a faux-Tudor commercial complex called London Square. I then explained what I was looking for.

"Have you talked with Clyde Snow?" he asked.

"Who's that?"

Wilkerson provided a quick primer. One of the world's most renowned forensic anthropologists, Snow was an expert both on mass graves and on identifying human skeletal remains. He had confirmed that the bones discovered in an unmarked grave in Brazil were those of the notorious Dr. Josef Mengele, the Auschwitz "Angel of Death," and he had helped to uncover the first graves of the disappeared in Argentina. Snow had trained teams of forensic scientists to uncover the mass graves of victims of political violence and ethnic cleansing in Guatemala, El Salvador, the Congo, and Bosnia. He'd studied the skeletal remains of Kurdish victims of Saddam Hussein's terror campaign in Iraq, and he frequently testified on human rights cases before the International Court of Justice at The Hague in the Netherlands. In time, however, I would learn much more, perhaps the most important lesson being that Clyde Snow was anything but uncomplicated.

The son of a small-town Texas doctor, Snow had graduated from the New Mexico Military Institute, a no-nonsense training school set on the dry and windy plains of Roswell, whose corps of cadets lived by an honor code that stated, "A cadet will not lie, cheat, or steal, nor tolerate those who do." But after he flunked out of Southern Methodist University, with the Korean War draft breathing down his neck, Snow took off for a remote cabin in the mountains of northern New Mexico, living off of jackrabbits and rainbow trout until the danger of his conscription passed. Eventually earning a doctorate in anthropology at the University of Arizona, he caught the eye of both law enforcement agencies and human rights activists with his pioneering work. He was so adept at finding clues in human remains about a person's identity or cause of death that other experts missed that for many years the Chicago Police Department had a standing arrangement in which they would fly him up to town twice a year, book him a suite at the Ambassador West Hotel, and have him look at cases that had stumped their own experts. Usually, Snow found things that the others had missed.

On the surface, Snow would often joke about his work. He kept a human skull in the center of the dining room table in the ranch house that he shared with his wife, Jerry, in the country outside Norman, Oklahoma, and at cocktail hour, he would raise a glass and offer a toast of "Homicide is good." And when he helped lead the team that identified the remains of the victims of the 1995 Oklahoma City bombing, Snow, like many of the other forensic scientists, often made light puns to get them through their day. It was the same dark humor used by ER nurses and others whose working lives are often filled with death. But the comedy was all a mask. "You don't look at the world quite the same," he told me one day, "once you've seen how the wrists of an eight-year-old boy were bound by wire right before a Guatemalan soldier put a bullet through the back of his head." He saw the end results of other horrid crimes as well, children who had been raped and tortured, pregnant women who had been set on fire, innocent lives snuffed out for no good reason at all. I once asked him how people who see things like this—especially police detectives and medical examiners—cope with visions that can't be unseen.

"That's what alcohol is for," he replied.

Clyde Snow and I first spoke over long-distance telephone, him from a hotel in Guatemala City. "Oh, hey, Scott," came his deep Okie drawl, crackling over the less-than-ideal connection. I explained to him about the riot commission, my role, and my decision, after discussing it with the survivors, to begin looking for the unmarked graves of riot victims. Snow loved the idea, and immediately jumped on board. Then he added his own twist. "When we locate those graves," he said, "we will exhume the human remains. We can use skeletal analysis to determine the race, age, and sex of each victim, and how they died. And we might even be able to extract DNA from the remains, and use that information not only to connect them with living descendants but also to identify them by name." The search had now changed. Not only would we be looking for the unmarked graves of riot victims. If and when we found them, we would also exhume the remains that were buried there.

Any doubts that Clyde Snow wasn't the ally that was needed disappeared the instant I stepped through the front door to his home on Blue Creek Parkway, about five miles outside of Norman, some weeks later. His wife, Jerry, and three huge friendly rescue dogs, all tails and slobber, greeted me at the door, while Clyde, with his round face, sparkly eyes, and white hair that gave him something of the look of an émigré poet or composer, tended a brisket on an Oklahoma Joe's smoker out back. By the time we all sat down at the dining room table with the centerpiece skull, we were fast friends, while the dogs took turns resting their chins on my lap, hoping for stray bits of brisket. When I drove back to Tulsa the next day, there was no question that the search had already moved to a higher, more professional level.

Doors soon began to open as well. Snow arranged a meeting with the state medical examiner, who signed off on the search. He would also eventually introduce me to Lesley Rankin-Hill, a professor of physical anthropology at the University of Oklahoma. An expert in African American burial traditions, Rankin-Hill had been a member of the team that conducted the scientific survey of the African Burial Ground, a colonial-era cemetery in New York City that had been rediscovered in the early 1990s. Others, including Bob Brooks, the state archaeologist, were also apprised of the project. Slowly and deliberately, Snow was seeding the ground for potential contributors and allies for the search. Looking for the riot dead was no longer an amateurish pipe dream. Rather, it was already taking on a shape all its own.

THE LADY WITH A CANE

All that fall, they were at it.

First came the rumble of the trucks, and the hollow slap of lumber being dropped to the ground. Then came the men's voices, low and matter-of-fact, followed by the sharp sounds of two-by-fours being cut by handsaws, and of tenpenny nails being hammered into joists and crossbeams. All that October, November, and December 1922, all across Greenwood, came a daily symphony of more than a dozen hired carpenters, plus their uncounted volunteer helpers, replacing hundreds of canvas tents with simple wooden shacks. More than a ton of nails would be used, along with over three hundred thousand feet of lumber, sixteen thousand feet of screening for windows and doors, a hundred and twenty-five rolls of roofing paper, and forty-one bundles of shingles. Less than five months after the fires of June 1, Greenwood was again on the rise.

In nearby work tents, African American women pieced together quilts, cut out patterns for dresses and undergarments, or stitched bed linens, baby blankets, and children's clothing on foot treadle sewing machines. At a newly erected wooden frame hospital, doctors and nurses tended to patients still coping with the wounds and trauma of the riot. Sixty-year-old Calvin Arnley, who had been shot in the ankle, was at risk of losing his leg, while twelve-year-old Arthur Morrison, whose mother had been murdered during the riot, was now homeless and suffering from pellagra. Not far away, classes were back in session at Booker T. Washington High School, which had escaped the torches of the arsonists, with the students using donated books and school supplies.

One of the architects of this rebirth, as it were, was a blue-eyed forty-five-year-old American Red Cross administrator by the name of Maurice Willows. Born in Canada, he had immigrated to the United States as a teenager and had fought in the Spanish–American War. When the riot broke out, Willows, who was living in St. Louis at the time, was immediately summoned to Tulsa, and for the next seven months he would lead the first-ever coordinated response by the American Red Cross to a man-made disaster. The needs of the African American community, of course, were immense. Hundreds required medical care, while more than ten thousand people were now homeless and possessed little more than the clothes on their backs. Navigating a still tense and supercharged political atmosphere, with the help of national Red Cross staff, the NAACP, and contributions from across the nation, Willows oversaw a relief effort that won the unqualified praise of Greenwood's beleaguered citizens.

A meticulous record keeper, Willows later chronicled the activities of the Red Cross in Tulsa for the headquarters staff in Washington, D.C. Special attention was given to medical statistics. Red Cross nurses and doctors made nearly three hundred field visits to families with maternity and infant health concerns, while more than eighteen hundred tetanus, typhoid, and smallpox serums were administered. Willows's report also noted that due to the riot, 183 persons "were in hospitals, practically all for gunshot wounds or burns," while another 531 were "seriously enough injured to require first aid, medical or surgical care." But there was one number that was missing, and that was the number of riot dead. "Figures are omitted," Willows wrote, "for the reason that NO ONE KNOWS."

That is still the case.

To this day, nobody knows how many people died in the Tulsa race massacre.

Despite claims to the contrary, there was never an "official" death toll. And even if there had been one, it would have likely been so low that, in some quarters, it would have elicited little more than sardonic laughter or bitter disdain. For while a handful of the dead were identified by name in the pages of the *Tulsa World* and the *Tulsa Tribune*, there was abundant evidence of casualties that never made it into the pages of either newspaper. Moreover, we don't know what the ratio was between Black and white casualties. While it is generally assumed that far more African Americans were killed than whites, not every riot survivor would have agreed.

I once asked W. D. Williams if, rather than use the term *race riot*, it would be better to call the events of 1921 a *massacre*.

He looked at me as if I was off my rocker.

"Hell, no" he declared. "We got as many of them as they did of us."

Nomenclature aside, it isn't difficult to come up with a range of estimates of riot deaths. The low end may well be the number cited in the textbook that was used in my ninth-grade Oklahoma history class:

twenty Blacks and nine whites. After that, the numbers keep going up and up. On June 1, 1921, the *Tulsa Tribune* reported that seven whites and sixty-eight Blacks had died. The next day, the *New York Times* declared, 85 WHITES AND NEGROES DIE IN TULSA RIOTS, while the front-page headline in the *Tulsa World* announced, DEAD ESTIMATED AT 100. One day earlier, the *Los Angeles Express* claimed that 175 people had been killed.

There was, however, one credible source of information who suggested that the actual casualty count was considerably higher. And that was Maurice Willows himself. For even though he did not give an explicit estimate for the number of riot dead in his report to the national office of the American Red Cross, he did leave some hints. Among his various "Relief Statistics," three, in particular, stand out:

> Total No. Families with no father (missing or dead) . . . 222
>
> Total No. families with no mother (missing or dead) . . . 87
>
> Telegrams sent or received (relative to riot victims) . . . 1350

Elsewhere in his report, however, Willows again addressed the question of riot fatalities head-on. This is what he wrote: "The number of dead is a matter of conjecture. Some knowing ones estimate the number of killed as high as 300, other estimates being as low as 55. The bodies are hurriedly rushed to burial, and the records of many burials are not to be found. For obvious reasons this report cannot deal with this subject."

Whether Maurice Willows counted himself among the "knowing ones" is unknown. But for my purposes in the spring of 1998, it did not matter. For twenty-nine to three hundred was a reasonable, if maddingly vague, estimate of riot deaths. Anyway, there was a much more pressing question, namely, where were these people buried? And as I began researching these questions, an unexpected accomplice soon appeared.

Dick Warner didn't exactly have the résumé of a seasoned researcher.

Especially when it came to African American history.

A former CPA and retired forklift salesman with a 1950s flattop haircut and thick glasses, he was a Sherlock Holmes fan who would often wear a checkered wool deerstalker cap, and even managed to have a treeless knob northwest of town, one that high school kids would drink beer or smoke dope on top of, renamed Holmes Peak. A lifelong Republican with a passion for St. Bernard dogs, Fox News, and a five o'clock vodka—or two—on the rocks, Warner had first shown up at an early riot commission meeting, where he buttonholed me for a question or two about the riot. We chatted a bit and discovered that I had gone to junior high school with his son Rick and daughter Betsy, and I even remembered when his wife, Mary, ran unsuccessfully for Congress. We ran into each other again a day or two later at the Tulsa Historical Society, where he worked as a volunteer. When I told him of my search for the graves of riot victims, his ears perked right up. Before the week was through, I had acquired a full-time volunteer assistant.

As it turned out, Dick Warner was a superb researcher. Not only had he read practically every book ever written about Tulsa, but he was a fount of arcane facts about the onetime Oil Capital of the World. Want to know where the all-metal house was in Tulsa? Dick knew. How about where J. Paul Getty lived when he was launching his career as a novice oilman? Ask Dick. Or where you could get a respectable chicken fried steak at two o'clock on a Thursday afternoon? Dick was your man. But more important, he had a way of opening doors that was magical. With a gift for gab and a slightly goofy smile, he could talk tight-lipped clerks into opening up their back rooms and suspicious office assistants into running off copies of odd-size volumes and oversize maps. In a Republican town, Dick would become my own secret weapon. And for the next two years, we would be in daily contact.

Though he was more than two decades older than I, Dick had heard some of the same stories about the riot growing up, especially the ones about bodies being dumped into the Arkansas River. But both of us were suspicious of that story from the start. To begin with, prior to the completion of the Keystone Dam in the 1960s, the river hardly ever had much water in it. As a child I had grown up a block away, and aside from one or two memorable floods, one could almost always walk across the riverbed, which was more great sweeps of sandbars than actual flowing current, all the way to the western bank without much difficulty. The river that Dick and I had grown up with was nothing like the Mississippi or the Columbia or the Hudson, mighty waterways that would sweep bodies away with their prodigious currents. The Arkansas River in the 1920s, we reasoned, had been more like the river that we'd grown up with: a timid, shallow snake, one into which any bodies dumped wouldn't go far, if anywhere.

There were other reasons as well. The science of public health was not exactly in its infancy in 1921. Military and civilian authorities alike knew that dead bodies needed to be buried in the ground in order to prevent the spread of disease. Some of these officials had served along the Western Front in France, where the disposal of bodies was a daily occurrence, while others would have been familiar with the spike in burials that had occurred as a result of the 1918 influenza pandemic. Dumping the bodies of riot victims in the Arkansas River would have run counter to everything that these men knew. The bodies of the riot dead had to go into the ground.

But what ground? And where?

• • •

One clue came from the writings of a man named Walter White.

He was, to say the least, a most unusual individual. Although he self-identified as African American, with his straight blond hair, blue eyes, and pale, buttermilk complexion, to all the world White looked white. "The traits of my race," he later wrote, "are nowhere visible upon me." But he would also use this to his advantage.

In 1918, White left his native Atlanta to move to New York City, where he took a job at the headquarters of the NAACP. There, despite his relative youth—he was only twenty-five at the time—he soon became one of the civil rights organization's most powerful assets. Traveling by train to the sites of some of the country's most brutal lynchings, often in the Deep South, White would first pass himself off as a white man. Sometimes he'd claim that he was a salesman for a company that manufactured hair straightener, and that he had to wait in town until the next shipment arrived. He'd chat up the local whites, including former members of the lynch mobs, who would sometimes brag about their role in the killings. Then, if he could, he'd slip across the tracks to the African American community and, revealing who he was, get details that only they would know. No other journalist in America had material like White had. Afterward he'd return to New York and write up his stories.

They were sensational. In the spring of 1918, he reported on how local whites in Estill Springs, Tennessee, a small town between Nashville and Chattanooga, despised Jim McIlherron, a so-called "uppity" Black farmer who refused to kowtow to whites and who would always travel about armed. One afternoon, outside a local store, three young white men started taunting him and pelting him with rocks. McIlherron pulled out his revolver and shot all three, killing two. He then fled to his pastor's home, hoping for some help in escaping the white mob that had quickly formed. First the mob murdered the minister. Then they captured

McIlherron and took him back to Estill Springs, where, White wrote in *The Crisis*:

McIlherron was chained to a hickory tree. The wood and other inflammable material already collected was saturated with coal oil and piled around his feet. The fire was not lighted at once, as the crowd was determined "to have some fun with the damned nigger" before he died. A fire was built a few feet away and then the fiendish torture began. Bars of iron, about the size of an ordinary poker, were placed in the fire and heated to a red-hot pitch. A member of the mob took one of these and made as if to burn the Negro in the side. McIlherron seized the bar and as it was jerked from his grasp all of the inside of his hand came with it, some of the skin roasting on the hot iron. The awful stench of burning human flesh rose into the air, mingled with the lustful cries of the mob and the curses of the suffering Negro. Cries of "Burn the damned hound," "Poke his eyes out," and others of the kind came in thick confusion from the mob. Men, women and children, who were too far in the rear, surged forward in an attempt to catch sight of and gloat over the suffering of the Negro.

Before he died, members of the mob castrated McIlherron and shoved the hot iron bars into his eye sockets.

A few days later, White was on his way to south Georgia, near the Florida line, where, over the course of two weeks, thirteen African American men and women had been lynched by white mobs, after a vicious white landowner was shot to death by an African American convict. The brutality of the Georgia lynchings defied belief. One victim, an innocent pregnant African American woman named Mary Turner, was strung up by her heels, splashed with gasoline, and then set on fire. Her executioners then cut her unborn baby from her womb and stomped it to death.

Walter White was showing the nation an America that most refused to see.

. . .

Three years later, in the aftermath of the riot, White came to Tulsa. He apparently didn't stay long, and the story that he wrote for *The Nation* was a brief, workmanlike overview of the violence. Seventy-seven years later, it also provided Dick Warner and me with clues about the riot dead and what might have happened to them:

It is highly doubtful if the exact number of casualties will ever be known. The figures originally given in the press estimate the number at 100. The number buried by local undertakers and given out by city officials is ten white and twenty-one colored. For obvious reasons these officials wish to keep the number published as low as possible, but the figures obtained in Tulsa are far higher. Fifty whites and between 150 and 200 Negroes is much nearer the actual number of deaths. Ten whites were killed during the first hour of fighting on Tuesday night. Six white men drove into the colored section in a car on Wednesday morning and never came out. Thirteen whites were killed between 5:30 a.m. and 6:30 a.m. Wednesday. O. T. Johnson, commandant of the Tulsa Citadel of the Salvation Army, stated that on Wednesday and Thursday the Salvation Army fed thirty-seven Negroes employed as grave diggers and twenty on Friday and Saturday. During the first two days these men dug 120 graves in each of which a dead Negro was buried. No coffins were used. The bodies were dumped into the holes and covered over with dirt.

White's estimates on the number of riot dead added some contemporary weight, albeit secondhand, to some of the higher estimates. And he added one more piece of evidence to the idea that city officials wanted to keep the death count low.

But more important, the information that White garnered from O. T. Johnson, the local Salvation Army commander, wasn't only detailed, but the details themselves—"thirty seven Negroes," "No coffins were used"—had an air of believability to them. We contacted the current local Salvation Army offices, but learned that they didn't have any records going back to the 1920s. Calls were also made to national headquarters, to see if there might be some records of activities by the Tulsa citadel in 1921. Again, no luck. But Allen Satterlee, who had written a history of the Salvation Army's efforts in the Southern states, tipped us off to a brief mention of the riot in his book. Again, one line popped out. "A candidate for officership," Satterlee had written, "Lt. Colonel Ruth Gibbs recalls feeding the black prisoners in leg irons who had been assigned to the gravedigging detail." It wasn't much, but it helped to confirm what O. T. Johnson had said.

Taken together, the two statements also hinted at other clues. The fact that the gravediggers were in leg irons suggested to Dick and me that they might have been African American prisoners who were held in the county jail, though it's possible that they were conscripted from the internment centers where Black Tulsans were being held under armed guard. And perhaps it was a minor point, but because the Salvation Army had been asked to feed the prisoners, and because roadblocks had been set up on the perimeter of the city, Dick and I concluded that these burials likely took place somewhere in town. Again, however, there was the question: Where?

The fact that *individual* graves had been dug seemed significant. And the numbers checked out as well. We had talked with both Clyde Snow and a retired funeral home director, and both of them had said that it took one man eight hours to dig one grave. Thirty-seven gravediggers on two days, plus twenty on two more, came out to 114 graves—not quite 120, but close enough. More important, however, was the fact that there had been a single grave dug for each victim, rather than a large hole or trench into which bodies were dumped. And where were individual graves normally found? In cemeteries. And that's where we started to look.

. . .

Located just off the edge of downtown at Eleventh and Peoria, Oaklawn Cemetery was a city-owned burial ground that predated the riot. Divided into African American and white sections, as well as a section that held the remains of early Muscogee Creek settlers, the cemetery included a larger potter's field, which was also divided by a Jim Crow line. And it was there that the only two headstones for African American riot victims in Tulsa were located, one for Reuben Everett and the other for Eddie Lockard. Everett was a day laborer who lived with his wife, Jane, on Archer Street, just off Greenwood. Lockard is thought to have been the brother of Joe Lockard, who, with his wife Rina, owned and operated a restaurant, also on Archer. Their headstones stand next to each other near the southwest corner of Oaklawn, in the African American section of the potter's field at the cemetery. Viewing them—then as now—is always a humbling experience.

Trying to find out anything more about either the headstones or the graves themselves led to one dead end after another. We soon learned that the early logbooks and maps for Oaklawn Cemetery were nowhere to be found. Lockard's headstone featured the letters *F*, *L*, and *T* enclosed in three links of chain, a reference to Friendship, Love, and Truth, a motto of the Grand United Order of Odd Fellows, an African American fraternal order, but no records could be found in Odd Fellows files relating to his membership. We also checked with a couple of monument makers in town to see if they recognized the style of each of the two headstones, in hopes they might be able to tell us who made them. But, again, no luck.

Then Dick had an idea.

Talking his way into the back rooms of the Stanley Funeral Home, a white-owned and -operated funeral services company that had been in existence since before the time of the riot, Dick found some astonishing evidence. In a set of dusty account ledgers, unseen for nearly eight decades, he found handwritten entries for the burial of African American riot dead that the then-named Stanley-McCune funeral home had billed to the county. All told, there were seventeen entries, seven of which were for "Unidentified Negro." And while Reuben Everett was not to be found, Eddie Lockard was. This is how one form read:

CHARGE TO: Tulsa County

June 2, 1921

NAME OF DECEASED	Unidentified Negro
DATE OF DEATH	June 1, 1921
PLACE OF DEATH	Tulsa
RESIDENCE ADDRESS	"
DATE OF FUNERAL	June 2nd, 1921
INTERMENT	Oak Lawn Grave #5
~~PHYSICIAN~~	County Attorney
CAUSE OF DEATH	Gun shot wounds (Riot)
OCCUPATION	Unknown
SINGLE OR MARRIED	"
DATE OF BIRTH	"
PLACE OF BIRTH	"
NAME OF FATHER	"
HIS BIRTHPLACE	"
NAME OF MOTHER	"
HER BIRTHPLACE	"
SIZE OF CASKET	
STYLE OF CASKET	
TOTAL CHARGES:	$25.00

Of the others, eleven had died of gunshot wounds and four from burns, while a stillborn infant was said to have died "probably from neglect." Sixteen of the victims, including all seven who were unidentified, were buried at Oaklawn Cemetery, in graves numbered from 1 to 19. Nothing in the ledgers, however, told where in the cemetery these graves were located. But this was still a huge breakthrough. We now had proof that African American riot victims, both known and unidentified, had been buried at Oaklawn Cemetery, all but one in an unmarked grave.

We hadn't located Walter White's 120 riot dead.

But we had found our first site. And soon enough, another heaved into view.

Located just north and west of downtown, wedged between the river and the old road to Sand Springs, Newblock Park had long since seen its glory days. Its nearest neighbors were a past-its-prime residential district, a set of long-dormant industrial facilities dating to the Second World War, a vacant youth detention facility, still surrounded by a razor-wire-topped chain-link fence, and the Cave House, a funky, Flintstones-like vernacular home, usually occupied by an artist, set into the side of a nearby hill. During the summer of 1975, I had drunk beer in a tough bar across the street from the park with some of the other members of the swing shift at Riverside Industries. But the park itself was usually unoccupied, a lonesome patch of city-owned property on the way out of town.

In 1921, however, Newblock Park wasn't a park at all, but the site of the municipal incinerator and a largely illegal dump, located near a polluted, slow-moving stream. Across the railroad tracks along its western edge, squatters lived in tents and makeshift structures along the river. Raw and uninviting, the land was an eyesore. But it was a place that kept reappearing time and again whenever the subject of riot graves was mentioned. More than once back in the 1970s, old-timers had told me, "I heard that they buried them at Newblock." Now, however, we began to hear different kinds of stories. Some claimed that the bodies had been burned in the city incinerator. But Clyde Snow nixed that idea.

"They couldn't have done it," he said. "They couldn't have got it hot enough. It would have been too hard to engineer."

Only Newblock refused to disappear.

In late February 1998, I interviewed Ed Wheeler, author of the "Profile of a Race Riot" story that Don Ross had published back in 1971. Ed and I had known each other slightly over the years, and in spite of the fact that we didn't see eye-to-eye on lots of things, we got along well. Most of all, I appreciated his candor and sincerity. We sat down together at his home in Tulsa.

"I have frankly no idea," he replied when asked where he thought the bodies of riot victims were buried. Then he told a story that made my ears perk up. During the winter of 1970 to 1971, when he was doing his interviews for what became his *Oklahoma Impact* magazine story on the riot, Wheeler had interviewed an older white man, whose name he could no longer recall. The man told him that on either Thursday, June 2, or Friday, June 3, he had gone to the old railroad bridge that was located just downstream from Newblock, near the site of the Eleventh Street bridge. The man walked out onto the bridge, and there, on a large sandbar that was located next to the Tulsa side of the river, he counted some fifty-seven corpses laid out in neat rows. Most, he said, were Black, though there were some white bodies as well. One day later, the man told Wheeler, either on Friday or Saturday, he came back to the bridge and again walked out onto it. The sandbar was still there, but the bodies were gone. What happened to them neither the old man nor Ed Wheeler had a clue.

. . .

A few weeks later, sitting in a sunny apartment filled with giltwood Louis XV chairs and other French antiques, I interviewed a man named Bruce Hartnitt. Like Ed Wheeler, Hartnitt was also a former US Army officer and an amateur historian of the race riot. Around 1970, when he had been director of evening programs at Tulsa Junior College, he had even entertained trying to write a book about the riot, and had started conducting interviews with old-time Tulsans. But it was Hartnitt's talks with his own father that caught my attention.

An automobile mechanic in the spring of 1921, Wylie Hartnitt had been in charge of the fleet of trucks for either the Mid-Continent or the Cosden oil refinery. A couple of days after the riot, the elder Hartnitt later told his son, he had been ordered by his boss to take trucks to the near north side of town, where the dead bodies of African Americans were loaded onto the truck beds and taken away for burial. Unlike some of the other drivers, who piled corpses on top of each other "like cordwood," Wylie Hartnitt only allowed bodies to be laid in a single layer on the bed of his truck. My handwritten notes for the interview continue:

> Although the father was reluctant to speak of this activity, Bruce Hartnitt was under the impression that the father had taken his truckload of bodies "somewhere near the Eleventh Street Bridge." When asked which side of the river, Bruce said he thought on the Tulsa side. It was understood that some of the other drivers may have taken their dead to other locations, and that this activity may have gone on for a couple of days. Wylie Hartnitt did not accept the "official" death toll for the riot. He thought that the death total was "in the hundreds."

The Wheeler and Hartnitt accounts were not the only ones to suggest that some kind of burial of riot victims took place somewhere in or near the Newblock corridor that ran alongside the river. A long-standing oral tradition, present in both the white and African American communities, held that there had been burials "around Newblock Park," while other elderly Tulsans related stories of trucks carrying the bodies of riot dead being seen headed west. Joe Welch, who ran a rock shop and antique store in Sand Springs, told me that his father, who was a housepainter and bootlegger, saw "truckloads of riot victims' bodies being taken to Newblock Park." There were others as well.

With every phone call and every interview, with every lead that was followed and every bit of evidence that was turned up, no matter how small, Dick and I were becoming more and more convinced that the old stories were true, and that some of the riot dead must have indeed been buried somewhere in the Newblock area. But, again, the problem was exactly *where*. "You can bury one hundred bodies in a ten-foot by ten-foot hole," Clyde Snow had once told us.

Among Dick's various acquaintances, particularly among his fellow Sherlock Holmes aficionados, was a man by the name of Bob Norris. Not overly burdened by what Tulsa-born country musician Garth Brooks would refer to as the social graces, Norris had a habit of parking himself in front of the hors d'oeuvre table at the semimonthly gatherings of the Baker Street Irregulars, and not moving until either the clam dip or the guacamole had been thoroughly decimated. A lawyer by training but a rare-book seller by profession, Norris also palled around with a group of gun dealers who sold Nazi memorabilia and military antiques. And it was here, through a dealer named George Washington Jr., that Norris heard a rather remarkable tale involving a Tulsa concrete finisher named Jack Britton.

The story went like this:

One day around the end of World War II, thirteen-year-old Jack Britton, who lived on the near west side of town, was walking along the railroad tracks between Newblock Park and the river when he came across some workmen who were, to his understanding, digging "some kind of swimmin' pool." The men had stopped their digging, however, as they had run into a large number of human bones. Apparently, they told the teenaged Britton that the bones were from the race riot. The next day, Britton was said to have come back to the site, where he retrieved a skull, which he tried to sell to another student at his junior high school. When he came back a day later, the hole had been either partially filled or maybe fenced off. Either way, he no longer had access to any more bones. But for years afterward, whenever Jack Britton would drive his family by Newblock Park, he would always point and say, "That's where they buried them riot people."

The story grabbed Dick's—and my—attention immediately. It had good detail and, taken on its own merits alone, the account made sense. But there was a huge problem with it, and that was the fact that Jack Britton was dead. There was no way to verify the details with the source. So we did the next best thing. We tracked down and interviewed as many people as we could who had known Jack Britton. We spoke to his adult children and other family members, and to friends and work associates, many of whom didn't know each other. Dick and I then discovered that not only had Britton independently told them the same thing, but the details were the same. Jack Britton had told a consistent story, over the course of several decades, about what seemed to be a mass grave from the race riot.

And then there was the swimming pool. While it was no longer in use, there had in fact been an outdoor pool at Newblock Park. As a kid, I had swum in it during the mid-1960s. Surely, it was when that pool was being constructed that the skeletal remains Britton remembered had been inadvertently discovered. It stood to reason that the rest of a mass grave might lie just beyond the perimeter of the pool. But in researching the history of the park, we learned that the pool had been built in 1927, well before Jack Britton had been born.

And then, when all the air felt like it would go out of the balloon, Dick had another brainstorm. Heading down to the offices of the city water and sewer departments, he cajoled out of one of the managers an older map of the water and sewer lines for Newblock Park. As it turned out, a sewage lift pump station had been built in Newblock Park in 1945, in a low spot that was just across the creek from the dump and the incinerator. And that lift pump station, which was essentially the size of a small building, required digging a sizable rectangular hole in the ground that a thirteen-year-old boy might have thought was a swimming pool. Not only did the construction of the lift pump station work timewise with the Jack Britton story, but a mass grave there could have also been the ultimate destination of the trucks that were seen heading toward Newblock. Indeed, even the bodies laid out on the sandbar could fit the narrative as well. The authorities could have simply had the bodies carried up the bank, across the tracks, and to a pit where, twenty-four years later, a group of construction workers accidentally stumbled upon them.

For the next two years, Dick and I kept at it.

Following leads. Chasing rumors. Dowsing for the truth.

While the riot commission lumbered along, Dick and I tracked down every lead that we could on where the victims of the riot might have been buried. More than three hundred people offered their stories, including riot survivors and eyewitnesses, city employees, undertakers, cemetery workers, construction engineers, police officers, and plain old regular citizens. Once, a man who said that his grandfather had been

the Imperial Wizard of the Ku Klux Klan proudly sho
billy club that, he claimed, had been made from on
state's first electric chair. Another time, I went to
interview a survivor who might have some valuable informau...,
been told by one of her former nurses, about riot fatalities. But the
woman grew so agitated when I mentioned the riot that I immediately
tried to change the subject and end the interview. It didn't matter. As
she looked at me with her tear-streaked eyes, I felt like the world's biggest heel. Despite what some people claim, PTSD doesn't always fade
with time. In her case, the riot had terrorized her for more than seven
decades.

As one source led to another, more and more potential burial sites
came to our attention. Some were patently ludicrous, others doubtful,
some possible but basically unprovable. One man, who had called the
Tulsa Historical Society but refused to give his name, insisted that the
bodies had been buried underneath Convention Hall, the theater that
had temporarily served as one of the makeshift internment centers for
African Americans. "About 123 blacks were clubbed and shot to death
in the basement of the Convention Hall (now Brady Theater)," Dick
wrote in his notes, "and buried in a tunnel under the theater. There are
three tunnels and they [the bodies] are in the coldest."

Others claimed that the bodies had been thrown down the shafts of
an old coal mine at 21st and Yale—a theory that was difficult to accept
since the mines were still operating in the spring of 1921. An amateur
historian of Greenwood named Robert Littlejohn told me that there
was a mass grave out on the Old Coyote Trail, between Tulsa and Sand
Springs. Elsewhere we heard stories about the bodies of riot victims being buried at the fairgrounds, under a sandbar near Jenks, out in the
country between Collinsville and Catoosa, along the Katy Railroad
tracks near Oneta, out near Chandler Park, near 36th and South Peoria,
and so on. All of those sites were possible. But none were very specific

erms of location, and most of the stories couldn't be traced back to a specific person who was alive in 1921.

There were, however, some exceptions.

Here are Dick's notes on a conversation with a man named Richard Gary:

> *He was 7 years old at the time of the riot. Someone came by their house and asked ("recruited") his father and a neighbor to get their guns and go to the shooting. They lived in a new house at 6th and South Yorktown Avenue. One man took a rifle and the other a shotgun and went to East Archer and Greenwood. The neighbor looked over a brick wall and was immediately shot in the neck and died. The father went home. Later the father took the family in their car to see what had happened. For some reason they drove south on Lewis and between 31st and 41st Streets they saw bodies being thrown in the ravines along the road. The paved road ended at 21st Street. A team of mules pulling a slip was used to cover the bodies. He saw at least thirty bodies of Blacks on a truck at the site. He recalled that there was trouble covering bodies because of the surface rock.*

On the one hand, the family history checked out. According to the 1921 *Tulsa City Directory,* Hugh Gary, a grocer, lived with his wife, Anna, at 556 S. Yorktown. And the details in the story made sense. On the other hand, was it reasonable to believe that Richard Gary, who was only seven years old at the time, could have concluded that the burials were made difficult because of the surface rock? I spoke with Gary as well, and found him to be credible. He did not, however, have any clear idea where the burials had taken place, while the area itself had been later developed into one of the city's wealthiest neighborhoods.

Moreover, there was no one spot along Lewis that presented itself as a likely candidate. The story may well have been true, but unless some more evidence was uncovered, there was no practical way for us to investigate it further.

There was another story, however, that offered more possibilities.

The way the cemetery workers told it was like this:

Of all the hundreds of African American men, women, and children who came to the newly renamed Rolling Oaks Memorial Gardens on Memorial Day, Monday, May 26, 1997, she was the one everyone would remember. Believed to be in her early nineties, she had a commanding, regal air about her, as if she was used to giving orders that she fully expected others to fully execute. She carried with her a distinctive, homemade walking cane fashioned out of PVC pipe and painted blue, which served, in her hands, as a pointer to indicate certain areas of the cemetery. She also used it to rap on the golf cart that a cemetery employee named John Irby was sitting in, instructing him to drive her up the hill to another part of the cemetery.

Long known as the Booker T. Washington Cemetery, and predating the riot, it had served as the burial ground of choice for many of Tulsa's African American families. John Hope Franklin's parents were buried there, as were those of hundreds of other early Greenwood residents. Located more than nine miles south and east of downtown, for much of its history, the cemetery had been surrounded by countryside. In the 1970s, white teenagers called it Sparky's, and used it as a clandestine spot to drink beer, make out, and tell ghost stories, oblivious to the fact that it was connected to an African American past. But by the 1990s, the endless southerly expansion of Tulsa's white neighborhoods, with development after development of brick homes with mansard roofs, two-car garages, and newly planted oak and Bartlett pear trees, had swept beyond it, leaving Booker T. Washington Cemetery as a Black island in a white sea.

As such, it was a most disorganized island. It had been owned and managed by a white couple for decades, and as the years went on and the caretakers grew elderly, the record keeping at the cemetery grew more and more erratic, leaving hired gravediggers to wonder whether they might encounter the remains of a previous burial when excavating a hole for a new one. The lack of accurate records concerned the new owners as well, though they also had some larger plans in mind. Looking to expand sales of burial plots to the residents of the newly established neighborhoods nearby, they had the cemetery grounds spiffed up, while a new name was selected that clearly seemed designed to appeal to a larger and more diverse demographic, aka white people. Added to this, the new owners very much wanted to know where previous burials had occurred—which was why John Irby and other employees were out in force in their golf carts, zipping from one section of the cemetery to the next in order to ask families where their loved ones, especially those without headstones, had been laid to rest.

The elderly woman with the cane, however, had a different agenda.

"Take me up there," she told Irby, pointing to a copse of trees at the south end of section three. On the way there, she had Irby slow down as she pointed out various headstones and talked about some of the families who were buried there. But once the golf cart reached the crest of the rise and the road turned to pea gravel and began to curve around to the west, she used her cane to indicate the place where a dozen or so trees had been planted—an area without any headstones. "That's where they buried the riot people," she said.

She then explained how she knew this to be true.

In 1921, her grandfather had owned a truck. Somehow, she said, it had not been destroyed during the riot. Perhaps it had been parked somewhere in the country, or maybe the white rioters couldn't conceive that a Black man could possibly own a truck and they had left it alone. Anyway, in the week or so after the riot, when African Americans began to return to where their homes and businesses had once stood, as they started to clean and sort through the ashes and charred debris, a few people found human remains. Not many, maybe five or six. The grandfather then took the remains, no doubt wrapped in blankets and tarps, out to Booker T. Washington Cemetery, along with a couple of fellows to help dig graves. And there, right where those trees are standing, was where they buried them.

The story made sense. While the Booker T. Washington Cemetery was located a long way from Greenwood, it was, first and foremost, a *Black* cemetery. This wasn't white people tossing the unidentified bodies of Black riot victims into a common grave. This was the African American community burying its own. But the account also bore with it some problems, the most important of which was the fact that John Irby couldn't remember the woman's name, and he hadn't written down her address or telephone number. So Dick and I called every survivor we knew and told them the story, hoping that small details like the grandfather with the truck, or her distinctive blue cane, might prompt someone to be able to identify her. For months, we tried to run down the identity of the mystery woman, but without any luck. So we decided to do the next best thing. Come the next Memorial Day, we'd be waiting for her.

One year later.

By seven thirty on the morning of Memorial Day, Monday, May 25, 1998, Dick and I had everything in place. A bright blue awning hovered over two collapsible tables of the sort that populate church basements and elementary school lunchrooms. On either side were two semicircles of chairs—the only ones in the entire cemetery—near which sat two large galvanized buckets filled with ice and bottles of water. On one of the aluminum tent poles holding up the awning was a sign that read:

NORTH TULSA HISTORICAL SOCIETY
TULSA COUNTY HISTORICAL SOCIETY

HISTORIC BOOKER T. WASHINGTON
CEMETERY

FAMILY REGISTRATION PROJECT

But the pièce de résistance of our plan rested in a large cut-crystal bowl that sat in the center of the other table. Inside were dozens of fresh white carnations, stemmed, wrapped in floral tape, and pierced by a hatpin, which were regularly refreshed by dozens more that were held in an ice chest beneath the table. Mary Warner, Dick's wife, had not only cut and wrapped each carnation, but she had even acquired a floral license in order to purchase them at a discount.

Come sit down and enjoy a cold bottle of water.
Sign the registry.
Tell us about your family.
And don't forget your carnation.
There was no way that we were going to miss her.

By ten o'clock that morning, as the temperature climbed into the low nineties, scores of families had already visited. Some came in vans, others in pickups or family cars, with Grandmama in the passenger seat in the front and the kids crammed in the back, laughing and talking. Some came with garden clippers and whisk brooms, others replaced sun-faded sprays of plastic flowers with brand-new ones, while the older generation told the younger ones who their people were.

Our setup was a hit from the start. Dozens of elderly African American women, often accompanied by a daughter or granddaughter, came over for a visit, a bottle of water, and a carnation. And once they realized that neither Dick nor I had anything to do with the new owners, they opened right up. Disgust over the new name—"*Rolling Oaks?* I mean, c'mon"—was usually followed by "But it does look better than it has, I'll give them that." With progress came erasure. "I think the improvements are great," wrote Evelyn Anderson in a guest book we had set out. "I wish you would have put Booker T. Washington Memorial Gardens. We Blacks need some history here." Others wanted to know why Dick and I were there. When we told them, there was both surprise and support. "For real? Here in this cemetery?"

The cemetery workers had also provided me with a walkie-talkie, just like the ones they carried as they rode about in their golf carts. Whenever one of them spotted an especially elderly person among a new set of arrivals, they would call me on the walkie-talkie. "There's a really old man that just showed up in section three, right in the middle. He's wearing a blue ball cap and a Hawaiian shirt." Or perhaps, "Section two, down the hill. Two old ladies." I'd then take off on foot for the area in question, introduce myself, and ask whether they knew anything about any riot victims being buried here at the cemetery—or anywhere else, for that matter. Almost all the time, folks said no.

Almost, but not always.

Up at the top of section two, a woman named Sarah Butler Thompson told me that her grandmother had told her that riot victims had been buried near "the big tree." But she didn't know how her grandmother knew about the graves. That part was lost.

The mystery woman never showed up.

Despite all our efforts and stratagems, the ice-cold bottles of water and the inviting chairs, the walkie-talkies and the carnations, the lady with the cane didn't come to Rolling Oaks Memorial Gardens on Memorial Day 1998. Maybe, we figured, she had passed. Or perhaps she lived in another state, and last year's visit had been a kind of farewell. Either way, as Dick and I started to pack up around eight o'clock in the fading twilight, we were both more than a little depressed. Then my walkie-talkie again crackled to life. "Scott, come to the top of section three."

It wasn't the mystery lady. Instead it was a diminutive elderly figure, dressed in a pink polo shirt, yellow pants, and a blue cap, with Jheri curls and double diamond stud earrings. Elwood Lett turned out to be a riot survivor who was on nobody's radar and had only recently moved back to Tulsa on a permanent basis. "Yeah," he said, "I heard something about those people." When the riot broke out, Lett's grandfather and a man named Billy Hudson gathered Elwood and the other children in a wagon and headed out for Nowata. "He threw blankets over us," Lett remembered, "because they were still rioting." Maybe two years after the riot, after his aunt had died, Lett had gone out to the cemetery with his grandfather to help decorate her grave. While there, the grandfather pointed out roughly the same area that the mystery woman had indicated, and told his grandson that that was where they had buried some of the riot victims. Not surprisingly, the young man found the spot to be immediately haunting. "To me, it was ghostly like," Lett said, "as if I could hear people's voices."

Talking about the riot itself, he then grew philosophical. "It's a sad kind of thing to know that they did that to the people, and to have nothing to show. Now, you take the Holocaust, they've got something to show. They got those bones, and clothing, and bodies of kids. But for the riot, they ain't got nothing to show." Elwood Lett was, of course, onto something. And while he and I would have many more conversations in the years to come, for right now, in the falling light of the cemetery, he had given a great gift. For if his grandfather was right, there was, indeed, something beneath those trees.

Something else had happened that day as well.

For more than a half century, most African American families in Tulsa had buried their loved ones at Crown Hill, a Black cemetery located on the north side. But, here, on the other side of the city on that hot and humid Memorial Day, with the temperatures climbing well past one hundred, something remarkable had occurred. The old Greenwood had once again stirred to life.

For out in the rows and sections of this cemetery, armed with garden tools and vases and flower boughs, were the direct descendants of those who had originally built the lost district. Here was a granddaughter of Loula and John Williams, who owned the Dreamland Theatre, the Williams Building, and the East End Garage. Over there were the great-grandchildren of the Vanns, a family of cooks and day laborers, porters and hotel maids who had lived and worked in pre-1921 Tulsa. In section two stood the headstone for B. C. Franklin, the attorney who had helped to defeat the city's attempted land grab of the Greenwood business district and had told his fellow citizens to start rebuilding with anything they could. And scattered about the cemetery were burial plots for families named Maxie and Washington, Vaden and Pitts, whose members had dodged the bullets and smelled the smoke and had been the targets of that white wave of hatred that had come crashing down upon them in the early hours of a June morning seventy-seven years earlier. The old Greenwood hadn't died after all. It was living and breathing in the descendants who walked the cemetery that afternoon, laid flowers on the graves of their ancestors, and signed their names in a guest book.

8

TULSA CALLING

Kelly Kurt was looking for a story.

A former member of the staff of the *Daily O'Collegian*, the student newspaper at Oklahoma State University, she had done stints at the *Tulsa World*, the *Tulsa Tribune*, and the *Times Leader* in far-off Wilkes-Barre, Pennsylvania, before landing a job with the Associated Press. The junior half of the two-person bureau, Kurt shared a cramped rented office on the sixth floor of the Tulsa World Building, right next to the telephone operator, furnished with a cast-off desk from the now defunct *Tulsa Tribune*. She was newly married and nine months shy of her thirtieth birthday, and the primary tools of her trade were a pager, a Toshiba laptop, and a Tulsa phone book. "I covered everything—crime, TU basketball, you name it," Kurt later recalled. "But as the number two person, I was looking to carve out a role for myself as a feature writer." While she often got assignments from the higher-ups, Kurt also spent time scouting for stories on her own. And in January 1999, as the countdown to the new millennium had begun and her fellow Tulsans shivered their way through the city's cold but brief winter, Kurt was again on the lookout for a scoop.

Back in 1996, she had written about the seventy-fifth anniversary of the race riot, including what turned out to be one of Don Ross's most memorable rhetorical touches. Standing in front of the about-to-be-unveiled 1921 Black Wall Street Memorial, Ross had pointed out how calls for a state or local government official to formally apologize for the riot had not been answered. Then noting how he was, as a state legislator, an official representative of the State of Oklahoma, Ross made the apology himself. "I ask you for your prayers and forgiveness," he said, "on behalf of the state of Oklahoma and the city of Tulsa." It was a brilliant bit of political theatrics. But what had happened, Kurt asked herself, since then? There had been nothing about the riot commission in the *Tulsa World* for more than a year, while the local television and radio stations had also been mum.

So Kurt called the chairman of the commission, Dr. Bob Blackburn, who was also the director of the Oklahoma Historical Society, and asked for an update. During their conversation, Blackburn mentioned not only the search for the mass graves but also some of the higher estimates of riot fatalities. Kurt was flabbergasted. "I had not heard anyone taking the three hundred number seriously until that point," she later remembered. Kelly Kurt had her story, which went out on the AP wire a couple of days later and was picked up by newspapers across the country. A second version, published in the *Daily Oklahoman* on January 30, 1999, was titled "Tulsa Race Riot Commission Searching for Mass Graves."

Mass graves. Those were words with power.

Practically overnight, the Tulsa race riot and the riot commission became national news. For Kelly Kurt's reporting unleashed what would become, over the next two years, nothing less than an avalanche of press attention to what had happened in Tulsa during the late spring of 1921. Alert production assistants and interns at the major television networks in New York took note of Kurt's AP piece and passed it on up the line as a potential story idea. Editors for daily newspapers in Los Angeles and Chicago assigned reporters to find out about what had happened in Tulsa in 1921. Film school students on both coasts tried to figure out how to scrape up enough dough to come to Oklahoma and start shooting documentaries, while riot-related book proposals began to arrive in the offices of literary agents in Manhattan. In time, not only did the nation's major media outlets run stories about the riot, but journalists from Sweden, France, Japan, and other countries came to Tulsa as well.

For the *Tulsa World*, the fact that the AP stringer in town had scooped them on the search for the mass graves was, if not a little embarrassing, then at least a compelling argument that they should at least start sending a reporter to riot commission meetings. As it turned out, they didn't have to wait long, for there was one scheduled for January 28, 1999. Moreover, Clyde Snow was to testify at the meeting. Whatever it had missed before, the *Tulsa World* was now very interested in the work of the riot commission.

Dick and I, however, sensed an opening. Why not use all the media attention as a way to give the public an opportunity, say, through a phone number that they could call, to share any knowledge they might have about where riot victims had been buried? We approached the *Tulsa World* and the *Oklahoma Eagle*, and they both agreed to help. On Friday, January 29, the *Tulsa World* included the following in their story about the commission meeting the day before:

Anyone with information about the Tulsa Race Riots or mass burial sites is asked to call either the Tulsa Historical Society at 712-9484, the Greenwood

Cultural Center at 596-1020 or the
office of Oklahoma state archaeologists at 405-325-7211. An additional search is on for sewer
workers who were working for the
city in the 1940s. Evidence exists
that the workers may have brushed
against a mass grave site near
Newblock Park while digging a
sewer line there.

Shortly thereafter, the *Oklahoma Eagle* ran a similar announce-
ment.

The calls poured in.

A woman named Virginia Styles phoned in to say that at the time of
the riot, her father was a private trash hauler who had his own wagon
and team of horses. She said that her father "was forced to haul six bodies to a hole in a low place in Oaklawn cemetery. He didn't want to do
it, but a deputy sheriff rode along with him." Alva Smith Jr. called to
say that his father, who had participated in the riot, was involved in a
shootout on a bridge during which some African Americans were killed.
The father said that some of the victims "were buried along the riverbank." Eunice McDaniel, age 88, remembered that her mother or aunt
took her down to the old Jenks bridge. A large crowd of people had
gathered there, and they were looking at the clouds of smoke over Tulsa.
"She thinks she saw one or two bodies float under the bridge," Dick
wrote in his notes. Cleo Quigley told me that in 1949, when he worked
at a millwork company near the Midland Valley Railroad tracks, a
freight agent for the railroad named Abernathy told him about a flatcar
loaded with bodies that was headed south from Pine Street. "He always

said that the bodies were laid out head-to-head on both sides and estimated that there were fifty or sixty bodies."

One after another, for nearly a week, the calls continued coming in. Most of the callers were white.

Carol Watteau, who had been a nurse intern at St. Francis Hospital in the late 1970s, spoke of a dying patient, an elderly white man, whom she had helped to care for. "He told her that he had been in the riot and had shot many Blacks," Dick wrote in his notes. "He was proud of this and said that he would do it again." Diana Aronson spoke of her father-in-law, Abraham Freed, who owned a furniture store on North Main Street. During the riot, some whites chased an African American into Freed's backyard, where they killed him. To Freed, it reminded him of pogroms in his native Latvia. Lillian Lough said that her grandmother, a Mexican immigrant who worked in a café near downtown, saw the bodies of Blacks "hanging from trees," while Lahoma Wilson said that her father, who was Cherokee, saw the bodies of African Americans who had been dragged to death behind automobiles. There was a confessional quality to many of the calls, as if they represented an unburdening of the heart.

In the end, we received 120 calls.

But one stood out from them all. It was not from a son, daughter, or grandchild remembering what a relative had told them about where the victims had been buried after the riot. Instead, it was from an eyewitness.

Clyde Joseph Eddy was the first child born in Tulsa in 1911.

"My birthday is easy to remember," he told me. "It's one, one, one, one." Tall and distinguished-looking, with snow-white hair and a carefully trimmed mustache, the former Oklahoma Tire and Supply

Company salesman was nattily attired in light brown slacks, a pale orange shirt, a striped tie, and a smart plaid trilby hat. But seventy-seven years earlier, on the evening of May 31, 1921, the then ten-year-old white youngster had gone with his parents to a program at Convention Hall, which included a school play. When his family was leaving to go home, they heard that there had been some trouble downtown. The next morning, with more rumors flying, Eddy climbed up a big pecan tree that was in the front yard of the family's home on Quaker Avenue, just off Tenth Street. "I was trying to see something," he recalled, but all he could see was some smoke. Later that day, he saw two or three airplanes. And on either June 3 or 4, Clyde Eddy saw something that he would never forget.

With his cousin Bennie, he had set out to visit an aunt who lived about a half mile to the southwest. To get to her house, Eddy would always take a shortcut through Oaklawn Cemetery. On this day, though, the two boys saw maybe a half dozen wooden crates along the southern edge of the cemetery, on what was then called Tenth Street. "Bigger and wider than a coffin," Eddy remembered. "I think one of them might have been a piano box. These crates were just lying helter-skelter." Nearby was a group of white workmen, dressed in overalls, standing near a substantial pit that had been dug into the ground, probably, he later figured, using a team of mules and a scoop. Eddy estimated that the pit, or trench, was maybe twenty feet long, eight to ten feet wide, and at least six feet deep.

Being naturally curious, he raised up the lid on one of the crates and looked in. "Inside were three bodies," he said, "all Black." He then walked over to a second crate and did the same thing. "There were at least four in that one," he recalled. "The smell was repulsive." About then, some of the men noticed Eddy and his cousin and chased them away. But the boys just walked to the other side of the wrought iron fence, right along Tenth Street. "We watched them for a while," Eddy added. "Then we walked on."

Just shy of seventy-nine years later, on a bright and windy March afternoon, Clyde Eddy is telling that same story to Bob Brooks, the Oklahoma state archaeologist, Dick Warner, and me. The four of us are standing one hundred yards or more from Reuben Everett's and Eddie Lockard's headstones, at the far eastern end of the potter's field. The trees and bushes are already in bloom, while near our feet stands a small black metal grace marker in the shape of a Scottie dog. Eddy, who again is sharply attired, in a glen plaid suit, London Fog trench coat, and wool hat, points out the spot where he says the bodies were buried. Dick and I take notes and draw crude maps. When asked how he knew for certain where the spot was, Eddy said it had to do with its relation to the front gates of the cemetery, and the proximity of the nearby sexton's house.

"Remember," he added, "I used to cut through here all the time."

"Come on in here."

The voice belonged to Elwood Lett, whom I would now always visit on my trips back to Tulsa. Invariably, whenever I'd walk into the tiny but tidy government housing apartment that he lived in, alone, off Greenwood Avenue, he'd be sitting on his sagging couch, a cigarette dangling from his small but strong fingers. We'd talk for an hour or two. Most of the time he would tell me stories of his life.

In 1940, at age twenty-two, he had moved back to Tulsa, living with his mother, stepdad, three brothers, and a sister, and working as a dispatcher for one of the African American cab companies, sending taxis, and quarts of bootleg liquor, to homes across the north side. When he filled out his draft card one year later—height 5'3", weight 125, complexion Light Brown—he was washing dishes and working as a cook's helper. Then he took off for good.

Hiring on as a cook for the Santa Fe Railway, he instead got the education of a lifetime. Working the Super Chief and the El Capitan, the luxury trains that ran between Chicago and Los Angeles, Elwood learned how to prepare oyster stew, broiled haddock, potatoes lyonnaise, smoked ox tongue sandwiches, and delicate cups of consommé for lunch, with relish trays of queen olives and watermelon cubes and mini-baskets of Ry-Krisp and melba toast on the side. For dinner he'd prepare fillets of red snapper with sauce anglaise, roast turkey with cranberry sauce, chicken à la reine, and baked sugar ham with Llewellyn sauce, all in a teeny rolling kitchen working shoulder-to-shoulder with three other guys. Come morning it would be boiled, poached, scrambled, and fried eggs, wheat cakes with maple syrup, French toast with orange marmalade, and gallons of coffee and hot tea with fresh cream and cubed sugar.

He'd cooked for GIs and movie stars, bankers and businessmen, politicians, cowboys, and families of four. After his shift ended, he'd head back to the cramped bunks that the cook staff shared with the Pullman porters and the baggage handlers. Here, there would be bull sessions and great debates, and pinochle and crap games, all washed down with half pints of Old Crow and Kentucky Gentleman. As he talked about those days, you could hear the wonder in his voice.

Elwood had crossed the Mississippi at midnight, watched the sun rise over the Great Plains, and glimpsed aspens and the Rockies in the cool Colorado rain. In Albuquerque and Gallup, New Mexico, he had seen Native American women, wearing blankets and bright-colored dresses, selling silver and turquoise jewelry and dolls made from lambswool and piñon wood. He had looked out upon the Mojave Desert by starlight, and rolled into Union Station in Los Angeles as the morning sun fell upon the breakers on the beach in Santa Monica. He'd eaten chop suey in San Francisco, listened to jazz on Central Avenue, and felt the winter wind off Lake Michigan in Chicago.

Only there was much more to Elwood than memories.

Armed with only a cheap electric iron and a spray bottle of water, he could iron a shirt better than anyone I have ever seen, before or since, with creases so perfect that they looked like origami. The highlight of his week was serving as an usher at First Baptist Church, dressed resplendently in a suit and tie. There were some things that he would talk about, and others that he wouldn't. He was an astute observer of local politics, and had an on-again, off-again opinion of Don Ross. He had no high estimate of white people in general, and was a blistering critic of American racism. He routinely dismissed my suggestions that there had been some racial progress in the past, say, forty years or so, and evinced very little hope for the future. This world, as his preacher at First Baptist would occasionally remind his flock, was not his home. Instead, Elwood looked to the Lord.

Despite it all, we got along. When I hadn't been back to Tulsa for a few weeks, he would send me letters, usually emblazoned with a "Jesus Is Lord!" return mailing address label. I started bringing him things as well. After he told me how much he missed the fresh seafood of the West Coast, I went to a local fish market in Oregon, bought ten pounds of fresh halibut, coho salmon, and wild Mexican prawns, double-wrapped it all in plastic bags and a fleece pullover, and stuffed it in my carry-on luggage for my morning flight to Tulsa. When he told me that he needed a new pair of white cotton gloves for his work as an usher, I found him a couple of pairs at a uniform store in Portland. Often cranky, sometimes falling-down funny, but always engaging, Elwood became a regular part of my life. And an impactful one as well.

He was not alone. A handful of other survivors, or relatives of survivors, had crossed over some unmarked border so that they had also become mentors. After Robert Fairchild passed away, I began a correspondence with his widow, Florence Fairchild, who was then living in Rustburg, Virginia, a small community less than a half hour's drive from Appomattox. In one of her letters, she first talked about her own experience regarding the riot, only to transition into a devastating cameo of the cost of white racism to her own family:

> *I didn't live in Tulsa, but about 60 miles away in Muskogee.*
> *I had just finished the ninth grade and it was summer so we*
> *had some free time. Soon the grown ups told us kids there*
> *had been a riot and victims who came walking with nothing.*
> *Sent us through the neighborhoods beg supplies for the*
> *victims. Guess who gave us supplies. Mostly the whites,*
> *& said come back if more is needed. Thanks again. I wasn't*
> *born in Okla. My father was killed by the night riders of the*
> *Ku Klux Klan and my mom brought us five kids to the*
> *Indian Territory. I'll keep in touch with you. Keep writing.*
> *You are a real historian. Thanks again.*
>
> *Florence Fairchild.*

Jewel Smitherman Rogers, who lived in Perris, California, outside Los Angeles, wrote to give me details about how her father, John Smitherman, an African American police officer in Tulsa, had been set up by the Klan eight months after the riot. "One day while he was on duty a man walked up to him and spat in his face for no apparent reason," Rogers wrote. "Needless to say, my Dad kicked him down." But it was also a planned action, with Smitherman's response being expected. By striking a white man, Smitherman had become a marked man, and it wasn't long before the Klan kidnapped him. "He was taken to a designated area, tied to a tree, beaten unmercifully, and had his left ear cut off, leaving only the ear lobe of the left ear," she added. "At some point there was an attempt to make him eat the portion of the ear which had been cut from his body." Stories like these only reinforced the fact that the violence that African Americans faced in Tulsa—and throughout the country—hardly ended with the riot.

As far as Kinney Booker was concerned, the threat of foul play was far from gone. The son of a chauffeur for a rich white oilman, Booker was eight years old in 1921. While he didn't have many memories of the riot, one stood out. As he fled the family home on North Frankfort the morning of June 1 amid the smoke and flames, his sister turned to him and asked, "Is the whole world on fire?" Later a music teacher and school band director, Booker had spent practically his entire life working in segregated schools and living in segregated neighborhoods, first in rural Oklahoma and Louisiana, then in Southern California. When he returned to Tulsa in his eighties, after a failed romance had drained him of most of his savings, he was angry, broke, and largely alone.

And fearful. The ways in which the civil rights movement had inspired and changed the lives of millions of African Americans had passed Kinney by—all the more so once he came back to Tulsa. One time, when I took him to lunch at a breakfast place on the east side of town, he stared in disbelief at an interracial couple sitting in a nearby booth. When I told Kinney's riot story to Brent Staples of the *New York Times*, he asked photographer Fred Conrad to shoot a portrait of Kinney. He did, but as the publication date for Staples's article neared, Kinney began to fret. "What if they come after me?" he asked. "Or my family?" The scars from the riot were far from healed.

But it was George Monroe who influenced me the most, especially on the subject of reparations. To my way of thinking, the whole point of both the riot commission and the search for the graves of the riot dead had been to try and create a way for the city to have a long-needed reckoning with its past. Initially, to me, this wasn't primarily about money. It was about wrestling with uncomfortable truths, facing up to the worst demons in our past, and trying to come to a new understanding about why things were the way they were today and, armed with that knowledge, having a better feel for where we needed, as a city and a nation, to go.

In my mind, the payments that the Federal Republic of Germany had made to the new nation of Israel after World War II neither atoned for the horrors of the Holocaust nor greatly contributed to the moral reawakening that the mass murders had necessitated. That came about through stories—Elie Wiesel's *Night*, films like *Night and Fog* and *Shoah,* and, of course, *The Diary of Anne Frank*. And it had been done through photographs and, especially, objects. The piles of children's shoes, eyeglasses, suitcases, toothbrushes, and prayer shawls at the former concentration camps would bring tears for decades. My hometown, I believed, needed to find a way to its own reckoning, and its own reawakening. An undue focus on money, I initially felt, could derail a deeply needed reappraisal of its turbulent past.

George Monroe convinced me otherwise. Even a symbolic payment, he believed, would be of real value if it came from either the city or the white community. "Just a little something," he would say, something that would acknowledge what had happened to his mom and dad, and all the others who had suffered from the riot, losing their homes, their businesses, and their loved ones. "Just a little." He also believed there wasn't a snowball's chance in hell that this would ever happen. "I've worked with those people all my life," he said. "And they're not ever going to pay one red cent of reparations." Amley and I disagreed and bet George ten dollars each that reparations would be paid. We all shook on it, with George adding, "You can kiss that money goodbye."

. . .

Tensions, meanwhile, had been slowly rising on the riot commission.

Some were a result of political differences. Others grew out of the increasing attention by the national media. As a rule, most newspaper and magazine journalists, as well as television news producers, tended to focus their interviews on riot survivors, Don Ross, and, for a historical perspective, usually either John Hope Franklin, commission chair Bob Blackburn, or me. Usually left out of the mix were the commissioners themselves, and for some, that stung. "When are the local people going to get to talk?" commission member Eddie Faye Gates asked. And for some, particularly those who were conspiracy-minded, their frustration was further fueled by a belief that their voices were deliberately being shut out and their interpretations unheard.

In truth, the feeling that the riot was not a riot at all but a pre-planned land grab by rich white Tulsans had a long heritage in Greenwood. In the early 1990s, however, it had gotten a considerable boost in the form of a book titled *Black Wallstreet,* by Jay Jay Wilson and Ron Wallace. In essence a novel, the book also contained passages that read like history. According to the authors, not only had it been "New York's Financial District" that had named Greenwood "the Black Wallstreet of America," but the community was "totally self-sufficient and operated independently of the white population of Tulsa." Indeed, Wilson and Wallace added:

> White businessmen would periodically come over into Black Wallstreet to borrow money from these wealthy blacks. Several black millionaires lived there during this time; six owned private airplanes in 1921!

The problem was that there weren't *any* African American million-aires in Tulsa in 1921. Nor did any Black Tulsans own airplanes before the riot.

But the authors were only getting warmed up. In their telling, the destruction of Greenwood was the direct result of a plot by the Ku Klux Klan and "high government officials" to destroy a unique Black eco-nomic model of success. In a later edition of the book, Jay Jay Wilson described the harrowing conditions under which *Black Wallstreet* had been researched and written. "The authors experienced incredibly hard times to get this story out," he wrote. "Their lives were threatened, they were followed, harassed, their phones were tapped; books were stolen—all done in an effort to stop this information from reaching the masses."

Wilson and Wallace had, in fact, tapped into a strong emotional current that ran through African American communities nationwide. For despite the near-unanimous support for the civil rights movement in the 1960s, there was no question that desegregation, along with ur-ban renewal and the restructuring of the American economy, had helped to put the nail in the coffin for numerous African American busi-ness districts that had thrived during segregation. Where, some won-dered, were all the Black-owned movie theaters, restaurants, hotels, and nightclubs that used to flourish in Detroit and Durham, Cleveland and St. Louis, Atlanta and Chicago? Why did so many Black professionals no longer live in the community? In Greenwood, those yearnings were potent and real. Why don't we have as many African American doctors and grocery stores as our forebears did?

Black Wallstreet offered a reason why. It may not have been a his-torically accurate one, but it more than made up for it in emotional terms. By transforming Greenwood into a fabulously wealthy and com-pletely separate enclave, kind of like a Wakanda before there was a Wakanda, the authors also built a rationale for the race riot. Who needed an incident in an elevator, or even the courageous seventy-five

African American war veterans trying to stop a lynching, when one could just go with white avarice and greed instead?

And while I didn't know it yet, the scholars were already on a collision course with the commission itself.

Out in the field, meanwhile, things had gone much better.

For three blisteringly hot days in July, state archaeologist Bob Brooks was back in Tulsa, this time accompanied by two technicians and a pulseEKKO 1000, a ground-penetrating radar unit. This state-of-the-art technology had been used, with success, by the petroleum industry and on some archaeological investigations, particularly in desert locations. Now we were about to see if the cutting-edge machine might also pick up on the remains of riot victims buried more than three-quarters of a century earlier. Dick and I, of course, were there, while Clyde Snow also drove over from Norman. And despite the fact that we wouldn't know the results until more than a week later, after Brooks and the team from Archaeo-Physics were able to crunch the data, it all felt momentous.

The pulseEKKO 1000 looked a bit like an elongated homemade lawn mower, though one without a cutting blade and six-horsepower engine. The two techs would slowly push it back and forth across the areas we'd designated as potential grave sites, as the machine silently collected data. At Oaklawn and Rolling Oaks, the work proceeded without any major issues, save for the need to maneuver the unit around trees and occasional headstones. At Oaklawn, we surveyed some fairly large areas, including virtually the entire southwestern corner of the cemetery, as well as the site that Clyde Eddy had indicated. At Rolling Oaks, our initial focus was on the headstone-free, tree-lined area that both the mystery woman and Elwood Lett had indicated as the location where riot victims had been buried. But we also surveyed some adjacent areas, particularly a large open field nearby, where Bob Brooks had seen signs of possible excavation.

At Newblock Park, however, we ran into trouble from the beginning. For even though from the street the park looked exactly like what it was, namely an underutilized parcel of public land, Newblock was crisscrossed by twentieth-century urban infrastructure. Sewer and water lines, as well as fiber-optic cables, snaked beneath the surface, while high-power lines floated above our heads. As a result, there was so much additional "noise" that the ground-penetrating radar operators worried that their readings would be hopelessly compromised. Undaunted, Bob Brooks then pulled out a probe, an eight-foot-long, tempered-steel rod, maybe a quarter of an inch thick. By feel alone, a skilled operator can shove a probe several feet into the ground and determine whether it hits a rock, a slab of wood, or a piece of bone. But bad luck lingered here as well. The ground was so dry and hard that for the first time in decades of fieldwork, Brooks broke the probe.

And with that, the survey ended. Brooks and the technicians packed up their trucks and started in on the two-hour drive back to Norman. Now there was nothing to do but wait.

The results were mixed.

Despite all the interference from buried sewer and utility lines, an area of disturbed response was detected at Newblock Park that, Bob Brooks and University of Oklahoma geophysicist Alan Witten later wrote, "might represent the walls of a shallow excavation (or pit)." At Rolling Oaks, another area of disturbed soil, measuring approximately twenty feet by nine feet, was picked up by the ground-penetrating radar that, Brooks and Witten wrote could, "potentially represent a pit such as one might find with a mass grave." The language was couched in uncertainty, but the possibility of riot victims being buried in both locations was alive and well.

It was the data from Oaklawn, however, that proved to be the most surprising. With some exceptions, practically the entire African American section of the potter's field, and especially the long-suspicious southwest corner, revealed nothing that resembled any kind of a trench or pit, or even, say, a series of contiguous individual graves that might fit with the one hundred or so graves described by Walter White. There were, however, some exceptions.

"We found a couple of locations," Bob Brooks told a reporter for the *Tulsa World*, "that are interesting in terms that there is something there. At this point we can't say exactly what." Moreover, an anomaly was discovered near where Clyde Eddy had indicated that he saw the trench and the large wooden crates with the bodies inside. Nothing was definitive, but so far, the oral traditions, the testimony by Elwood Lett and the others, as well as the written documents that Dick Warner had unearthed were holding up. While we weren't there yet, there was every reason to believe that the search for the dead of the 1921 Tulsa riot was on the verge of entering new territory. The next step, it seemed, would be to start digging.

REPARATIONS AND REPRISALS

Tonight we are going to report on a story that is almost eighty years old, but will come as news to most Americans as, frankly, it did to us." The speaker, dressed in an elegant striped gray suit, blue shirt, and red tie, was silver-haired Bob Simon, veteran newsman and frequent correspondent on CBS's hit television program *60 Minutes*. "A state commission has begun investigating the riot and is already raising tough questions about what today's citizens owe yesterday's victims." Two weeks before Thanksgiving, on November 9, 1999, millions of television viewers across America were about to watch their first primer on what had happened in Tulsa in 1921.

The segment, titled "Tulsa Burning," was a fourteen-minute tour de force. The producers, Mike Rosenbaum and Jill Landes, not only gave a detailed account of the riot but also covered what was going on at the moment, including both the search for the graves and the rising debate over reparations. Survivors George Monroe, Kinney Booker, and Veneice Sims gave powerful, riveting testimony about what had happened to them during the riot, and there were cameos by Clyde

Eddy, commission member Eddie Faye Gates, and me. A white Republican state representative, Bill Graves, who had opposed the creation of the commission, spoke out against reparations. "The sons don't pay for the sins of the fathers," he said. "They pay for only their own sins."

But the star of the program was the telegenic Don Ross, a master of dramatic timing. His was the testimony that millions of viewers from coast to coast looked up from their dinners to hear. No stranger to the power of a well-turned phrase—regardless of historical accuracy—at one point Ross even claimed that on May 31, the first night of the riot, African Americans had the clear upper hand. "We were winning!" he declared. "Only till they brought airplanes in, and dropped bombs and firebombs, and brought the National Guard in, could they subdue my people." Near the end of the program, Ross also staked out some territory.

> BOB SIMON: Don Ross says he doesn't need a memorial. He's already got one. His anger.

> DON ROSS: I feel, strongly, if I'm ever satisfied with whatever we do, that I will let down some people who educated me in my life. And who *died* angry. I am their living memorial. My anger is.

The riot had hit prime time. And it was about to hit some nerves.

Less than two weeks after the *60 Minutes* story aired, the riot commission approved our plan to do an excavation at the Clyde Eddy site at Oaklawn Cemetery. "We are convinced what we have found is a mass burial site," commission chair Bob Blackburn was quoted as saying in the *Daily Oklahoman*. Bob Brooks, the state archaeologist, was a bit more circumspect, stating that a group of vertical walls detected by the ground-penetrating radar might be the sides of the crates that held the bodies of riot victims. Clyde Snow would supervise the testing of any human remains that the excavation might uncover, including determining the age and cause of death of victims. Buttons, coins, bullets, and any other artifacts found with the remains, he added, could also serve as vital clues. "Once they find the grave, we will begin the excavation," Snow said. But he added that there was one clue that would be more powerful than any of the others. "The bones are always the best and last witness to history."

At the same meeting, the commission's subcommittee on reparations delivered its recommendations. At the top of the list were five hundred endowed college scholarships for north Tulsa youth, and, much more significantly, direct reparations to be paid to riot survivors, not to exceed $150,000 per family. The overall cost of the eight-point plan was estimated, at minimum, to be $33 million. Reactions were immediate. Robert Milacek, one of the state legislators on the commission, gave a grim assessment of the future of the eight-point plan. "If this is presented to the legislature, it is unlikely to get much support," he said. "People are going to say, 'If we do this for Tulsa, where does it stop?' What about the Mennonites whose homes were burned during World War II? And the American Indians? And we could go on forever." There was dissension from one wing of the commission as well. "Commission members Eddie Faye Gates and Vivian Clark," reported Randy Krehbiel in the *Tulsa World,* "said they believed that survivors and victims of the riot did not get high enough priority in the proposal."

None of this, however, came close to the reactions that appeared in the *World*'s Letters to the Editor feature. Here's a sampling:

> This is the most ridiculous thing I have seen in Tulsa in years. If this city or this state has to pay one dime to anybody in reparations for something that happened 75 years ago, it will be the most divisive thing that has ever happened as far as race relations in this state. I am appalled.

I am calling about the race riot reparations. I am Cherokee In-
dian. Do you feel like I should get my land back?

The Tulsa Race Riot Commission has shown the true reason for
forming the commission. It is not to gain recognition for a crime
against the black community. It's to see how much money they
can bilk from the hard-working people of Oklahoma.

If my state senator or representative falls for this scam, he will
never again receive a vote from me.

While there were a handful of letters that supported reparations,
most of the letters fell in line with what polling data revealed. A December poll sponsored by the *Tulsa World* revealed that 57 percent of the
state's citizens opposed reparations. In Tulsa, the figure was even
higher. There it topped 62 percent. Supporters on the commission, however, were defiant. "To me, it's a matter of conscience," Eddie Faye
Gates told a reporter for the *Dallas Morning News,* dismissing the notion that paying reparations to a small group of survivors would create
a large financial burden. "It's not a big thing," she added. "There's only
74 of those people. It's not like the billions paid to Holocaust victims or
millions to Japanese internees."

Perhaps. But that was also a poor way to try and sell the concept of
reparations for African American survivors in a state dominated by
white conservatives. The successful effort to win reparations for Japanese Americans whose property had been wrongfully seized, and who
had been sent to internment camps during the racist hysteria following
the attack on Pearl Harbor, had been a well-funded campaign. But its
architects had also crafted a sophisticated appeal to win white support
by focusing on the patriotism and sacrifice of Japanese American soldiers during World War II, as well as on the experiences of families in
the camps. By highlighting sacrifice—the all–Japanese American 442nd
Infantry Regiment, which fought in Italy, France, and Germany, was

the most decorated US military unit during the war—and unfairness, they hit upon themes that could resonate across a broad spectrum of the public. Whether such a message could be successfully crafted on behalf of *African American* victims of injustice was another question in white-dominated America. But what was certain was that the proponents of reparations for Tulsa riot survivors had neither money nor, in most cases, extensive political experience.

Nonetheless, they made sure that their voices were heard.

And on Friday, February 4, 2000, the riot commission voted in favor of reparations. Payments to survivors and descendants were listed as the top priorities, followed by a scholarship fund, tax incentives for the Greenwood business district, and the construction of a riot memorial. The 7-to-4 vote wasn't just a cannon shot. It was also national news. PANEL RECOMMENDS REPARATIONS IN LONG-IGNORED TULSA RACE RIOT, read the headline in the next day's *New York Times,* where it landed above the crease on the front page. The naysayers, meanwhile, had their voices heard as well. State Senator Milacek, according to the *Tulsa World,* said that "direct payments would have virtually no chance of winning the Legislature's approval."

Don Ross, meanwhile, seemed undaunted. "They told me I couldn't take down the Confederate flag over the Capitol," he said. "But the legislature changed its attitude. They told me I couldn't pass a Martin Luther King holiday, but the legislature changed its attitude." Three days later, appearing on *ABC News Nightline,* Ross debated reparations with Representative Bill Graves, a prominent Republican legislator. "If he signs on," Ross said, referring to his colleague, "it's a done deal." Beneath the surface, however, a lot more was going on.

For starters, all the media attention given to the riot was raising blood pressure in parts of the white community. "It used to be if you'd travel out of state somewhere and told people that you were from Tulsa," the neighbor of a friend told me one afternoon, "they'd ask about Indians, or say, 'Isn't that where Garth Brooks is from?' Now they say, 'Isn't that where they had that terrible riot?'" When the first calls came in to the Tulsa Historical Society following the news that a search was on for the graves of riot victims, some folks weren't calling to offer any information. Instead, they phoned in to complain. Mike, a thirty-nine-year-old white male, left a message on the answering machine saying that the riot was a dark part of Tulsa's history and that the commission should leave it alone. "You are stirring up memories about something that doesn't need to be discussed anymore." Another caller claimed that the work of the commission was "self-serving," and that the real intent of all the historical research was merely to sell books.

Indeed, one local white history buff, an acquaintance of Dick's named Bill O'Brien, was so incensed at all the press attention given to the riot that he started writing his own book. "Those now trying to sensationalize what happened have chosen to ignore all actions by the militant blacks who started the race war," O'Brien wrote. "In addition to television, derogatory articles are being published through magazines, newspapers and they saturate the internet. The damage to Tulsa's future economic development, tourism, convention trade and credibility will adversely reflect on the lives of every citizen living in the greater Tulsa market for years to come."

There were rumblings from city hall as well. Mayor Susan Savage had straddled the fence when it came to the question of reparations. In a private meeting with commission members in her office, she had indicated her openness to the idea, but avoided the subject in public. There was no doubt, however, that Savage was starting to feel the heat from disgruntled white citizens—the "Who will speak for us?" crowd, in Bill O'Brien's words. Not long thereafter, Bob Brooks, Dick, and I started hearing about "concerns" of the city regarding the planned excavation at Oaklawn.

The truth was that the search for the graves, the call for reparations, and all the national media attention given to the riot had laid bare the simple fact that on matters of race, Tulsa was still a divided city. By bringing these matters not only to the front page of the newspaper but also to prime-time television, deeply held emotions and opinions started to emerge into the light of public discourse. And as they did, it soon became clear that there was plenty of dissatisfaction among the ranks of the riot commission as well.

On the same day the vote took place in favor of reparations, the conspiracy-minded wing of the riot commission, calling themselves the Investigative Subcommittee, delivered their own preliminary findings. "The 'Tulsa riot' was not a riot," read their report. "It was a well-planned ouster of the Tulsa Natives from their stomping grounds by grafters who saw the advantage of making the lands owned by the Tulsa Blacks in the Greenwood area into a commercial district." There was more. Dick Rowland, they claimed, wasn't even in Tulsa on May 31. Instead, he had been taken "to Kansas City, Missouri, to stay with some of Sarah's relatives"—Sarah, as in Sarah Page. It may have been an emotionally satisfying interpretation, but it was unsupported by the available historical evidence.

More important, however, it was a sign of a growing rift between the scholars and certain members of the commission. Clyde Snow, with Dick's help, had been working on a list of *confirmed* dead from the riot. This did not mean every person Snow believed had been killed. Rather, it was a listing of named and unnamed individuals for whom we had been able to find a death certificate, funeral home or cemetery records, or other contemporary written evidence, so far, that showed they died as a result of wounds sustained during the riot. But when Snow presented his preliminary findings, which featured twenty-six African American men and thirteen white males, some commissioners were upset that there were so many whites listed. "Perhaps the commission can let us know," Snow snapped back, "what the politically correct ratio of black to white deaths is."

Don Ross, meanwhile, had begun to talk less about reparations and more about creating a riot memorial in a park off Greenwood that would feature, he said, "the largest monument depicting African American history in the world."

The rift between the scholars and the riot commission eventually developed into a pitched battle. John Hope Franklin and I had agreed to edit and helped to write a fully researched and footnoted report for the commission, which we were nearly finished with. I had already written a longish account of the riot, while individual chapters on riot fatalities, African American property loss, the use of airplanes during the riot, and our geophysical surveys at the various suspected grave sites around town were being written by Clyde Snow, Bob Brooks, Lesley Rankin-Hill, Phoebe Stubblefield, Larry O'Dell, Alfred Brophy, and other professionals. In other words, as with other governmental commissions, we would deliver our report to the riot commission. Hopefully, our "expert testimony" would help them as they made their final recommendations. In reality, however, they could accept it, reject it, publicize it, or bury it. The one thing they could not do is change our words.

Only this wasn't good enough for the new chair of the commission and his allies. Instead, I was informed, the riot commission would have the right to rewrite *anything* that we delivered. To me and the other scholars, whose names would appear next to our work, this was simply unacceptable. So we fought back, threatening, among other things, to release our report directly to the public at large. In the end, after Franklin had told the new chair in no uncertain terms that the words of our report were not to be altered, the other side blinked. We had won.

Then we lost.

Angered by the fact that the scholars had retained control over our report, the riot commission shut down the search for the graves of the victims of the riot, including the planned excavation at Oaklawn. "Acting on the recommendations of state Rep. Don Ross, D-Tulsa, and Commissioner Eddie Faye Gates," Randy Krehbiel wrote in the *Tulsa World* on June 30, 2000, "the panel voted Thursday to permanently shelve the project unless compelling new evidence is found." Ross said, "I'm not comfortable with Oaklawn as a mass burial site." While pointing out that it was a matter of record that African American riot victims were buried at Oaklawn, Krehbiel wrote, "So, Ross said, finding unidentified blacks would add to the commission's work, while not finding them might damage its credibility." There may have been other reasons as well. But the uncomfortable truth of the matter was that it was the riot commission that stopped the search for the graves. A couple of days later, the city followed suit. The search was over.

Three months later, I hand-delivered three copies of the scholars' report, *The Tulsa Race Riot: A Scientific, Historical, and Legal Analysis*, to the chair of the riot commission. Compiled and edited by John Hope Franklin and me, and running to 284 pages, it was the most comprehensive study of an act of racial violence in the United States prepared for a governmental commission in at least thirty years. The American Library Association would name it one of the most significant government documents issued worldwide that year. Nearly twenty years later, Brent Staples, one of the guiding hands of the 1619 Project at the *New York Times*, had this to say: "You guys did a wonderful job on the original riot report. Reading it (again) fills me with admiration—including the full extent of your candor."

As far as the riot commission was concerned, however, the scholars were now fully personae non gratae. Not only would we not be invited to attend the official delivery of the report at the state capitol, but the commission had gone ahead and hired a new historian to craft its own preface to our report, a Tulsa resident named Danney Goble. But even that move did not entirely satisfy the conspiracy-minded commissioners, as Goble ended up defending the scholars and our findings in his own carefully crafted introduction.

And then it was over. Before the floodlights of the press, members of the riot commission delivered their findings and recommendations to the governor and the state legislature. These were taken under advisement, and after committee markup and debate, including an impassioned call for reparations by Don Ross on the floor of the legislature, in June 2001, the governor signed the 1921 Tulsa Race Riot Reconciliation Act.

It included no reparations or payments of any kind for survivors.

John Hope Franklin called it "scandalous." Riot commission member Currie Ballard was incensed that the state government wouldn't even give the one hundred or so survivors "$10,000, or whatever token amount" for the nightmare that they had endured. Instead, the State of Oklahoma gave each of the survivors a gold-plated medallion that hung from a red, white, and blue ribbon.

"I had heard about you on television," said the brief note that arrived in George Monroe's mailbox one day, "and I was saddened by what had happened to you. My family too had suffered a great wrong. And so please accept this small token." Inside the handwritten letter, sent from back east, was a check for one hundred dollars. "Well, I'll be," George said. "Can you imagine that?" Then he looked at me. "You still haven't won the bet," he reminded me, then broke out into a laugh.

By the summer of 2001, there had been less and less to laugh about at George's house on East Young Place. Amley still came over to hold court in the Spin Room, while Patricia now had one of their two daughters, either Amecia or Latrecia, walk over with a warm dinner plate every night. Sometimes it would be fried chicken, steak, or fish, usually accompanied by greens, corn, broccoli, or mashed potatoes. "His preference was for soft foods because of his dentures," Patricia remembered. "On holidays I would send him cakes or pies. Sweet tea would be his drink, but most of the time he had his own." Lovingly wrapped in foil, with a napkin and plastic fork and knife, the dinner plates were often the only food that George would eat.

He was also losing weight and losing strength. Once-easy chores like keeping the branches of the sweet gum trees in his yard trimmed at least six feet off the ground—"I like to be able to see if anyone comes onto my property"—had grown taxing. Often when I pulled up into his driveway for a visit, he'd be sitting alone in a chair on the porch. And even on warm afternoons he'd be wearing a hat and a faded corduroy jacket. Then a smile would bust out on his face and with a twinkle in his eye he'd say how good it was to see me.

There was no question, however, that I got the better end of the bargain. For George Monroe taught me more than I could ever repay him. Like W. D. Williams and Elwood Lett, Jewel Smitherman Rogers and Robert and Florence Fairchild, Kinney Booker and John Hope Franklin, he was a member of a generation that had lived more life, and experienced more changes, than almost anyone I had ever met. Born during segregation, they had come of age during it as well, getting their first jobs, becoming parents, and navigating American life during the age of Jim Crow. In their forties and fifties, they had been in awe of the courage and brilliance of the young men and women of the civil rights movement, and seen their children and grandchildren break barriers of their own. Their lives had spanned horses, wagons, and kerosene lamps, as well as television, computers, and men walking on the moon.

But what George really gave me was a model of how to live. Though he had experienced a lifetime of tragedy, including burying his wife and two of his sons, that went far beyond the events of the riot, he was not consumed by hate, crippled by rage, or burdened by self-pity. He had no shortage of strong opinions, but he also knew how to smile, how to laugh, and how not to take himself too seriously. He had worked hard all his life, yet he had never found work to be a burden. His secret? "Find out what you like to do," he'd tell me, "and do that. It's that simple."

He also loved to joke, and to rib me whenever possible. A few weeks after he had met my wife, Betsy—whom he hit it off with immediately—for the first time on a visit to Tulsa, he sent me a postcard of a rainbow framed by a pair of Hawaiian palm trees. "Thanks for the birthday card," he wrote in his scrawly handwriting, "and say hello to Mrs. Ellsworth. Personally I don't know why she picked somebody like you. It wasn't for looks. She could have done much better."

But George Monroe also had a secret.

And another hole in his heart.

The photograph was of a little girl.

She was maybe one and a half years old. She was wearing a white knit dress and Mary Janes with ankle socks, and she was smiling at the camera with her left hand placed over her heart. On the back of the photograph, the girl's mother had written, TO MY DARLING DADDY, HOPING YOU'LL NEVER FORGET. SO UNTIL I'M OLD ENOUGH, BYE BYE. ALL MY

LOVE, YOUR DARLING SUSAN. XXXXXXXX One afternoon, sitting in the
Spin Room, George handed me the picture. Then he told me the story
behind it.

It went like this:

In 1943 or early 1944, when he was in the US Army, George had
been stationed with his unit in a rural outpost in Staffordshire, England. While there, he met an Englishwoman who lived in Cannock, a
colliery town in the flatlands north of Birmingham. Her name was Iris
Hickinbotham, and she lived with her five-year-old son. Her husband,
a British soldier, was fighting overseas. George and Iris fell in love, and
when George shipped out to fight in France right after D-Day, Iris was
pregnant. She then gave birth to a daughter, whom she named Susan.
Remarkably, when Iris's husband came back home at the end of the war
and learned of his wife's infidelity, he not only forgave her, he agreed
to raise Susan as his own. And because the husband had a dark complexion, strangers had no trouble believing that little Susie was his
daughter.

Of course, George and Iris knew otherwise, and for maybe two
years they kept up a correspondence with each other. Iris secreted away
a photograph of George from the *Oklahoma Eagle*, from when he ran
his sandwich shop. And when Susan was about a year and a half old,
she mailed George a photograph of their little girl. But maintaining the
correspondence was too difficult, especially after George got married in
1948. The letters stopped.

Only George had not forgotten his "little Susie."

"I haven't done right by her," he told me.

So I reached out to Ian Potts, a London-based BBC journalist who
had done a story about the riot. I explained who George was, and
that he was trying, for honorable reasons, to track down the English

daughter he had fathered while stationed in Britain during the war. "He'd like to send her some money," I said. Ian then found a man named Ken Brewster who ran a missing-persons bureau in London and did that kind of detective work. So right before Christmas in 2000, I hired Ken, told him everything I knew, and crossed my fingers. Not wanting to get his hopes up too much, I casually mentioned to George that I had contacted some people in England who were going to see if they could find Susan.

"That," he said, "would be the best thing that could ever happen to me."

Eight months later, Ken found her.

FROM: BrewsterInt@cs.com
DATE: Sun, 26 Aug 2001 10:00:59 EDT
SUBJECT: George M.
TO: Betsy.Ellsworth@reed.edu
CC: Ian.Potts@bbc.co.uk

Hi Scott

It was nice speaking with you and I wanted to report that Susan has received the photograph from us and we have spoken on the phone. As suspected, she was totally unaware of the matter and in fact, since Iris's husband was olive skinned the circumstances of her origin were never questioned. She tells me that she was very close to her "father" and was very proud to share his skin colouring.

Susan tells us that as a consequence of our letter and sending the photograph she spoke to her late mother's relatives. I now know that Iris died a couple of years ago, and when pressed admitted that the man she knew as father was not so, and sadly her brother

Terry and other family members were aware of this but chose not to tell her.

Susan has sent me a photograph found amongst her late mother's papers and it is thought that this could be George M. There is also a photograph of Iris holding Susan as a baby and a further photograph of Susan taken, I think, prior to the one you provided, most likely taken late 1945. We also have a newspaper cutting of Susan taken in 1970/71 when she was entered for a beauty contest. Susan has asked me to get these to George M. and to say that although she is much saddened that her mother did not tell her the truth, she is very excited and looking forward to hearing from George.

Please let me know where to send the photographs.

Scott, I hope all this makes sense and please get back to me if you need more Information or any assistance with this matter.

Sincerely
Ken
BREWSTER INTERNATIONAL, LONDON

Attached to the email was a scan of the same photograph of George that had appeared in the *Oklahoma Eagle* in the advertisement for his sandwich shop.

The email came too late. George had died three days earlier.

The funeral was on a Thursday. The weather, for the end of August, already had a touch of fall. The morning was wet and overcast, with little squalls of rain blowing in from the west through the headstones at Crown Hill Cemetery. George Monroe had survived the murder and mayhem of that terrible spring night in 1921, and seventy-five years had brought the immediacy of that event to the world. Newspaper readers and television viewers in New York and Los Angeles, London and Geneva, Paris and Tokyo had all been touched by the little boy whose fingers had been stepped on while he hid with his sister beneath their parents' bed. There had never been a better or more powerful spokesperson for the horrors of the riot. And it had been George who had encouraged the search for the graves and, despite his pessimism on the matter, had fully supported reparations. But that was not all he was. For those who gathered in the small chapel that morning, George had been a brother, a father, a granddad, a neighbor, a friend.

After the brief graveside ceremony had ended and the closed casket had been lowered into the ground, Amley and I lingered for a few minutes, while the others said their goodbyes, climbed into their cars, and drove away. As soon as it was just the two of us, we walked over to the grave, which the gravediggers wouldn't fill in until later that afternoon. Then, one by one, we each dropped ten new one-dollar coins into the wet earth alongside the casket and walked away in the light, on-and-off rain.

BOOK THREE

THE STEPS TO NOWHERE

ere is a traveler's tip. A small bit of inside information.

Along the southern face of Standpipe Hill, just west of Martin Luther King Jr. Boulevard, a visitor to Tulsa today can see a curious set of architectural remnants. They are a series of concrete steps, some with gently sloping sidewalls, of the type that one might see as part of a walkway leading up to the front door of a house. Some have five steps, others eight, and at least one has ten. A few are connected to knee-high concrete retaining walls that flare out perpendicularly. The staircases are strewn about in more-or-less level rows. Created by cement masons using wooden forms to block out the steps and finishing trowels to smooth the wet concrete, the steps have stood the test of time. They are as safe to walk up and down today as they might have been eight decades earlier.

Only the houses they once led to are completely gone.

Instead, there are only grass and overgrown clumps of trees, oaks and elms and an occasional mimosa, leading all the way up to the treeless, grass-covered summit of Standpipe Hill. The area has the feel of an archaeological site, which indeed it is. If the ruins of an ancient temple or a sacked cathedral were to suddenly appear just over the horizon, you would not be at all surprised. For nowhere are there any other obvious traces of the people who once lived here, the lives they led, and the dreams and aspirations that they once held on to. All that is left is the sturdy concrete handiwork of some long-forgotten cement masons.

Locals call them the Steps to Nowhere.

And if there was ever a fitting metaphor for what happened to Greenwood after the riot, these are it.

Hard as it may be to believe, Greenwood came back.

Rather than perish forever because of the riot, or reemerge as only a shadow of itself, Tulsa's Black district eventually came back as vibrant as ever. Despite the murderous intentions of thousands of its fellow white citizens, Greenwood stubbornly refused to die.

A nearly exact copy of the Williams Building, where John Williams had scared off the white rioters on the night of May 31, 1921, with a .30-30 rifle and a repeating shotgun, rose up at the corner of Greenwood and Archer within two years' time. Caver's French Dry Cleaners, which had been torched the next morning, returned in even fuller glory, this time with state-of-the-art machinery and two delivery trucks. Tulsa's African American merchants harnessed ingenuity and elbow grease, and made miracles out of charred bricks and ashes. One by one, lot by lot, business by business, year by year, they fought their way back. By the 1940s, Greenwood's commercial district was even bigger than before.

Call it Greenwood 2.0.

Not all of the businesses, of course, made it. J. B. Stradford, facing arrest, took off for Chicago, and his famed fifty-four-room hotel was never rebuilt. But by 1941, Greenwood could boast of the Hotel Small, with *seventy-seven* rooms, a dining service, and a telephone in every suite. Loula Williams didn't resurrect her confectionery. She never got over the massacre and died before the decade was up. But there was now a Williams Drug Company, one of three African American pharmacies in the district. "Values Today and Everyday," ran an advertisement in the *Oklahoma Eagle*, "Phone 3-6034." And while many of the old, pre-1921 restaurants did not survive the decade ahead, others rose up to take their places, including coffee shops, lunchrooms, sandwich bars, and sit-down dining establishments. FINE CHILI—DELICIOUS COFFEE—HOME MADE PIES—ICE CREAM were available from ten A.M. to two A.M., six days a week, at Art's Chili Parlor at 110 N. Greenwood, while out on North Lewis, customers were drawn to the mouthwatering aroma of ribs, brisket, and hot links at Latimer's One-Stop Barbecue. And you could fill up on chicken, steaks, and Louisiana gumbo at Tan's Place.

Only Greenwood's businesses did not end there. At Cannon's Dry Goods, shoppers could purchase everything from cosmetics and school supplies to candy and hosiery. Do-it-yourself-oriented homeowners could buy wiring, insulation, and conduit boxes at the Tate Electric Company, while sittings for wedding photos and senior class portraits could be had at the Potts Photo Studios on Archer. You could pick up the latest 78 rpm records by Jay McShann, Helen Humes, and Billy Eckstine at Berry's Radio Service, and you could catch a live show by Greenwood's own Ernie Fields and His Orchestra and other national acts at the Down Beat Ballroom at 120½ N. Greenwood. And scattered throughout the district were beauticians and barbers, shoe repair shops and clothing stores, and the offices of doctors, lawyers, and real estate salesmen. For folks to get around, Greenwood had its own Black-owned bus line, run by Simon Berry Sr., who also owned an airplane.

The churches took longer to come back. As late as two decades after the riot, the women's circle at Vernon AME Church was still raising money for the building fund. But Greenwood's clubs and social organizations, including the Elks Club and missionary societies, had come back strong. In addition to chapters of professional organizations, such as the Ladies Auxiliary to the Oklahoma State Medical, Dental, and Pharmaceutical Association and the local NAACP chapter, there were dozens of neighborhood groups, including the Vogue Art Club, the Sans Souci Club, and the Jolly Wives Club, that mixed charitable work with plain old-fashioned camaraderie and fun. The Maids Domestic Club hosted an annual semiformal dinner, while the Fifteen Fellows club raised money for medical equipment for a local clinic. Indeed, there were those who felt that by the end of the Second World War, Greenwood was even bigger than it had been before the riot. Mozella Jones called it Little Black Wall Street.

Only it would not last.

For by the end of the 1950s, when Don Ross graduated from Booker T. Washington High School, bustling Greenwood was already on the decline, the victim of forces large and small. Though the United States had emerged from World War II with the strongest economy on earth, the nature of American business was rapidly changing. In 1921, the city of Tulsa claimed more than 110 hotels, including four in Greenwood, almost all of which were individually or family owned. By the 1960s, nearly all the city's mom-and-pop hotels were gone, while its lodging industry was now dominated by Holiday Inn, Hilton, and other national chains. The same applied to other sections of the economy as well, as small, family-owned businesses—which most in Greenwood were—simply could not offer the same prices for the goods and services that national chains, such as Target and Kmart, Denny's and McDonald's, Walgreens and Kress, could. In the new retail model for the American economy, independent Black businesses were hit especially hard.

Desegregation had an economic cost as well. Even by the early 1940s, some white-owned businesses in Tulsa, including at least one downtown department store, were already advertising in the *Oklahoma*

Eagle, seeking Black dollars. As more followed suit, African American families discovered that not only was the selection of products more varied in white-owned businesses, but prices were often lower as well. And as more and more white merchants began to welcome, or at least not oppose, Black customers, businesses in Greenwood took an economic hit from which many could never recover. By the end of the 1970s, the Greenwood commercial district was in a deadly free fall.

But that is only part of the story.

Because the decimation of the second, reborn Greenwood can also be laid at the feet of men and women who sat in air-conditioned offices and did their work with pencils and calculators, blue-line maps, real estate estimates, and government statistics. For the efforts to carve up the city's historic African American district had not ended with the attempted land grab for a new railroad terminal back in 1921. Now they had new names. Urban renewal. Redlining. Slum clearance. Model Cities. Opportunity. Progress.

The most visible, if not the harshest, blow came in the early 1970s when a massive new eight-lane interstate highway, I-244, plowed its way, east to west, through the city's near north side. While the highway designers could have steered it around the African American district, instead they had the highway bust right through the heart of the Greenwood business district, right across Greenwood Avenue. Not only did the new interstate deal a death blow to a number of family-owned businesses that were trying to stay afloat in an age of franchises and national chains, but the highway cut off north Tulsa's Black and poor white neighborhoods from the city's booming south side. "It was like the Berlin Wall," a former pastor at First Presbyterian Church once told me.

After that, the spiraling down of some of Greenwood's oldest neighborhoods only accelerated. The churches—Mount Zion, Vernon AME, and First Baptist among them—held their ground, as did the first, and now lonely, block of Greenwood Avenue running north off of Archer.

But elsewhere, especially in some of the residential neighborhoods, the lack of opportunity, jobs, and ready capital led to leaky roofs and cracked sidewalks, missed rent and mortgage payments, utility shutoffs, foreclosures, and repossessions. In time, hired work crews would strip abandoned homes and buildings of lead pipe, copper wires, glass door-knobs, and leaded windows, while bulldozer operators finished the job. On the very same blocks where African American men and women once fought off an army of invading whites, no one could stop the slow tide of heavy trucks hauling away roll-off dumpsters filled with dry-rot wood, roofing tiles, and busted cinder blocks, as well as the remaining pieces of foundations that had withstood the onslaught during the district's darkest days. And in some neighborhoods, they took everything but the steps.

And if you know where to look, you can still find them.

Yet despite all the demolition, by the 1990s Greenwood could lay claim to some bright new additions as well. The Greenwood Cultural Center, a beautiful multipurpose community center, opened its doors on Greenwood Avenue, right across the street from the new Vernon AME Church, while ground was broken for a brand-new multi-university complex just to the north. And Don Ross had gotten his memorial. Anchored by a massive, twenty-seven-foot tower that depicted the African American experience in Oklahoma from slavery and territorial days, through the riot, and into an imagined future of peace and coop-eration, John Hope Franklin Reconciliation Park was a stunning oasis of carefully manicured plantings, evocative sculpture, and a vibrant history lesson. Whether it featured the largest Black history sculpture in the world was up for debate, but there was little doubt that it was the largest public sculpture in the city of Tulsa. Ross himself, meanwhile, had decided against running for reelection in 2004 and had retired from public life. But just as his star was receding, the riot had once again become a topic of conversation across north Tulsa, this time through a lawsuit that had been filed in US District Court in 2003.

The brainchild of Charles Ogletree, an attorney and professor at Harvard Law School, *John Melvin Alexander v. State of Oklahoma* sought reparations, in the form of unspecified financial payments, on behalf of more than one hundred elderly riot survivors, aged 89 to 105. Ogletree, a gifted speaker and advocate for racial justice, quickly won the support of the Greenwood community, who filled the seats whenever the Massachusetts professor came to town. The lawsuit also augured potentially national implications, for a victory in Tulsa might prove to be a legal stepping-stone for a much larger case arguing for reparations for slavery. And if *Alexander v. Oklahoma* could prove that the State of Oklahoma, the City of Tulsa, and the Tulsa Police Department were complicit in the murders, theft, arson, and other acts of violence that took place during the riot, it could open the door for similar Jim Crow–era lawsuits. There was a lot riding on the outcome, and Ogletree did not skimp on seeking help from fellow attorneys, including Johnnie Cochran Jr. of the O. J. Simpson case, plus a bevy of academics. This was no small-time effort.

But Ogletree, his team, and the plaintiffs had a very large legal hill to climb. On the one hand, it would not prove to be too difficult a task to establish the horror and injustice of the riot, including the contributions of the police and local National Guard units to the violence, as well as the lingering psychological effects of the tragedy on the survivors. Eric Caine, a psychiatrist at the University of Rochester Medical Center, testified as to how the riot had had a profound effect on the survivors. "It was above and beyond anything they could have imagined," he said, "seeing your home burned down, seeing your parents dragged off, having to escape in the woods." When Leon Litwack, a Pulitzer Prize–winning historian from the University of California,

Berkeley, took the stand, his testimony about lynching was so powerful that, according to a reporter for the *Los Angeles Times,* "several elderly women held their hands over their ears."

Overcoming the statute of limitations was another matter. In order to do so, Ogletree took a two-pronged approach. To begin, he argued that because of racism and segregation, both of which prevented African Americans from serving on juries in Tulsa, there was no way that Black plaintiffs could ever have received just treatment in the courts immediately following the riot. But more important, Ogletree asserted that because the story of the riot had been suppressed for so long, including by state and local government, the clock on legal remedies for the riot should not start ticking until 2001, when the report of the riot commission was delivered, first to the governor, and then to the public at large.

Attorneys for the city and the state argued otherwise. And in the back-and-forth of the case, both John Hope Franklin and I found our words being used by lawyers on both sides. I ended up filing an affidavit on behalf of the plaintiffs, detailing how the story of the riot had been deliberately suppressed, the threats of violence against those who dared to bring it up, and even how difficult it was to find copies of *Death in a Promised Land* in Tulsa after it first came out in 1982. "Time, of course, is clearly not on the side of the survivors, and their chance for their day in court is quickly passing," I wrote. "And while I am neither a lawyer nor an authority on the law, it strikes me that even delayed justice is justice nonetheless. In closing, as both a historian and as a native son of Tulsa, let me state my profound hope that the remaining survivors of Tulsa's darkest day will finally have a chance, in a court of law, to tell their story."

It didn't matter. Ogletree and the survivors lost the first round. An appeal was filed, and while they lost that as well, a split decision allowed them to submit the case for possible review by the US Supreme

Court. Only the Supreme Court refused to hear the case. Nonetheless, while Ogletree's effort had ended in failure, he had raised the hopes and honored the humanity of the last generation of survivors. Moreover, he had reminded the legal machinery of the state that the survivors weren't just some ancient relics of a time long past, but that they *mattered*. When it came to what to do with the survivors and their descendants, and how to try and right the wrongs that they had suffered, the country hadn't changed yet. But it was changing.

All you had to do was to look. And to listen.

In a middle school auditorium in rural Massachusetts, an eighth-grade girl adjusts the sleeves on her dress, goes over her lines one last time, and walks out to the center of the stage. Behind her is a backdrop, which she and her classmates made that winter, depicting the ruins of the Dreamland Theatre. As the stage lights come up, she is sitting in a chair at stage center:

> [*Loula Williams takes a deep breath. EXHALES. Pauses. Sits up straight.*]
>
> [*Raises one hand with an open palm to compose herself.*
>
> *She drops the hand and lowers her head.*]
>
> [*Then she raises her head (slowly and dramatically) and stares out at the audience (broken by these events) for a couple seconds for maximum effect.*]

LOULA: This is STILL my town. My FAMILY'S town. We're staying.

As the houselights come on and the audience explodes into applause, Izzy, Bella, Jack, and Sofia, all students in Mr. Howley's eighth-grade social studies class at Norton Middle School, take their bows. Since the semester started up again, all through the bleak New England winter, they researched and wrote their own play about the Tulsa riot. They also built their own sets and props, including a replica of the May 31, 1921, edition of the *Tulsa Tribune,* a hand-painted backdrop of the Tulsa County Court House, and the elevator at the Drexel Building, complete with a sliding cage door. And while they will win third place in the National History Day Massachusetts State Competition, just missing going to the finals in Washington, D.C., they have done something that once would have been unheard of. They have brought to life the tragic events in Tulsa in a small town that is fifteen hundred miles away.

They are not alone. In National History Day competitions, students across the country had tackled the massacre as the subject of their entries. A California sixth grader created a ten-minute documentary, while students at a Houston high school made it all the way to the Texas state championships. Larger stages have beckoned as well. Beneath the brilliant stars above Santa Fe, New Mexico, in July 2018, mezzo-soprano Alicia Hall Moran performed "Black Wall Street," a chamber piece she cowrote with her husband, jazz pianist Jason Moran. One year later, the Alvin Ailey American Dance Theater premiered "Greenwood," an ensemble piece by renowned choreographer Donald Byrd.

For in the wake of the seventy-fifth anniversary, the riot commission, the reparations lawsuit, and all their attendant media attention, the events in Tulsa in 1921 had finally entered, if not most American history textbooks, then at least a portion of the national consciousness. Between 1997 and 2002, eleven books were published about the riot, ranging from novels like Jewell Parker Rhodes's *Magic City* and Rilla Askew's *Fire in Beulah* to historical and journalistic accounts like Hannibal Johnson's *Black Wall Street,* Tim Madigan's *The Burning,* and James Hirsch's *Riot and Remembrance.* As of early 2021, Amazon shoppers could purchase nearly two dozen books about Greenwood and the race massacre, including *Dreamland Burning* and *Reconstructing the Dreamland,* as well as *Tulsa's Black Wall Street, The Rise and*

Fall of Black Wall Street, and *Black Wall Street Historic Picture Book and the Commission Report.*

Hollywood, television production companies, and graduate students in film studies programs had come knocking as well. Only their initial amazement at hearing about the riot for the first time—"I can't believe there hasn't been a film about this!"—has almost always been followed up with more practical concerns. How can one tell such a dark story? Where are the heroes? And how much is it going to cost to reenact the destruction of Greenwood, especially prior to the advance of digital film techniques? Hollywood hasn't quite figured out yet how to tell the story of the Tulsa riot.

It would be at the National Museum of African American History and Culture in Washington, D.C., where the massacre would find its largest in-person audience. When the new Smithsonian museum opened on the National Mall in the fall of 2016, to massive crowds and advance ticket sales, it featured an exhibit about Greenwood and the massacre—which included two of the burned "riot pennies" that George Monroe had pressed into my hands before he passed. There was no question that Greenwood and the massacre were working their way into the country's historical memory book.

Back in Greenwood, all this attention was taken in stride. For despite the welcome tidings that the community was gaining national renown, there were far more pressing matters to attend to. And on a warm September evening in 2016, Tulsa and its long and difficult history with race relations was suddenly back in the news.

It all began innocently.

Shortly before eight o'clock on September 16, 2016, a silver Lincoln Navigator suddenly came to a stop on East 36th Street North, a largely rural two-lane road along the city's far northern edge, its wheels straddling the double yellow lines. Terence Crutcher, a middle-aged African American man dressed in a white T-shirt and khaki trousers, exited the vehicle and started walking toward Lewis Avenue. A couple of motorists slowed down and asked Crutcher if he needed any assistance, but he waved them off, saying he thought the car was going to explode. "Somebody left their vehicle running in the middle of the street with the doors wide open," one woman told the 911 dispatcher. "The doors are open, the vehicle is still running. It's an SUV. It's like in the middle of the street, it's blocking traffic. . . . There was a guy running from it, saying it was going to blow up. But I think he's smoking something."

He had been. A toxicological analysis would reveal that Crutcher had PCP in his system.

But there was much more to his story than that. Having turned forty years of age just one month earlier, Terence Crutcher had experienced a series of ups and downs throughout his life. The son of a minister, he had struggled with drugs for years, and had even spent four years in prison for selling five grams of crack cocaine. Crutcher was also a loving father to his four children, and a devoted churchgoer whose beautiful tenor voice would enliven the services at New Heights Christian Center, where he sang in the choir. Warm, funny, and affable, he would light up family gatherings. He also had a soft spot for the city's homeless population. "Terence would always have someone on our sofa. We would wake up, and there would be someone with a blanket on them because they didn't have a place to go," his twin sister, Tiffany, said. "Terence was always feeding the homeless." And he had just enrolled in a music course at Tulsa Community College. Crutcher was wrestling hard with his demons to gain control of his life. But now, as he walked alone on East 36th Street North, with the late summer sun dipping below the horizon, his future had suddenly taken on a much different trajectory.

A few minutes after the first calls came into the 911 dispatcher,

Tulsa police officer Betty Jo Shelby was driving alone along East 36th Street North, responding to a domestic disturbance call, when she came upon Crutcher. A ten-year veteran of the TPD, she stopped her cruiser, got out of the vehicle, and asked Crutcher what was going on. "Hey, man," she said, "is this your vehicle?" Crutcher mumbled something, and then put his hands in his pockets. When Officer Shelby told him to take his hands out of his pockets, Crutcher raised his arms over his head, turned, and started walking back toward the SUV. His twin sister, Tiffany, later recalled that he was doing exactly what their father had told them to do if they were ever stopped by the police, to "put your hands in the air, and put your hands on the car." Shelby then told Crutcher to stop, and when he didn't, she called for backup.

By then, a police helicopter was hovering over the scene that was rapidly unfolding on the ground, with Terence Crutcher walking slowly toward his car while Shelby unsuccessfully ordered him to stop. "That looks like a bad dude," the pilot told the officer in the chopper, who, of all people, was Shelby's husband. While the helicopter slowly circled around the silver SUV, another Tulsa police officer, Tyler Turnbough, pulled up behind Shelby's cruiser with his lights on. By the time Turnbough ran up to Shelby, she had her gun out and was aiming at Crutcher. Exactly what happened next is difficult to know with complete certainty, as the helicopter was on the far side of the SUV, and Turnbough and Shelby were partially blocking the view from the dash cam on Turnbough's cruiser. According to Shelby, Terence Crutcher lowered his arms and reached into the SUV, and she opened fire, hitting him in the chest. She was later asked by *60 Minutes* journalist Bill Whitaker why she didn't try to shoot Crutcher in the foot or the leg. "I'm not trained," she replied, "to shoot someone in the foot."

The result of her action was painfully visible in the footage from the police helicopter as it circled around to the side of the SUV where Crutcher and the officers had been standing. Terence Crutcher lay now on his back in the street, a huge dark red stain spreading along his upper right chest. Other officers, just arriving on the scene, can be viewed running to Shelby. According to Tiffany Crutcher, her brother lay alone and unattended on the street while the police on the scene gathered around Betty Jo Shelby, comforting her. "Nobody went to check on him," she said. "They let him lay there, like an animal." By the time an ambulance brought Terence Crutcher to the St. John Medical Center, he was declared DOA, dead on arrival.

The shooting split the city, largely, though not entirely, along racial lines. "If he had just followed the directions of that police officer," one of my white Central High School former teammates told me, "he'd be alive today." A newer acquaintance, a Black detective, told me that he supported Shelby 100 percent. As the case blew up on social media and her name was revealed to the public, Betty Jo Shelby said that she started to receive anonymous death threats, causing her to move from her home. "My situation," she said, "was no different than a lynch mob coming after me."

African American community leaders viewed the tragedy in a much different light, especially in regard to Shelby's actions. "Race had everything to do with her pulling the trigger that day," Reverend Ray Owens of Metropolitan Baptist Church told reporters. "Is she a racist? Does she . . . have some ill will toward Black people? I doubt it. But if she is like so many people in our nation, she assumes too quickly that a Black male, especially out on the streets at night, is a threat and not a citizen. Is a suspect and not—a decent human being." There was no question, in many minds, that had Terence Crutcher been white, he'd still be alive.

Six days after the shooting, Betty Jo Shelby was charged with first-degree manslaughter and placed on unpaid leave. The case, meanwhile, had become national news. The Reverend Al Sharpton came to Tulsa to lead a protest march from city hall to the Greenwood Cultural Center, with many of the four hundred marchers chanting "Justice for Crutch"

and "Hands up, don't shoot." Many national news outlets r
the Tulsa race riot in their coverage. Yet despite the presenc
African Americans on the jury, eight months later, Betty Jo Shelby was
acquitted. She would later form a consulting business offering advice to
other officers caught up in what she called the Ferguson Effect—namely,
she said, "when a police officer is victimized by anti-police groups and
tried in the court of public opinion."

For the Crutcher family, the verdict was a hammer blow.

"Let it be known that I believe in my heart that Betty Shelby got
away with murder. I don't know what was in the mind of that jury, how
they could come to that conclusion," Terence's dad, the Reverend Joey
Crutcher, said. "You did your job, but I'm wondering what you were
thinking about." Sister Tiffany echoed her father's sentiments. "Betty
Shelby," she said, "murdered my brother."

If nothing else, the Terence Crutcher–Betty Jo Shelby case revealed
just how divided Tulsa was when it came to matters of race. But it also
revealed, once again, how the 1921 race riot was ever hovering in the
background when racial matters came to the fore. The unvarnished
truth of the matter was that since the seventy-fifth anniversary and the
days of the riot commission, the elephant in the room—the city's once-
buried tragedy—could no longer be ignored. Whoever attempted to
bridge the city's gaping racial divide would, by necessity, have to grap-
ple with the unresolved issues of the past. Like it or not, that was now
a given. But what few could have predicted, as the Obama era ended
and the age of Trump began, was where the next effort would begin.

ROLEXES AND PICKUP TRUCKS

"G T was a dork."

The speaker is Suzie LaFortune Bynum. She is referring to her son, the mayor.

"He loved Mister Rogers," she said, describing a routine that her then-three-year-old son would go through every time he watched his favorite television show. "We got him a little coat for Thanksgiving or Christmas. On his own, he'd go get the coat with the little hanger. He'd take it off and button it up, and we have him on video singing along." In high school he once had a job selling Cutco knives door-to-door. "One of his early sales meetings was with my parents. GT was demonstrating the ability of a particular knife by cutting through rope, and he cut off the end of his thumb."

Others have focused on G. T. Bynum's looks, still boyish even in his early forties. "He looks like your classmate who made money tutoring in graduate school," quipped Tulsa writer Barry Friedman. "Your co-worker who's now your boss." Superficiality aside, there's something to this. His cheery smile, peaches-and-cream complexion, and perfectly pressed blazers and slacks remind one more of an awkward teen in his first dress clothes at the big family wedding than of the chief executive of the forty-seventh-largest city in the country. But appearances are often deceiving, and doubly so in the case of George Theron Bynum IV, nicknamed GT. For behind the Annie Hall eyeglasses and the often seemingly bepuzzled expression lies a shrewd politician, a confirmed believer in right and wrong, and an advocate for conciliation and compromise in an age of distrust and take-no-prisoners partisanship.

Born in 1977 to a family steeped in business and local politics, Bynum grew up in a world of privilege on the city's near south side. An Eagle Scout, he had been voted most likely to succeed at Cascia Hall, Tulsa's premier Catholic high school, when he graduated in 1996. But it was at Villanova University, outside Philadelphia, where Bynum began to find his calling. Not only did he help establish the campus chapter of the Young Republicans, but he also became deeply interested in public policy issues. "It sounds kind of dorky for two college guys," he told a reporter for the *Philadelphia Inquirer* about how he would discuss education policy with his roommate for hours. "We would be up until 2 or 3 in the morning." During his senior year, he was elected class president. When he graduated in 2000, as befitting his Clark Kent image, he wore a Superman T-shirt under his graduation gown.

His next stop was Washington, D.C., where for six years he worked on the staffs of two different Oklahoma senators, Don Nickles and Tom Coburn, eventually rising to the position of legislative aide. But if his experiences on the Hill gave Bynum a front-row understanding of Washington politics, the prospect of a career as a congressional aide was not for him. In 2006, he returned to Tulsa, where he worked for a real estate auction company before starting a lobbying firm of his own. But the call of politics was too strong, and two years after coming back home, Bynum ran for, and won, a seat on the city council.

In truth, politics had been a family tradition. Not only had one of his uncles served as the city's mayor, but so had his maternal grandfather, Robert LaFortune, a former chemical engineer who became one of the city's most beloved politicians. "Growing up, I would go to places with him and my grandmother," Bynum later recalled, "and if we ever went anywhere in Oklahoma, someone would stop us to say hi to him and tell me about what a great job he'd done." But equally important was a family ethos, grounded in Catholicism, that placed a high premium on public service. "All of us have been involved in . . . the Catholic Church and its philanthropic and charity efforts," Bynum said. "Everybody in our family has been involved in building up the city and community in one way or another." And they had done so despite the fact that Tulsa was overwhelmingly Protestant. But perhaps even more remarkable for an energetically churchgoing, Protestant city was that Tulsa didn't have just one powerful and successful Catholic political family. It also had one other. And in 2016, G. T. Bynum decided to aim straight for it.

The first Dewey Bartlett hadn't exactly been cut from the same cloth as most of the Sooner State's politicians. Born in Ohio, he had attended prep school at Lawrenceville and was president of his class at Princeton. Following service as a Marine Corps dive-bomber pilot in the Pacific during World War II, he set out for Oklahoma, joined the family oil business, and struck it rich. By 1962, he had been elected to the state senate. Four years later, at age forty-seven, Bartlett was elected as Oklahoma's second Republican governor. Even more important, perhaps, was the fact that he was also the state's first Catholic chief executive. For not only was Oklahoma fiercely Protestant, but the Ku Klux Klan had literally run the state government for a while back in the 1920s, when the order was also vitriolically anti-Catholic.

Tulsa, in particular, had become a huge Klan center following the riot. They owned their own building, an impressive brick auditorium nicknamed Beno Hall, on the city's north side, and held massive parades downtown. Tulsa was also one of the few places in the country that had both a women's auxiliary and an active chapter of the Children of the Ku Klux Klan. Speaking of the Klan in the city's white neighborhoods during the years immediately following the 1921 race riot, Ed Wheeler likened it to the Nazi Party in 1930s Germany. "Almost everyone," he said, "had to belong." When the police officer father of future radio commentator Paul Harvey died in the line of fire, it was the Tulsa Klan who paid for his funeral. Given such a heritage, Bartlett's election as the state's chief executive was no small accomplishment. A writer for the *Washington Post* even claimed, at the time, that Bartlett's gubernatorial victory represented "the end of religious bigotry in Oklahoma." It wasn't, as the state's Muslims, Sikhs, and other religious minorities could attest, particularly post-9/11. But it was significant nonetheless.

By the standards of the Age of Trump, Bartlett's politics were scandalously moderate. A huge proponent of strengthening the public school system and of bringing new industry to Oklahoma from out of state, Bartlett also moved to open up opportunities for minorities—while also being a loyal supporter of the oil industry. Oklahoma voters liked Bartlett, and picked him to serve a second term in the governor's mansion, followed by electing him to the United States Senate in 1972. But his career on Capitol Hill was cut short when, five years later, he was diagnosed with lung cancer. Resigning from the Senate, he died two years later.

The family's political legacy was now up to the son.

Only Dewey Bartlett Jr. had a different upbringing. Instead of Lawrenceville and Princeton, he attended Bishop Kelley High School in Tulsa and Regis University in Denver before joining the family oil business. At age forty-three, he ran for Tulsa's city council and won, only to be defeated two years later when he ran for mayor. Twelve years later, he lost another race, this one an especially bitter contest, widely considered to be the most expensive legislative race in Oklahoma history, for the state senate. Finally, five years after that, at age sixty-two, Dewey Jr. was elected mayor of Tulsa. "We have a lot of challenges ahead of us. But not tonight—because we won!" he declared at his victory party. "I appreciate your vote for one Tulsa, for one good Okie, Dewey Bartlett." He was reelected in 2013, and three years later, he set out for a third term. Dewey Jr. knew how to work a room, he loved his hometown, and he wanted to make it a better place. Everything, it seemed, was finally coming up roses.

G. T. Bynum had grown up in awe of Dewey Jr.

"I grew up looking up to him," Bynum said. "The first campaign I ever worked on was his race for the city council," he added. "His parents lived next door to me when I was a kid. His dad was my grandfather's political mentor."

But in 2015, while he was still serving as a Tulsa city councilor, G. T. Bynum was also charting his own political future. And that December, his political team commissioned a poll that looked toward the next year's mayoral election. Not surprisingly, Dewey Jr.'s personal approval ratings were high. "His personal approval ratings were in the sixties," Bynum said, "but his re-elect numbers were in the high twenties." They had found a chink in the armor. Bynum then announced that he was running for mayor. The city's two Catholic political dynasties would be going head-to-head.

Bartlett ran an old-school campaign, attacking Bynum and offering very little in terms of an actual platform. "I went to his announce party," one experienced local political hand later told me. "It was almost all old white men. But I went to Bynum's as well. It was fun, and young, and upbeat." So was the Bynum campaign, which attracted the support of younger voters, people of color, and members of the city's increasingly visible LGBTQ community. "I think of myself as a conservative, but it's in the Barry Goldwater school of conservatism, which is about minimizing government intervention in people's private lives," Bynum told a reporter. "There's a group of conservatives who do not like me because I'm not anti-gay." When a political neophyte jumped onstage during a televised debate and tried to make a case for his own candidacy, GT could be seen smiling, while Dewey Jr. reached for his cell phone. The polls all had Bartlett winning handily.

Bynum beat Bartlett by eighteen percentage points.

It had been an impressive campaign. Bynum had cobbled together a coalition of Democrats, Hispanics, African Americans, young voters, and moderate Republicans to topple a two-time incumbent who was widely predicted to win a third term. In Tulsa, the election did represent a turning of the page, perhaps, for how the city's politics might emerge in the future. With a thirty-eight-year-old mayor-elect, and with new construction starting to take place downtown, Tulsa suddenly seemed younger and more vibrant than before.

Only this wasn't any kind of revolution or palace revolt.

"I'm more conservative than you think," Bynum once told a group of onlookers.

And in Oklahoma, conservatism wasn't just a feature of the state's dominant politics. It had practically become a prerequisite for wielding any kind of significant political power. In the 2008 and 2012 presidential elections, Oklahoma was the only state in the union where not a single county voted for Barack Obama. And in the earthshaking presidential election of 2016, Okie voters stayed the course. Not only did all seventy-seven counties vote for Donald Trump, but the new face of the GOP carried the state by a whopping 36 percentage points. While there were pockets of reliable Democratic Party supporters in Tulsa, including African American voters, the truth of the matter was that for much of the past half century, the city was a reliably Republican town in a reliably Republican state.

Hand in hand with such rugged conservatism, however, is a deep and not at all ironic sense among many white Tulsans that, in its heart of hearts, the city is both progressive and urbane. Part of this thread comes directly from the oil industry itself, a global enterprise that has sent generations of Tulsa-based petroleum geologists, drilling engineers, riggers, and mechanics all over the world. Another part derives from the very wealth of the city. Not only did the early oilmen build mansions, stock them with grand pianos and Renaissance art, and do their banking on Wall Street, but they sent their children off to East Coast boarding schools and Ivy League colleges before bringing them back home to help run the family business, a tradition that continues to this day.

In the city's high-end shops and boutiques, one can find the latest fashions, the most up-to-date home appliances, and elegant and sophisticated furnishings for either a beloved 1920s architectural gem in the elegant Maple Ridge neighborhood, or a McMansion on the far south edge of town. But most Tulsans are also unpretentious, and are happiest in a pair of jeans and a T-shirt. In the wealthiest parts of town, Rolexes and pickup trucks aren't an oxymoron.

But as both the nation and the world have grown smaller, this combination of rock-ribbed conservatism and urban aspirations has caused something of a problem for the city's business leaders. In brief, in their efforts to attract the Amazons and the Teslas of the world to establish new facilities in town, Tulsans have consistently fallen short. One reason is fairly simple: The city has to offer more than a place to make money. Left-leaning millennials from Brooklyn and Seattle and Silicon Valley may drool over the real estate prices in Tulsa, but would be aghast at how the public schools have been gutted by the state government, raise their eyebrows at the lack of bike lanes and mass transit, and fret over a political climate in which, between 2011 and 2019, Governor Mary Fallin ordered National Guard facilities to deny benefits to same-sex couples, signed a law that required restaurants to place antiabortion signs in their restrooms, and called upon the state's Christians to "thank God for the blessing created by the oil and natural gas industry and to seek His wisdom and ask for protection." To attract the kinds of industries and growth that the city wants in the decades to come, a new kind of leadership would be needed, one that could not only envision a new future for the city, but attempt to cope with its haunted past. This would be no small order.

Nor would trying to heal the city's stubborn racial divide.

And before G. T. Bynum's term as mayor was only a little more than half finished, the city's turbulent 1921 history would, once again, start to work its way back onstage.

"What the hell is a deputy mayor?"

The speaker is standing next to a large metal gate on a lonesome stretch of East Ute Street in north Tulsa. Most of the nearby lots are vacant patches of brown Bermuda grass surrounded by barbed wire or decades-old chain-link fence. The few houses that remain have ancient roofs and chipped paint, overgrown shrubbery, and WARNING KEEP OUT signs. It is difficult to tell, from the outside, whether anyone lives in them or not. This is a neighborhood on life support.

Except, that is, for the house behind the gate, a low-slung affair, painted a cheery shade of orange with royal blue trim. Several times a week, more during weekends, cars will pull up opposite the gate, and drivers and passengers will emerge, pulling out their cell phones from purses and pants pockets. They are not here, however, for the house. Instead their eyes are fixed on the three-story-high, seventy-four-foot, fifty-ton steel Chinese junk that is being constructed in the front yard.

It is a dazzling sight, complete with hand-forged brass propellers and hatch covers. The brainchild of Doug Jackson, a stocky walkabout and jack-of-all-trades, the completed boat, the SV *Seeker,* will be towed to the Port of Catoosa, outside Tulsa, and will make its way down the Arkansas and Mississippi Rivers to the Gulf of Mexico, the Atlantic Ocean, and the rest of the world. A sign on the gate says for one to beware of the dogs, but in this case they are an elderly basset hound and a German shepherd, both of whom are wagging their tails. With them is Betsy Warner, she of the question about the deputy mayor.

In her early sixties, with brown eyes and silvery hair, she is the daughter of the late Dick Warner, my old research partner from the riot commission days. Betsy is also the keeper of her late father's archives, which she has sorted and refiled in a set of bright plastic file boxes that she keeps in a small room at the back of the house. Nearby, in a bookshelf, are some of Dick's books on the history of Tulsa, which she now adds to. "I just found a copy of Ron Trekell's *History of the Tulsa Police Department* on eBay," she proudly tells me, "that didn't cost sixty-five dollars."

Only I am not here to talk books, or dogs, or Chinese junks.

Instead, there is a new priority. The search for the riot dead has started up again.

The email arrived on a Wednesday.

The mayor, it said, had announced his intention to reopen the search for the mass graves from the 1921 race riot. "We are highly interested in the work that you did to identify those locations," the brief message read, "and we appreciate any information you are willing to share with us." The email came from Amy Brown, deputy mayor, City of Tulsa. The date was April 10, 2019. While I had quietly hoped that someday someone would be interested in all the work we'd done to try and locate the graves of the riot victims, there was certainly no guarantee that this would happen during my lifetime. But here it was. Eighteen years after the riot commission had shut down our search, the city was knocking on the door.

Much, of course, had happened since then.

To begin with, the riot had a new name. Now it was the Tulsa race massacre.

There had been keenly felt grumblings in the past over the term *race riot*. Some felt that the term implied guilt on both sides. Others were unhappy with lumping what had happened in Tulsa in 1921 with, say, the urban racial rebellions of the 1960s, or the violence that broke out across Los Angeles following the not-guilty verdict given to the Los Angeles police officers who had beaten Rodney King. Still others asserted, without any evidence to back it up, that the violence in Tulsa had been intentionally called a "race riot" by powerful whites as a way to ensure that the claims of African American property owners against white-owned insurance companies would be denied. So by the opening months of 2019, from the pages of the *Tulsa World* to the stationery for the 1921 Tulsa Race Massacre Centennial Commission, the riot had now become a massacre.

Seven weeks after Amy Brown had sent her email, I met with both Mayor G. T. Bynum and the deputy mayor inside a conference room in Tulsa's sleek new city hall building to discuss the history of the search for the graves. For Bynum, this was not a new area of interest. Back when he had been on the city council, he and a fellow councilor had tried to get the city government to reopen the search for the graves, only to be stopped by then-mayor Dewey Bartlett Jr. Now, as mayor, Bynum wanted to start up the search again, and had already contacted the Oklahoma state archaeologist, Kary Stackelbeck, and was in the process of putting together a Public Oversight Committee, composed primarily of African American leaders, elected officials, and Greenwood

community activists, to oversee the effort. After listening to my chronicle of the original search during the riot commission era, Bynum asked
me to lead the team that was to conduct the new investigation.

All of which is why, one month later, I have come to see Betsy Warner. For in restarting the search, the first thing that I need to do is to
look again at her father's old files, which I hope either to borrow or to
borrow and photocopy. Only Betsy has other ideas. She lets me know
right off the bat that she is *very* interested in helping out on the revived
search for the graves, and it becomes obvious that if I want access to the
files, she is part of the package.

As it turns out, Betsy Warner is a talented amateur historian. She is
great with names and faces, and, like her dad, she is a creative and
dogged researcher. She will bring plastic containers of homemade cook-
ies to secretaries and records managers in obscure city offices to sweet-
talk her way into seeing old maps and logbooks locked away in gray
metal filing cabinets. And while about half the time she is mad at me,
she has a good eye for relevant detail. And most important, it is Betsy
Warner who reminds me of the memorandum that her father sent me
about his interview with Bob Patty, a former Tulsa police officer, and
the photograph he had seen of riot victims being buried in a trench. As
soon as I reread the seventeen-year-old memorandum, there is no question that the mysterious photo is of interest. So is the onetime police
officer.

Bob Patty had been no choirboy.

Long and lanky, with piercing blue eyes and muddy brown hair, he
had been a difficult child and a rowdy teenager, one who ran along the
edges of what passed for the fast crowd in Coweta, Oklahoma, a sleepy
country town on the outskirts of Tulsa. His dad, a master machinist at
McDonnell Douglas, had died when Patty was twelve. His mother was

a research librarian at the University of Tulsa, and while she tried to rein her son in, young Patty missed his father greatly. One thing his dad had taught him, though, was how to shoot. And he was a natural. He could shoot the top off of a pop bottle at a hundred yards. "I grew up chewing on a gun barrel," Patty said. He joined the Marine Corps reserves while still in high school, and one week after graduating from Coweta High School in 1966, he went on active duty.

Sent to Vietnam as a counterinsurgency sharpshooter, he ended up with the Third Battalion, Fifth Marine Regiment in Quang Tri, the northernmost province in South Vietnam. "We were up in the corner, near the fence," Patty said later. "Things were heating up in '66." Part of a six-man patrol that worked the dense, enemy-choked terrain near Khe Sanh, Lang Vei, and the Ho Chi Minh Trail, he was tasked with picking off Vietcong or North Vietnamese army artillery spotters. And he was good. But on October 28, 1966, when he was out on patrol, his world changed forever. He had spotted an enemy bunker on a hillside and had radioed in for an artillery barrage, when everything went haywire. "We were boogying down off the ridge, and a lieutenant redirected fire on my squad. It killed both observers and two of my men, screwed me and another guy up, and left one walking." Wounded, and racked by survivor's guilt, he was now haunted by all that he had seen and done, including a stint with the Phoenix Program, a political assassination campaign that had been organized by the CIA. "When you're nineteen years old, you don't know what the fuck is going on. All you know is a front sight, a whole bunch of leaves, and Ho Chi Minh's eyeballs behind every fuckin' one of 'em," Patty later recalled. "But it's the most alive you'll ever feel."

Discharged from the Marine Corps, he came back to Coweta. Following in his dad's footsteps, Patty used his GI Bill money to take classes in diesel mechanics at a nearby technical college. "Graduated in '69. Got a job, got to working. Found out I was allergic to diesel fuel,"

Patty said. "So, I grabbed my old gun, headed to Tulsa, and got on with the police department."

When Bob Patty signed on as an officer, the Tulsa Police Department was engulfed in change. A spate of new buildings had recently been erected, including a new headquarters, police academy, and adult detention center. Police cars had finally been air-conditioned and officers were no longer required to provide their own handguns, while further efforts were underway to professionalize the force. But the pay was abysmally low, with Tulsa police officers receiving the thirty-second-lowest salaries in a study of thirty-three similar-size American cities. In August 1969, nearly two hundred uniformed officers launched a protest march over pay. At the end of the protest, a reporter asked one of the officers what *Amity*, a brand-new, $35,000 stainless steel sculpture that the city had mounted on a pedestal on the new civic plaza, meant to him. "About two years' salary," he replied.

There were other issues as well. Despite the presence of a handful of Black patrolmen on the overwhelmingly white police force, police relations with the African American community continued to be poor. Civil rights activists had picketed police headquarters in 1963, while an effort to create a Police–Community Relations Department in north Tulsa three years later was quickly shelved. As the decade of the seventies dawned, there was precious little evidence that the Tulsa police were going to abandon some of their old ways.

Consider the case of the Pigelle.

A low-rent African American bar located in an unadorned cinder block building on Pine Street just north of Latimer, the Pigelle was a favorite watering hole for north-side hustlers, dope dealers, and small-time crooks. "It was a place you didn't want to hang around in for long," Bobby Eaton Jr., a longtime musician and radio personality, told me. But the Pigelle was also a place that the Tulsa police would raid from time to time, not just to catch people with outstanding warrants but also to remind the community who was in charge. During one raid in the early 1970s, twelve officers swept in on the bar all at once, led by a police sergeant carrying a 12-gauge. First, he shotgunned the jukebox. Then he blasted the mirror behind the bar. "After that," a former officer who had been in on the raid told me, "the only sound you could hear was that of knives, brass knuckles, and pistols hitting the carpeted floor of the bar, as the customers emptied their pockets."

While brutally dramatic, the raid on the Pigelle wasn't all that surprising, at least in Greenwood. "In those days," Eaton continued, "the police could do anything they wanted. They could haul you out to Mohawk Park and beat you up. Then they would take you downtown and report that you were resisting arrest." African Americans in Tulsa lived in fear of a police cruiser with flashing lights pulling up behind them. Eaton, who played club dates in Tulsa in the 1970s until the bars closed, said that his fellow bandmates would have to drive home on the back streets. "The cops would wait along Peoria in order to pull you over," he said. "They could do whatever they wanted."

Bob Patty fit right in.

Assigned to Charlie Squad, he patrolled the near north side, including the fading Greenwood business district, during the late night–early morning shift. Working alone in a squad car, he routinely tailed suspicious vehicles, cruised the back streets and alleyways for prostitutes and drug deals, and, acting on tips, would burst, alone, into all-Black bars, looking for a perp with an open warrant. Fearless and stoked on adrenaline, he thrived on taking action and found police work to be the closest he would ever come to reliving the electric, highly charged emotions that he had experienced in Vietnam. His methods were far from gentle. When too many of his arrestees ended up in the ER, Bob Patty was fired from the Tulsa Police Department.

He drifted after that, first to the Wagoner County sheriff's office, where, he said, conditions were so bad that "the worst crooks in

Wagoner County wore a badge." Later he worked for an outfit that provided private security for Tulsa-based oil companies, including armed work overseas. He was married and divorced and had children, but ended up living alone in the house in Coweta that he'd grown up in. And despite his less-than-stellar record as a police officer, especially when it came to Tulsa's African American community, he was still haunted by the box of photographs from the 1921 riot that Sergeant Cotton had shown him in the break room at police headquarters that night back in the early 1970s.

"Those people need to be found," he said. "They need to be reburied with respect."

Nearly a half century later, it was time to find out what Bob Patty knew.

It was Betsy Warner who found him.

She had ferreted out a phone number and the address of a country house outside Coweta, a white clapboard home with a green roof, overgrown bushes, and a couple of broken windows. But no matter how many times she called, nobody picked up the phone, and the one time she drove by, she was reluctant to enter the gate and head up the long drive to the house. "I figured somebody might shoot me first," she said. A retired private investigator volunteered to help track down Bob Patty as well, but he got nowhere. No one in Coweta, he claimed, had ever heard of the guy. Then, one afternoon, somebody picked up the phone when Betsy Warner called. It was Bob Patty. Three weeks later, I was headed out to Coweta with Joe Rushmore, a talented photojournalist who was doing a series of portraits of people connected with the race massacre for the *New York Times*.

The house was as advertised, a once-charming family home that was slowly sinking into disrepair. Books and curios lined the walls of the living room, while parts of the house were more or less inaccessible. Bob greeted us at the door. He was in his stocking feet, wearing a reddish-brown sweatshirt and a pair of camo sweatpants. With his shoulder-length gray hair and beard, he looked like a cross between Leo Tolstoy and a member of ZZ Top. His mode of transportation was a bicycle, and he had recently been driven off the road by a hit-and-run driver. He was healing OK, though he now walked with a cane. Bob had no problem with Joe being there or shooting pictures, but there was a question of where the three of us could sit. Finally, we settled on his bedroom, where Bob and I sat on the bed. Nearby, on the wall, hung an Uzi submachine gun and a commemorative brass plaque, from the Fraternal Order of Police, Tulsa Lodge 93. On it was inscribed, PRESENTED TO ROBERT PATTY FOR MERITORIOUS SERVICE PERFORMED IN THE YEAR OF 1974. Joe lingered in the doorway, firing away.

Bob Patty then told me the story of Sergeant Cotton and the box of photographs. Ninety percent of what he said matched what he had said before. That was key.

With Joe tagging along, I then drove Bob to Tulsa. He insisted on going armed, and stuck an ivory-handled semiautomatic pistol into the waistband of his sweatpants. Walking was difficult for Bob, so we couldn't get quite as close to the Canes, the homeless camp alongside the river, as I had hoped. Instead we parked along the railroad tracks beneath one of the nearby overpasses. The area had changed so much since he had been down there that Bob was hesitant to point to a specific spot of ground. But there was no question, at least in his mind, that we were in the correct general vicinity. Afterward, we went out for lunch at the White River Fish Market, a legendary seafood spot in a tiny strip mall on the north side. Bob had a catfish platter with hush puppies, fries, and coleslaw, and he ate it all with relish. It was probably the biggest meal he had had in weeks.

By the time I finally got Bob home, he was sundowning, rambling on about meteorites and a coming flood that would cover most of the earth. According to Bob, the only dry land wouldn't be in the Himalayas, the Alps, or the Andes, but would somehow be in Arkansas. "All the top navy brass have already bought property there," he assured me and Joe. But his story about the photograph of the bodies felt credible, and I was convinced that he was telling the truth. Soon, I hoped, it would be time to find that out. At least, it seemed, we knew where to begin.

Reminding a City of Her Sins

The auditorium was packed.

Up at the front of the room, in a huge arc, a row of folding tables had been set up, congressional committee style, for the members of the Public Oversight Committee, whose names had been prominently printed on large cardstock placards placed in front of their seats. Vanessa Hall-Harper, who represented north Tulsa on the city council, was there, as was Regina Goodwin, whose grandfather had established the *Oklahoma Eagle*. She was now the state representative for District 73, which included Greenwood, and served as the chair of the seven-member Black Caucus in the Oklahoma legislature. Other seats were filled by various African American activists and community leaders who made up the majority of the committee. One seat, however, was empty. It was for former state representative Don Ross, who, while named a member of the committee, attended no meetings. Off to the side sat Mayor Bynum, state archaeologist Kary Stackelbeck, and Scott Hammerstedt of the Oklahoma Archeological Survey, as well as Lesley

Rankin-Hill and Phoebe Stubblefield who, like me, were veterans of the first search some twenty years earlier.

The local press had also shown up, setting up their lights and cameras facing both the podium and the committee members. But it was the public who filled the back of the auditorium of the Rudisill Regional Library on that warm Thursday afternoon in late July 2019. Talking among themselves in the sea of folding chairs, some were already standing quietly in line in front of the floor microphones that had been set up for their use when it became their turn to talk. And while there were a few white faces scattered among the crowd, it was the citizens of Greenwood who had come to express themselves. And once the short presentations were made about the various suspected grave sites, that is exactly what they did.

"Just give us our land back," said a young man who identified himself as a descendant of the Creek Freedmen, former African American slaves of the Muscogee (Creek) Nation who had been forced to come to Oklahoma on the Trail of Tears. "We had the richest land in the world, and everything that we needed. Just give it back." Some members of the audience nodded enthusiastically, while others tried to get the young man to sit down, especially when he began to interrupt others.

A middle-aged Black woman, her voice shaking with nervousness, told how she was descended from massacre survivors who lived in a house right on Greenwood Avenue and had lost everything. She then described in vivid detail a dream that she'd had about that particular address. "I believe that there is a mass grave right there," she said. Other members of the audience spoke of bodies being thrown into the Arkansas River, of airplanes bombing Black Wall Street, and of how the massacre had been covered up.

"They don't want the truth to come out!" came a voice from the audience.

"Amen!"

"That's right!"

From speaker after speaker, an electric charge ran through the audience, causing some to clap and cheer. "And I know that I have power," spoke one woman at the microphone, "for I have the Lord Jesus Christ behind me, and that is the greatest power of all."

That the public meetings of the Public Oversight Community were going to be passionate and emotion-driven was no surprise. The massacre, by its very nature, called forth deep, soul-shaking feelings. But what most of the scientific team hadn't expected was just how politicized the meetings were. More than a few of the members of the public who took their turns at the microphones used their time to pointedly criticize Mayor Bynum, the white business community, and city hall. And there was plenty to complain about. Even by the city government's own statistics, in social indicator after social indicator, African Americans in Tulsa faced far greater challenges than whites. Black unemployment was double that of whites, Black youth were three times more likely to get arrested by the Tulsa Police Department than white youth, while African American infant mortality was fully four times higher. And in north Tulsa, life expectancy was ten years less than on the city's south side.

But the massacre brought out its own share of impassioned commentary as well. "They're still covering it up!" one woman shouted. "It's a conspiracy of silence," said another. Other community members extolled Black Wall Street, claiming that white greed was the sole reason for its destruction. Members of the Public Oversight Committee, meanwhile, made their own stump speeches, vying to see who could best represent the will, and perhaps win the votes, of the community. None, however, had a bigger voice and a larger footprint that evening than the current pastor of Vernon AME Church, the Reverend Robert Turner.

* * *

A gifted orator, Turner had been a young man in a hurry. Born and raised in Tuskegee, he had been an honors student at the University of Alabama, where he helped to win official recognition for two slaves, Boysie and Jack, who had been buried on campus. Graduating in 2004, he interned for Senator Richard Shelby and went on to law school—only to withdraw while trying to find his life's calling. He found it on a mission trip to Kenya, where he helped to bring two hundred new converts to Christianity. When he came back home to the United States, he enrolled in seminary, earning both a master's and a doctorate.

His career as a pastor, however, was not without its challenges. Turner served at five different churches in seven years, all of them small AME congregations in his native Alabama, where he launched membership drives, sanded floors, raised funds for computers and kitchen appliances, created youth choirs, stocked food pantries. And as he counseled and got to know his parishioners, especially in Selma, Birmingham, and Tuscaloosa, older members taught him, firsthand, the history of the great civil rights struggles in the 1960s, of Jim Clark's nightsticks and George Wallace standing in the schoolhouse doorway, of Bull Connor's police dogs and fire hoses and the sickening explosion that claimed the lives of four schoolgirls at the Sixteenth Street Baptist Church.

Then came Tulsa.

Selected as pastor of Vernon AME Church, right on Greenwood Avenue, he arrived in town during the late summer of 2017, less than a year after Terence Crutcher had been killed, and only three months after former police officer Betty Jo Shelby had been acquitted. Emotions in north Tulsa were still raw, but rather than step away from what had already happened, Reverend Turner used it as fuel to push forward. Every Wednesday afternoon, rain or shine, he led a sparsely attended protest march from his church to city hall, where, with megaphone in hand, he would call upon the mayor and the city council to pay reparations for massacre survivors and their descendants.

"Every time we hear an elected official talking about 'We want to have unity,' you're a liar, because you cannot have unity until you truly unite with all God's children. And every time I hear somebody talk about 'We need reconciliation,' you're a liar, because you cannot have true reconciliation without having first reparation," Turner would tell his small group of supporters and anyone else who would listen. "And so God has sent me, as he has every week, to remind this city of her sin—of her sin that she tried to destroy and bury and put even in mass graves. I come to remind this city of her first sin, of her original crime and that is the Tulsa race massacre of 1921."

Reverend Turner hadn't just come to Tulsa to feed his flock.

He'd also come to rattle the temple walls.

But he had also signed on, enthusiastically, to the idea of restarting the search for the graves, which Vanessa Hall-Harper had begun pushing for the previous fall, especially as the one-hundredth anniversary of the massacre drew near. "In honor of the centennial," Hall-Harper had told *Washington Post* reporter DeNeen Brown, "I think that we, as a city, should look into that, and ensure those individuals are laid to rest properly." While Mayor Bynum, on the one hand, and Reverend Turner and Councilor Hall-Harper on the other, were rarely political allies, in this case they had all reached the same conclusion. Black and white Tulsa were, for the moment, working together. It was time to find the dead of 1921.

After I'd met with Bob Patty, the Canes looked more and more promising as a burial location. Not only would the lower level have been out of the sight lines of the houses across the railroad tracks in Crosbie Heights, but it was also only a short walk up the bank from the sandbar where the man whom Ed Wheeler had spoken with back in 1971 said that he had counted fifty-seven bodies laid out in a row. When I told forensic anthropologist Phoebe Stubblefield about my theory, she readily agreed. "They would not have wanted to have carried those bodies very far." Plus, if any bodies had been transported to the area by either trucks or railroad cars, it would not have been especially difficult to carry them down to the lower level. But there was potentially a big problem with the area as well, at least as far as the photograph that Bob Patty had described. Simply stated, it was unclear whether the authorities could have gotten a steam shovel down to the lower area.

And there was another problem—namely, where exactly to look?

My original go-between with the residents of the Canes, Noe Rodriguez, had moved on to another job. In his place now stood Scott Blackburn, a stocky, six-foot-two bear of a man who served as a homeless outreach worker for the Mental Health Association of Oklahoma. A former drug runner for a cartel, Blackburn had turned his own life around after his brother, Justin, who had been a combat medic in Iraq, died of a methamphetamine overdose. No matter the day of the week, or even the time of day, Scott would meet me in the parking lot behind the fire station next to Newblock Park, and together, in his white Ford F-150 4x4, we would cut through the park, skirt past a nearby dirt bike track, drive up onto the levee, and head to the Canes. One warm late fall afternoon in the homeless camp, while we discussed what would need to happen before we could get a ground-penetrating radar unit to survey the lower level, a familiar face suddenly emerged from a sagging green tent.

It was Angel.

"When I heard somebody talking about graves," she said, "I knew it was you." She seemed genuinely happy to see us. But it was also abundantly clear that the streets had started taking their toll. Her clothes were now wrinkled and dirty, while her complexion was red and mottled. Angel was soon joined by a skinny fellow, wearing only a pair of filthy jeans. He stayed in the shadows, refusing to look anyone in the eye. Angel then asked me a question. "If someone, say, found an old gun," she said, "do you think that there might be some reward money?"

I never saw her again.

Angel had not, however, been the only resident of the Canes to talk about bodies being buried there. Later that fall, a rail-thin guy named Smoke said that he always felt there was something evil about the area where the thick stand of Spanish cane bisected the camp. "They's something wrong," he said. "I can feel it when I'm in there." Another resident told me that his dog wouldn't go into the canebrake. And Angel hadn't been the only one to hear the voices. Two other homeless men told me the same thing. "You got to keep your eyes open," one said, "'specially when it be dark." The feeling among the residents at the Canes was near unanimous. Something bad had happened here.

But what did it mean? As a historian and nonfiction writer, my stock-in-trade is evidence and facts. And while I am both a Christian and a spiritual person, I also believe in rationalism and the scientific method. Yet there was something about the insistence by the homeless population at the Canes that *something* had happened there that I couldn't so easily dismiss from my mind. After all, myths and tall tales often have origins in the truth. And I had lived long enough to believe that while most things can be readily explained by logic and the perceived order of things, others exist on a different plane. Like it or not, truth isn't always black-and-white. Sometimes it changes shape as it is told and retold over time. Maybe, I thought, the homeless were onto something.

Once the winter weather moved in and the leaves and underbrush disappeared, I could finally get a good look at the landscape of the Canes. And when that happened, one spot jumped right out. It was a long, shallow depression that ran for maybe sixty feet or so along the very end of the lower level of the now deserted homeless camp. Standing at its downstream end and looking up, I could see a slight berm that ran along its left flank, separating it from the final drop down to the river, while on the right side, the ground rose quickly to the upper level. And cutting right across the middle of the depression was the Spanish cane itself, its now brown leaves scratching against the dry stalks in the breeze. Practically invisible during the summer, the depression looked like a long, shallow trench.

Betsy Warner, meanwhile, had been trying to unlock the secrets of Oaklawn.

Because the original maps and logbooks of the cemetery had gone missing, trying to figure out who had been buried in the African American section of the potter's field had been extremely difficult. Some of the headstones were missing, others damaged, while the various surveys that had been done of the section did not always match what was actually on the ground. Taking a cue from her father, all that fall Warner carefully walked the section, row by row, marking in a notebook every bit of information she could read off the old grave markers. Then, using a copy of an earlier section map of the cemetery, she created a new, ground-proofed map of the potter's field. And when she did, she made a simple if important discovery, namely that the sextons of the cemetery had largely buried the dead in the potter's field by year. In other words, there was a 1918 row, a 1919 row, a 1920 row, and so on. And right along the southern edge of the 1921 row were the headstones for Reuben Everett and Eddie Lockard, both of whom were murdered in the massacre. But south of these headstones was a lot of empty space, running all the way to the iron fence along Eleventh Street. Was it here, we wondered, where the rest of the Original 18, or maybe other massacre victims, were buried?

Betsy Warner had made a second discovery as well.

For in trying to determine who the various sextons had been over the years at Oaklawn, she ended up speaking with nearly every surviving one. And while none of them went back to the years before World War II, more than one of them passed on something remarkable. While this had never been discussed in public, there was an oral tradition among the sextons, passed down from one to the next, that a bare area along the northwestern corner of the African American section of the cemetery was where massacre victims had been buried. This wasn't in the potter's field, but was located between a section reserved for Black veterans and the fence along the western edge of the cemetery. One sexton during the late 1990s and early 2000s, a man named Tim Mills, had even planted a row of crepe myrtles just inside the fence, as a quiet memorial to the victims. Later on, I asked Mills why he had never volunteered this information during the riot commission days, when we did our first ground-penetrating radar scans at Oaklawn. "Oh," he said, "I figured that someone would eventually ask me."

According to the official Oaklawn records, no one had been buried in this area. Nor were there any grave markers present. But the oral tradition among the sextons was too powerful to ignore, and plans were quickly drawn up to have Scott Hammerstedt and Amanda Regnier of the Oklahoma Archeological Survey bring their ground-penetrating radar unit to Tulsa. They would survey not only the bare end of the 1921 row in the potter's field but also what was now called the Sexton's Site.

We weren't yet digging. But we were getting closer.

"It's unbelievable. I've never seen anything like it."

The voice on the phone belonged to Scott Hammerstedt, who was describing to me the results of the geophysical survey work that he and Amanda Regnier had done at Oaklawn Cemetery. And while anomalies had shown up both at the Original 18 and the Clyde Eddy sites, the big news was what the ground-penetrating radar had revealed at the Sexton's Site. "I showed the results to a buddy of mine who's an expert in these matters," Hammerstedt told me. "And what he said was, 'If this isn't a mass grave, I've never seen one before.'" Moreover, the anomaly itself, which was located in the northwest corner of the site, was quite large, perhaps ten feet by thirty feet. Doing the math quickly in my head, depending on how the burials had been performed, this could either be the remains of the Original 18 or even, conceivably, the one hundred–plus dead that the Salvation Army commander had spoken to Walter White about. I immediately called Betsy Warner and shared the news with her. This was potentially a huge breakthrough. And while the news of the ground radar results wouldn't be released until the next Public Oversight Committee meeting, we were both ecstatic, and deeply moved.

I did, however, want to call Tim Mills, the former sexton who had planted the crepe myrtles for the dead of the massacre that he firmly believed were buried there. He didn't pick up on his cell, so I left a message that told him what Hammerstedt had discovered, and asked him to keep it under his hat for now. Mills called back maybe an hour and a half later. He'd been driving to his home, he told me, which was located about forty-five miles from Tulsa. Near the end of the call, he said something that I didn't understand.

"I went and told them that everything would be OK."

"Told who? Where?" I asked.

"At Oaklawn."

I still couldn't figure out what he was talking about.

Then it hit me. Tim Mills had turned his truck around and driven all the way back to Tulsa. He had gone straight to the cemetery and, standing in the Sexton's section in the rapidly gathering fall twilight, he had left his own personal message for the dead.

. . .

We were, it seemed, on our way.

We were also national news. Interest in the massacre had mush-roomed during the fall of 2019 with the release, on HBO, of a new dramatic series based on the bestselling graphic novel *Watchmen*. Set in Tulsa in a futuristic alternative reality where Robert Redford was president and the United States had won the war in Vietnam, the series opened with a re-creation of the massacre, complete with the invasion of Greenwood on the morning of June 1, 1921. Not only did *Watchmen* introduce the story of the Tulsa massacre to millions of viewers glob-ally, but interest in our search for the graves skyrocketed. After the ground-penetrating radar data from the Sexton's Site at Oaklawn was released, *Time* magazine reported that "Archaeologists Have Located a Possible Mass Grave Associated with the 1921 Tulsa Race Riots." The *New York Times*, *The Atlantic*, *CBS This Morning*, *People*, Fox News, *USA Today*, *The Root*, *HuffPost*, and National Public Radio ran stories as well.

By January, plans were already well underway to begin an excava-tion at Oaklawn in late March 2020. While some potentially promising anomalies had turned up in the data from the area near the Everett and Lockard headstones, all eyes were now firmly fixed on the Sexton's Site. Kary Stackelbeck, the state archaeologist, would be running the dig, which was expected to take one to two weeks. The City of Tulsa would provide the lion's share of what would be needed, including funding, hotel rooms, a specially trained excavation crew, security, food, electric power, lighting, tents, and worktables. Neither the media nor the public would be allowed inside the cemetery, but they could observe from along the iron fence, where plans were made to bring in some bleacher-type seating. Members of the Public Oversight Committee would be allowed inside the fence to observe the excavation, as would official representatives of the Muscogee (Creek) Nation. Most of the analytical work would be done by archaeologists and archaeological graduate students from the University of Tulsa and the University of Oklahoma, though plans were being formulated to allow members of the Greenwood community to help with the excavation as well.

Then everything fell apart.

On January 6, 2020, the *New York Times* published its first story about a new, pneumonia-like illness that was sickening dozens of people in Wuhan, China. Less than three weeks later, the first case of what was then called the coronavirus had been reported in the United States. And from then on, with a steadily rising drumbeat of new cases, deaths, and news stories likening COVID-19 to the 1918 flu pandemic, the possibility that we were going to be able to start the excavation at Oaklawn in early April grew dimmer and dimmer. On March 6, the first case was reported in Tulsa County. "Well, things certainly seem to be moving very quickly on the coronavirus front," I wrote to Kary Stackelbeck five days later in what was surely the understatement of the year. A week and a half later, the curtain came down. "I regret to announce that OU has issued new guidance that would preclude our staff's participation in the forthcoming test excavations as scheduled," Stackelbeck emailed on March 23. The dig would have to be postponed. At least it wasn't canceled.

But other problems had been brewing as well.

Despite their common ground when it came to the search for the graves, relations between the Bynum administration and local African American leaders had continued to fester. And following the killing of Terence Crutcher and acquittal of Betty Jo Shelby, the relationship between the Tulsa Police Department and the north Tulsa community, which was never great to begin with, had taken a nosedive. So when it was announced that the city would soon have a new police chief, Greenwood activists demanded that they play a role in the vetting process. That did not happen, and on the first of February, Wendell Franklin, who had served for twenty-three years on the TPD, became the new chief. That Franklin was African American did little to still the simmering anger and frustration in Greenwood. And one month later, at the Public Oversight Committee meeting, those feelings were on full display.

In truth, the committee meetings had grown smaller and smaller, and the March 2 gathering reflected the trend. Unlike the packed auditorium at the Rudisill Library some eight months earlier, where members of the public stood in line for their turn at the microphones, this meeting was held in a modest room where empty chairs far outnumbered occupied ones. Moreover, far more POC members were missing than were present.

At the beginning of the meeting, Kary Stackelbeck gave an overview of the excavation that we planned to conduct at the Sexton's Site at Oaklawn the next month. She detailed the processes of the dig. She talked about security and what the media would and would not be allowed to do, and she explained how members of the Public Oversight Committee could serve as observers during the excavation. Stackelbeck then introduced a representative from the Muscogee (Creek) Nation, who would also have a tribal monitor present. Long-standing federal law gave Native American tribes the right to be present when human remains were uncovered during an archaeological investigation. And in the case of the dig at Oaklawn, the interest by the nation had been elevated by the fact that some Creeks had been buried not far from the Sexton's Site. The representative gave a brief presentation. But when she asked for questions from the audience, the fireworks began immediately.

Kristi Williams, a descendant of Creek Freedmen, went into detail about how the Creek Freedman had also suffered along the Trail of Tears, including members of her own family. And then she got to the heart of the matter, namely when the Creeks kicked the descendants of the Creek Freedmen off the tribal rolls, and she unleashed a withering and impassioned critique. The Muscogee (Creek) Nation representative looked like she'd been bushwhacked, saying that she had not expected this to be on the agenda that evening. Then it was Reverend Turner's turn, and the atmosphere in the half-empty community room soon felt like a spring storm.

First, Turner questioned why the Public Oversight Committee was only *now* hearing about having tribal monitors at the upcoming dig at Oaklawn. Why are we just learning about this now? How come whenever Black people finally get close on something, others take it away? He then went after Amy Brown, the deputy mayor, for not yet having cut a deal with the owner of Rolling Oaks to allow for ground-penetrating radar scans to be made there. "You're just incompetent!" But the climax came when Reverend Turner lay down on the linoleum floor of the meeting room. There are bodies lying out in the cold ground, he said, while other people are just standing around. Then he threatened to quit the Public Oversight Committee. A photographer from the *Tulsa World* began shooting away, while one of the reporters scribbled notes. It was all high drama.

Only the meeting wasn't quite over. Phoebe Stubblefield explained that nobody was trying to stop the excavation, and Stackelbeck retook the podium and tried to address federal law and Native American claims. But the anger, and the seemingly growing divide between the majority African American Public Oversight Committee and the largely white scientific team and city representatives, was evident. Neither Reverend Turner nor Kristi Williams, of course, spoke for the entire Greenwood community, and there were other African American pastors, I had been told, who had expressed concerns that the search for the graves was being politicized. "This is sacred," one preacher had allegedly warned. But there was no denying the anger and frustration that simmered beneath the surface, not just in Greenwood, but in communities of color across the nation. And two months later, following the murder of George Floyd in Minneapolis, that anger and frustration were evident in marches and protests from coast to coast.

Tulsa had a protest march as well, perhaps the largest in the city's history. Nearly a thousand people joined a procession that wound through Greenwood and ended up at John Hope Franklin Reconciliation Park. But the protest soon went off-script, or at least followed multiple playbooks. One group peeled off and blocked traffic on Interstate 244, until the Oklahoma Highway Patrol—and an angry white driver, hauling an empty horse trailer—shut that down. Other groups fanned out downtown or moved into the white neighborhoods on the south side. A few windows were broken, some tear gas canisters and pepper balls were fired off by police, but on the whole, the local protests were largely uneventful. Only the city wasn't yet done with its season of political turmoil.

On June 10, 2020, the Trump campaign announced that the president would hold his first post–corona outbreak rally in Tulsa on June 19, which also happened to be Juneteenth, an unofficial holiday that African Americans in the southwest had long celebrated as the date when news of the defeat of the Confederacy and the end of slavery had finally reached Texas. Criticism quickly erupted and three days later, the campaign moved the rally to June 20. Only that did not stem the outcry, as pundits for CNN, MSNBC, and various East and West Coast newspapers saw the selection of Tulsa for the Trump rally as a clear racist dog whistle—much in the way that Ronald Reagan had kicked off his presidential election campaign in Philadelphia, Mississippi, the site of the kidnapping and murder of three civil rights workers. As a result, the massacre received another jolt of attention in the national press.

President Trump's campaign rally turned out to be a complete bust. Not only did the imagined overflow crowd fail to appear, but the BOK Center was demonstrably less than full with a rather meager assemblage of MAGA-hatted supporters. Afterward, the president stormed out of town, while the imagined clashes between Molotov cocktail–hurling antifa militants and gun-toting militia members failed to materialize. Indeed, when the Tulsa police arrested a white-haired grandmother for staging a one-woman sit-in too near the entrance to the BOK Center, one wag suggested that the Trump campaign might want to bail her out and invite her inside. Meanwhile, shortly before the rally, a group of local artists and activists had painted a huge BLACK LIVES MATTER sign on Greenwood Avenue in case the president or Vice President Mike Pence visited the district. They did not.

Life in Tulsa moved on.

Four weeks later, we were digging in Oaklawn.

BREAKING GROUND

Shortly after seven o'clock, two bright red pickups, each emblazoned with the official seal of the Oklahoma Archeological Survey, pushed through the back gate at Oaklawn Cemetery. The morning was warm and overcast, with a curtain of low, gray clouds hovering over the downtown skyline to the west. Betsy Warner was already on-site, while the rest of us slowly trickled in. The night before, Phoebe had refused to stay at the hipster hotel that the city had put us up in after she had determined that there were no individual window air-conditioning units in the rooms, and that we would thus all have a higher risk of contracting COVID-19 because of the recirculating air. "We're just a bunch of middle-aged people, trying to stay alive," she told the desk clerk, before heading over to the Hampton Inn. On the drive down from Michigan, I had noted that once one hit southern Indiana, face masks started to disappear. Tulsa was no different. There would be plenty of people in town during the next two weeks who went about their lives unmasked. Even the bars were open.

At the cemetery, we were all issued orange hard hats and bright green safety vests. One by one, we also had the backs of our throats swabbed by a Tulsa police officer, who then snapped off the end of the plastic probes and sealed them in a test tube, which he placed inside plastic bags with our names on them. Later that day we all learned that none of us had tested positive for the coronavirus. Soon afterward, the heavens opened up and we all dashed to our cars to wait out the rain. But by late morning, the grid had been laid out and the city workers had arrived with the track hoe, while a smattering of television and print reporters and camera operators stood along the other side of the iron fence on the western edge of the cemetery, waiting for something to happen.

And at exactly 11:17 a.m. on Monday, July 13, 2020, something did.

After first carefully relocating a butterfly bush and three baby garter snakes that were curled up among its roots, the first bucketful of dirt was removed in the search for the graves of the missing of the Tulsa race massacre. It had taken decades of work to get to this moment, years of digging through old papers, maps, and newspapers. Years of speaking with scores and scores of people, white and Black, who had seen something as a child, or whose parents or grandparents had told them stories in the dimming evenings of their lives. Years of ups and downs. Whatever the end result would turn out to be, this was an important step for Tulsa, a clear and unbroken marker along the city's long struggle to face up to its past.

But even more important, this was an unprecedented moment in American history as well. For the dead of the Tulsa massacre were hardly alone. Over the course of four centuries, thousands of African Americans had been the victims of murderous racism. Slaves had been shot, stabbed, and tortured to death, their bodies tossed in unmarked graves. Lynchings had claimed hundreds more, as Black men and women had their life force stolen from them beneath railroad trestles, telephone poles, and ancient oak and elm trees, their limbs creaking and swaying beneath the extra weight. And then there were the ones who simply disappeared, into labor camps and county jail cells, or patches of woods or swamp, lit only by the pine knobs and kerosene lamps of their executioners. The victims of racism weren't few. They were legion.

But here, in this aging cemetery in the heart of the country, was the first time that an American government—federal, state, or local—had ever *actively* set out to locate the remains of victims of American racism. While highway and construction projects occasionally uncover the boneyards of anonymous slaves and prison farm laborers, some of whom were undoubtedly worked to death or murdered, such discoveries were unplanned and incidental.

No, this was something new.

The rest of the afternoon proved to be seemingly uneventful. Inch by inch, the track hoe driver scraped away the top layers of soil, forming a rectangular pit that was maybe twelve by twenty feet. And while the hole was still only a couple of feet deep by the end of the day, there had been an odd discovery or two, including a large piece of rusted metal, a relic of another age, that appeared to be the door to a house furnace. The archaeologists who hovered near the slowly deepening pit wrote it off as something that might have come with fill dirt, perhaps from a construction site, that might have been hauled to the cemetery at some point. But no one seemed overly concerned. By quitting time, the sun had finally come out. After everyone else left, Angela Berg, a forensic specialist with the state medical examiner's office, quietly set up a series of imaging tools, known as target spheres, around the perimeter of the pit. Looking like an elementary school model of the solar system, with each of the spheres mounted on its own tripod, the device quietly traced the depth and dimensions of the newly excavated ground.

. . .

The city workers were back bright and early in the morning. Led by a tall Russian-German from South Dakota named Tim, whose multicolored brown-gray hair hung in a nearly two-foot-long ponytail down his back, the crew was both skilled and enthusiastic. Most had heard of the massacre, but none had ever participated in an archaeological investigation before, and all were eager to learn. After Tim, the two stars on the crew were Dave and Twinkie, the track hoe operators. Both were big and blond-haired. Dave sported a pair of titanium steel earrings, while Twinkie—so named because he demolished an entire box by himself when he spent the night at a friend's house as a boy—was covered in tattoos. Sitting in the track hoe, carefully maneuvering the controls with subtle movements of their wrists, each looked to me like a Grateful Dead version of the Buddha. On the other side of the cemetery fence, along the berm rising up to the freeway, a homeless man played a ukulele while his dog slept nearby.

The day brought one discovery after another.

At eight o'clock sharp, two small pieces of leather emerged. Black and musky, they were pieces of a shoe or boot. The copper eyelets had turned green. Heather Walsh-Haney, a forensic archaeologist from Florida, stood inside a white City of Tulsa dump truck where Dave or Twinkie deposited each bucketful of dirt from the deepening pit. Using a shovel and a heavy garden rake, Heather and one of the city workers sifted through each load of dirt, using hand signals to communicate with the track hoe operators. A half hour later, work stopped when Heather found a piece of wood. Bob Pickering, an archaeologist from the University of Tulsa, took a look, and decided that it was probably from a fence post.

"Not a finished piece of wood like a coffin part," he said.

Between the cemetery fence and the freeway ran a bike path. During weekdays, however, most of its users appeared to be either the homeless or people out for a stroll. An older white man on an adult tricycle asked Randy Krehbiel, a reporter for the *Tulsa World,* what was going on inside the cemetery. When Krehbiel told him that we were looking for victims from the 1921 race riot, the old man was dismissive. "They're in the wrong place," he said. "My granddad told me that they dumped the bodies into the Verdigris River, and that they floated down to Muskogee."

At a quarter past nine, Greg Maggard, an archaeologist with the Oklahoma Department of Transportation, found a bullet cartridge. Center-fire, it had been shot. Bigger than a .22, it was probably from a .32 pistol. Carlos Zambrano, an investigator with the Office of the Chief Medical Examiner, emailed photos of the cartridge to a firearms expert at the J. M. Davis Arms and Historical Museum in Claremore, about a half hour northeast of Tulsa, for identification. A few minutes later, Angela Berg spied a sliver of bone, possibly from a rib, though it was uncertain whether it was of human or animal origin. Nevertheless, the discoveries of the bullet cartridge and the piece of bone electrified the team. Voices were now lowered to a whisper, while all eyes were trained on both the deepening pit and the buckets of dirt that were being hauled upward. Along the fence, camera crews started aiming their boom mikes toward small clusters of archaeologists, hoping to catch a scoop by picking up on what they were saying.

A quick lunch was followed by a noon press briefing in the nearby Tulsa Fire Museum. At least six camera crews had set up their gear in the ornate Art Deco building, built ten years after the massacre, which originally served as the central dispatching station for the city's firemen. Print journalists, some representing the *New York Times,* the *Washington Post,* and *National Geographic,* had claimed the available folding chairs, their iPhones and notepads at the ready. Kary and Phoebe spoke briefly. Despite the discoveries of the morning, there were still no head-lines. No evidence of a mass grave had been discovered, nor had any clearly identifiable human remains been found.

More discoveries came after lunch.

A pair of horseshoes. A temporary metal grave marker. Bricks. Bits of crockery.

An older white woman appeared at the fence and handed over a spray of lavender and other flowers, wrapped in brown paper. It was a small remembrance, she said, to those who died in the massacre. One of the city crew placed it along the corner of the hole.

The soil was now growing uniform in color, a chocolatey brown, sometimes lightening to a sandier shade. The pit, now the size of a child's bedroom, was fully eight feet deep. Along its eastern end it had been benched, with three large steps, two feet wide and nearly as deep, leading down to the bottom of the hole. By now it was clear that we had hit a large deposit of landfill dirt, likely deposited in the 1930s.

This was not welcome news. This, and not a mass grave, is what had shown up on the ground-penetrating radar readings. Some members of the team were still optimistic. While dictating a podcast narration into his phone, Kavin Ross related how he had heard that there was a connection between horseshoes and African American graves. But I was far less hopeful. Since the GPR data had been discredited as indicating a mass grave, we now had only one piece of evidence, namely the oral tradition among the former sextons, that suggested massacre victims had been buried in this area. I was ready to stop digging here and instead move to the site near the 1921 headstones. But I was not in charge of the excavation. At half past three, the city workers had been on the job for eight hours. It was time to close up shop for the day.

Twinkie took one more bucket of dirt and dropped it in the dump truck.

Then he turned off the track hoe and started heading for the exit.

Kary now had a new plan.

We would extend the original hole, now referred to as Site A, to the south. This extension would be known as Trench B. The city crew, cheerful and businesslike, got right to work while a light, unsettled wind swirled in from the south. West of downtown it looked like rain. Of course, it was just my mood, but the skyline that morning felt grim. Rising up behind the freeway, the Bank of Oklahoma, the First Place and Mid-Continent Towers, and the old Fourth National Bank building reminded me of a group of bishops, all miters and frowns, from some half-remembered painting or movie. In the trench itself, however, the forensic scientists and other archaeologists were anything but gloomy.

"We're gonna make this stuff up as we go," said Carlos. "Like we usually do."

Greg lightly chuckled. "You're onto me," he said.

Bucketful by bucketful, the trenching unfolded. But with it came head scratching more than anything else. Instead of easily defined horizontal layers of soil, what was revealed looked more like abstract art.

"This is the damnedest profile," said Greg, rubbing his temple. "It's incredibly mixed. There's not a homogenous fill episode here."

"It's crap," Angela replied. "Well, that wasn't the word I was going to use."

"This is not natural in any sense of the word. You don't get marbled clay over sand."

As the son of a geologist and the younger brother of a seismologist, I was not completely lost in the conversations, though much of it was well above my pay grade. As the digging, and the day, wore on, however, the general drift of the emerging analysis became clear. This part of Oaklawn had been originally much lower than it was now. And over the years, both before and after the massacre, loads of fill dirt, possibly from construction sites, were dumped onto the area. One possible reason for this, geoarchaeologist Deb Green explained to me, is that a nearby underground stream kept eroding the soils. "It looks just like a dump," Greg added. "There doesn't seem to be any rhyme or reason to it."

A few artifacts turned up. Bits of glass and brick. A woman's hairpin.

The most exciting find was a woman's metal cosmetic case. Inside was tucked a 1913 silver dollar, three Mercury dimes, a nickel, a penny, and a one-dollar silver certificate, all in remarkably good shape. But nothing was found that could be immediately tied directly to the massacre. We called it a day at eleven minutes after five. Ten minutes later, all of us, city workers and scientists alike, gathered in a circle as Brenda Alford, the chair of the Public Oversight Committee, led us in a moment of silence.

Day Four. Thursday, July 16.

Disappointment was now growing. Phoebe, Brenda, and I had become concerned when there was talk of taking "a pause" in the excavation. Emotions were starting to fray as well. As if on cue, the wind picked up and dark clouds quickly rolled in from the west. While the Florida contingent, veterans of that state's deadly hurricanes, took off for their cars, the rest of us Okies stood beneath the lightweight nylon awning put up by the city, marveled at the show in the sky, and swapped tornado stories. We'd all seen much worse.

Once the weather passed, it was back to work. Lee Bement, another OU archaeologist, was down in the trench now, carefully observing the newly turned earth whenever Twinkie or David scooped out another bucketload. Lee's tools were the custom-made, flat-ended shovels that archaeologists prefer, along with a World War II bayonet that he kept in a leather scabbard. He'd poke and prod at anything that looked of interest. Most were just bits of crockery. But when an air pocket was uncovered, a jolt of excitement surged through the ranks of the scientists. Air pockets often result when something has decayed, say, a body. But nothing of interest was found. A little later, I was speaking with Deb Green when her eye was caught by a small flake in the east wall of Trench B, which she extracted with her trowel. It was colored a dull, light gray.

"Is that a piece of stone?" I asked. "Or bone?"

"The way to find out," she told me, "is to place it in your mouth. If it sticks to your tongue, it's bone."

Along the fence, meanwhile, a handful of regulars had kept vigil.

Tall and bearded, John Patrick Kinnear was a real estate salesman who had returned home to Tulsa to help take care of his aging father. But during his years in Los Angeles, he had also skirted along the edges of Hollywood. In *The Outsiders,* Francis Ford Coppola's movie version of S. E. Hinton's classic young adult novel, he played a Soc. "I was the tall one," he told me, "driving one of the cars to the rumble." Now he was out bearing witness to his hometown tragedy. So was Terry Baccus, an African American entrepreneur who'd been raising money to produce a new film about Greenwood. A descendant of Creek Freedmen, Baccus believes that the real history of indigenous peoples has never been told. "You know why they won't ever dig up the Spiro Mounds?" he asked me. "Because all of those people look like me." He gave me a business card and encouraged me to check out his website.

Reverend Turner also stopped by.

"Hey, good to see you!" he called out to me.

"Good to see you."

But not all encounters were so positive. A middle-aged white woman in designer sunglasses came storming up to the fence. "Are my tax dollars paying for this?" she demanded to know. I responded that most of us were volunteers, which threw her for a loop. Afterward, Mike Simons, a staff photographer for the *Tulsa World,* pulled me aside. "You know," he told me, "I've worked on dozens and dozens of murder and missing-person cases, where investigators work their tails off trying to locate the bodies of the victims. Sometimes they'll dig in ten or twelve places. And not once has someone like that woman ever asked whether her tax dollars were involved. They only ask this about the riot people."

Only the visitors weren't done yet. Near the end of the day, the president of the local archaeological club, an elderly white woman, came up to the fence and inquired about a couple of the OU archaeologists. She then started talking about the massacre, and she asked me whether I had known Bill O'Brien, a now deceased local history buff, who claimed that "blacks were coming from the south to attack white Tulsans." I said that I did, but that I didn't think much about the quality of his work.

"Well," she said, "it's mostly just rumor anyway."

My jaw immediately stiffened. "What is just rumor?"

"Well, all that happened back then."

It was a tired refrain that I had heard many times. If you don't like parts of your history, then claim it's controversial, or unproven, or unknown. Or maybe just a rumor. The conversation left me with a sour taste in my mouth. But the old lady and the selectively tax-conscious woman in sunglasses weren't the only reasons. For by Thursday afternoon, Trench B had already grown to more than forty feet in length and six feet in width. We had also dug down to a depth of nearly fourteen feet. But we couldn't dig our way out of disappointment. And it was abundantly clear to me that the excavation at the Sexton's Site was likely turning out to be a bust.

Five days later, on Tuesday, July 22, the curtain finally came down.

Despite yet a third trench being started, this one extending toward the east, and a huge coring truck being brought in to drill out core samples at other locations in the Sexton's Site, the archaeologists had found zero evidence of a mass grave, or even of any individual burials.

At the closing press conference, the mayor, however, was steadfast. Stating that it was a moral imperative that we find the remains of the massacre victims, he made it abundantly clear that despite our first failed attempt, we would continue our work with the full blessing and tax dollars of the city. It was an impressive performance. Bynum wasn't backing down, and the entire dig team was fully grateful for his support. But we also knew all too well that the stakes were now higher than ever before. There was no question that we would get at least one more shot at an excavation. But if we came up empty again, all bets were off.

Meanwhile, across town, another drama involving the massacre was already taking shape. And before the summer was through, it wasn't just cemetery soil that would be laid bare. So too would be the divide that neither press conferences nor city-owned bulldozers could begin to cover up.

BODIES OF EVIDENCE

On the Wednesday that the cosmetic case containing the one-dollar silver certificate and a half dozen old coins was unearthed in Trench B at Oaklawn Cemetery, the Reverend Robert Turner set off on his weekly pilgrimage to city hall to call for reparations. The weather was warm and breezy, with bright shafts of sunlight breaking through the uneven cloud cover. Turner was wearing a patterned white polo shirt and black slacks, shoes, and cap. Taking up his familiar position at the corner of Second and Cincinnati, the pastor of Vernon AME Church lifted a battery-powered fifty-watt megaphone and began to again remind the city of its great uncorrected sin. Only this time, he was not alone.

For gathered on the sidewalks leading up to the entrance of city hall was a crowd of around seventy-five to eighty people who had a different agenda. Carrying handmade signs that read, LET FREEDOM BREATHE, MY RIGHTS DON'T END WHERE YOUR FEAR BEGINS, and MANDATORY MASKS = TYRANNICAL OVERREACH, they had come to register their displeasure over the recommended use of face masks as a tool to fight the quickly spreading coronavirus pandemic. All of the anti-mask protesters were white, and most were women. Many carried plastic water bottles, and had their purses strapped crosswise across their upper torsos. What they hadn't planned on was an African American minister interrupting their protest.

"Hey, sweetie, let us have our voice. We'll let you have yours."

This was said by a thirtysomething woman dressed in white leggings and a tie-dyed top, her hair pulled back beneath a blue ball cap, who reached out and put her right hand on Turner's forearm as she spoke. But when the pastor didn't respond and kept on talking, she reached up into his megaphone and tried, unsuccessfully, to unscrew the horn. Other members of the crowd tried to block Turner's vision with their signs and a black-and-white golf umbrella, or tried to drown him out with chants of "LIBERTY!" "FREEDOM, FREEDOM!" and "USA! USA! USA!" Only Turner was not about to be stopped. "An angry, racist mob descended upon Greenwood, and dropped a bomb upon Greenwood, and killed Black people. And not one of those angry, racist, white thugs went to trial for their crimes," he said. "And it is a travesty that you care more about a face mask than you do about justice for people whose bodies are still in mass graves." But when Turner called for "REPARATIONS NOW," he clearly touched a nerve.

"How much do you need?" asked a skinny white male in a T-shirt, who then pulled a wad of cash from the back pocket of his shorts and began waving a couple of one-dollar bills at Turner. The young woman standing next to him, wearing a cotton dress and a silver necklace, had a different take.

"You are racist," she shouted at Reverend Turner. "*You* are."

Reparations were now back on the table.

This time, however, the social landscape of the massacre had changed radically. Unlike the days of the riot commission and Professor Ogletree's lawsuit, when there were more than one hundred known living survivors, by the first days of August, there were perhaps as few as two or three. Hal Singer, who went on to become a noted jazz musician and who lived in Paris, had been eighteen months old in the late spring of 1921. He would die on August 18. Lessie Randle was still spry and talkative, and Tiffany Crutcher had recently helped to restore and upgrade her home. But Randle was now 105 years old. The last survivors of the massacre were flickering out.

But the call for reparations was no longer aimed solely at those who had experienced firsthand the horrors of 1921. Now the focus was on their children and grandchildren and great-grandchildren, and the long shadow of lost homes and looted businesses, missing inheritances and vanished opportunities. "This isn't just some passing thing that we're doing," said Regina Goodwin, who represented Greenwood in the state legislature. "We're thanking God Miss Randle survived. We're also thinking about all the unborn children that could have been and we will never forget and we're going to keep fighting." In north Tulsa, there was also a new catchphrase: NO RECONCILIATION WITHOUT REPARATIONS.

Here was an issue that, perhaps more than any other, went to the heart of Tulsa's stubborn racial divide. For there was no longer any question, even in white neighborhoods, that the massacre had happened, that Greenwood had been destroyed, and that the looters and arsonists and murderers of the spring of 1921 had gotten away scot-free. That a great wrong had been done was no longer up for serious debate. But how to respond, a century later, to the long-term devastation caused by the massacre was the sticking point. In the white neighborhoods on the south side of town, there was a familiar litany of "It happened so long ago" and "I wasn't even alive then, so why should I have to pay?" And, as always, on the internet, far harsher sentiments were on display.

"We could tear down every statue, change our holidays and our currency, pay billions in reparations," tweeted someone named Jake. "And in a few years they will be back with more demands, as full of hatred and envy as ever."

Reparations would be no easy sell in Tulsa.

But some were willing to try.

Damario Solomon-Simmons once had dreams of being in the NFL.

Born and raised in Tulsa, the son of a single mom, he could dissect for you every memorable run that Barry Sanders had made at Oklahoma State, or explain, on any given play, why Lawrence Taylor of the New York Giants slanted right or held back. Out on the practice field at Booker T. Washington High School, or in crosstown battles with rivals Central or McLain, his heart would race. But when he tore his ACL his senior year, his dreams of gridiron glory disappeared like yesterday's newspaper. His grades were abysmal, and though he managed to graduate high school, a year later he was working in a warehouse in Dallas.

Coming back home to Tulsa, Solomon-Simmons was determined to turn his life around. He put in two years at a community college before he landed at the University of Oklahoma. He even made it as a walk-on to the Sooners football team his senior year, but his football days were soon over. Setting his sights on being an attorney, he was accepted at the OU College of Law and spent a summer studying abroad at Oxford. But it was his second year of law school, in 2003, that helped change the trajectory of his career. While interning at the Department of Commerce in Washington, D.C., he was asked to give a speech for an MLK Day event. In the audience was Adjoa Aiyetoro, a civil rights attorney and reparations activist. When Aiyetoro learned that Solomon-Simmons was from Tulsa, she connected him with Charles Ogletree's legal team, who had just launched a reparations lawsuit on behalf of more than one hundred survivors of the Tulsa massacre. Though the suit failed, for the young law student, this was heady stuff. And when he returned home to Tulsa upon graduation and set up his own law firm, Solomon-Simmons was determined to both enact change and make a name for himself.

Both would eventually come true.

Solomon-Simmons litigated for tribal citizenship rights for the descendants of Creek Freedmen and helped to file a wrongful death lawsuit against the City of Tulsa on behalf of the family of Terence Crutcher. He also represented nearly a half dozen first-round NFL and NBA draft picks in contract negotiations, and he created his own foundation to help address the needs of young African American males. A dynamic advocate with sharply tailored suits and a million-dollar smile, by the time he turned forty Damario Solomon-Simmons had become not only one of the best-known lawyers in Tulsa, but was edging toward a national reputation as well.

On September 1, 2020, those stakes were raised considerably.

For on that day, in Tulsa County District Court, Solomon-Simmons filed a race massacre reparations lawsuit on behalf of nine plaintiffs, including survivor Lessie Randle, six descendants of massacre survivors, Reverend Turner's Vernon AME Church, and the African Ancestral Society. Equally broad were the defendants in the suit, which included the City of Tulsa, the local chamber of commerce, two planning authorities, the Tulsa County Board of Commissioners, the sheriff, and the Oklahoma National Guard. At the heart of the case was the allegation that the defendants were, in effect, still improperly making money off the massacre. "The defendants are working to bring business to Tulsa using the Massacre and Black Wall Street as a 'cultural tourism' draw," read the petition for the lawsuit. "The problem is not that the Defendants want to increase the attraction to Tulsa, it is that they are doing so on the backs of those they destroyed, without ensuring that the community and descendants . . . are significantly represented in the decision-making group and are direct beneficiaries of these efforts. This exclusion appears intentional, not a happenstance."

On the surface, the lawsuit was nothing short of remarkable. Not only did it in essence allege that the most powerful governmental and quasi-governmental institutions in the city were out to make a buck off the tragic events of 1921, but that, in effect, the story of the massacre belonged to the descendants. Equally noteworthy, however, was the legal tack that Solomon-Simmons and his legal team were taking—one that had its roots in, of all things, the opioid crisis.

A little over a year earlier, the State of Oklahoma had won a landmark $507 million case against Johnson & Johnson, the drug manufacturer, for launching "false, misleading, and dangerous marketing campaigns" that resulted in an explosive increase in opioid addiction and overdose deaths in the state. The evidence in the case was both stark and powerful. "From 2000 through 2011," the *New York Times* reported, "members of Johnson & Johnson's sales staff made some 150,000 visits to Oklahoma doctors, focusing in particular on high-volume prescribers." In a state that had been hit hard by the opioid crisis and its attendant broken homes, suicides, and children put up for adoption, here was an evidence trail that was difficult to ignore.

The ultimate success of the lawsuit, however, depended upon some novel legal interpretations, beginning with the court's finding that Johnson & Johnson had violated the state's "public nuisance" law. "Under Oklahoma law," the *Tulsa World* would later report, "a nuisance is defined generally as the performance of an unlawful act, or the failure to perform a duty, that renders an individual insecure in the person's life or ability to use property or endangers the person's comfort or safety." Only there was one other twist, and that was that the statute of limitations did not start running until *after* the nuisance was abated. This was, for Solomon-Simmons, the key to getting around the issue that had doomed Charles Ogletree's efforts at winning reparations for riot survivors.

Announcing the lawsuit at a press conference at the Greenwood Cultural Center, where he was joined by both Reverend Turner and Greg Robinson, a Tulsa native and community organizer, Solomon-Simmons was, by turns, emotional, defiant, and unbowed. "We are so excited to finally get justice for Greenwood after 99 years," he said. "No one to this day has been held accountable. They got away with it. Until today." There was more. "The City of Tulsa destroyed an entire community and displaced its citizens," he added. "The question is: Does the massacre and its effects continue today? The answer is an unequivocal yes." Reverend Turner then fired off some salvos of his own, accusing the City of Tulsa of profiting off the misery of 1921. Greenwood isn't just a tourist site, he said, "It's a crime scene." Later, Solomon-Simmons offered a more sobering assessment of the road ahead. "We know this is going to be a long fight," he told a reporter for the *Tulsa World*. "Could be three, four years. But I think we have a really good shot."

The search for the graves, meanwhile, continued.

A few weeks after I had seen Angel for the last time, arrangements were made to survey the long, trenchlike depression at the Canes. Scott Hammerstedt and Amanda Regnier had driven over from Norman in their bright red Oklahoma Archeological Survey truck, with the ground-penetrating radar unit in the back. The morning was bright and clear, and while none of the homeless were seen, an unattended campfire smoldered near the upstream end of the site. The two archaeologists worked quickly, marking the coordinates on their iPhones and setting up their grid. Soon, the only noise to be heard beyond the low rumble of the traffic rolling across the I-244 overpass was the hollow sound of the plastic wheels of the ground radar unit scraping over the now bare ground, its dirt as fine as chocolate powder, mixed with ash and cane. But the subsequent data revealed nothing suggesting a mass grave. Wherever the burial pit was that Bob Patty had seen in the old black-and-white photograph, we seemingly hadn't yet found it.

And we needed to find something.

We needed to do so for the sake of the victims and their families, and there was a largely unspoken sense among the archaeological team that the clock was ticking and the window of opportunity might not last long. In August, G. T. Bynum had been elected to a second term as mayor, and there was no reason to question his support of our efforts. But in the middle of a pandemic, with its stresses and strain on the economy, there was no guarantee as to how long we could rely on sufficient funds to continue our work. We couldn't afford to throw away our shot.

As a result, once again, all eyes turned to Oaklawn. For even though the geophysical data for the Sexton's Site had not, in fact, indicated the presence of a mass grave, the anomalies that had been detected near Reuben Everett's and Eddie Lockard's headstones looked promising. Moreover, if we began an excavation in this area, soon dubbed the Original 18 Site, there was little question that we would encounter human remains. In other words, whether they were massacre victims or not, any excavation in that area would quickly turn into a recovery effort. And as the pandemic summer of 2020 turned into the pandemic fall, and the likelihood of such an excavation increased, responsibilities on the scientific team subtly shifted. For a forensic investigation required a forensic expert. And fortunately, we were not lacking in that regard.

Los Angeles, Fall 1983.

Located at 108th and Denker in South Central L.A., George Washington High School had long since waved goodbye to its glory years.

Drugs were openly dealt in the hallways, while wannabe Crips and Bloods flashed their colors and alluded to all the heat that they were capable of bringing. Not too many years later, Denzel Washington would even star in a made-for-TV movie called *The George McKenna Story,* about a reform-minded principal who would eventually change the culture at the embattled school. But for sixteen-year-old Phoebe Stubblefield and her identical twin sister, Peggy, Washington High was a gauntlet that the two brand-new tenth graders would somehow have to navigate. "It was horrible," Phoebe later recalled. "Being smart was seen as either a sign of weakness, thus making you a target to be exploited, or as trying to be white." Both girls were placed in the highest-level classes, even as tenth graders, but they were still miserable.

Born in Los Angeles in 1968, the girls were the daughters of two Tulsa-born transplants who had sought a better life fourteen hundred miles west of Greenwood and Archer. Their mom was a housewife, while their dad worked as an engineer for Northrop, where he'd hired on in 1958. But after seventeen years of steady employment, with the Vietnam War winding down, he was suddenly laid off. The stress on the family was great, as the parents tried to make ends meet. "We had some really weird dinners for a while," Phoebe recalled. Eventually, however, their dad caught a break and found work at Hughes Aircraft. There, the most amazing thing happened. "He got pay raise after pay raise, practically with every paycheck," Phoebe said. "Finally, they asked him why he never joined the management program at Northrop. My dad replied, 'They never asked me.'"

Growing up in South Central L.A. in the 1970s and early 1980s, Phoebe and Peggy lived in an all-Black neighborhood and attended all-Black schools. But their immediate environs also presented their own challenges, particularly the growing prevalence of drugs and the rise of gang violence. In the seventh grade at Horace Mann Junior High School, the girls and their parents caught wind of an organization called

A Better Chance, which offered scholarships for students from low-income areas in Los Angeles to attend one of the city's elite private schools. For three years in a row, Phoebe and Peggy carefully filled out the detailed application forms for the scholarship and turned them in to the school's guidance counselor. And a few months later, after asking the counselor again and again whether they'd won the scholarships, they'd always get the same answer.

No, the counselor told them, they'd been turned down.

The next year, at Washington High School, Peggy wanted them to try one more time for a Better Chance scholarship, the last year that they would be eligible. Phoebe was reluctant, but her sister eventually wore her down and, together, they once again filled out the forms. Almost immediately they were accepted. Moreover, they were contacted by the foundation *at home*. Then it hit them. They hadn't been denied before. Their junior high school guidance counselor had never bothered to send in their applications.

The Westlake School for Girls may as well have been on a different planet. The student body all wore uniforms—white blouses, gray skirts, navy sweaters—and were dropped off each morning by a line of Mercedes-Benzes, Porsches, and Lincoln Continentals. Well-coiffed, tanned, and overwhelmingly white, they were the daughters of motion picture studio executives, physicians, lawyers, and investment consultants. There was an equestrian club, a ski team, and a winter formal, and packed houses for dance recitals and an all-school production of *A Midsummer Night's Dream*. At the much-anticipated ring ceremony, senior girls wore pearl necklaces and white dresses of lace and chiffon, and had garlands of fresh cut flowers in their hair. Perched between Beverly Hills and Bel Air, the elite private school was seven zip codes and a million miles from the streets of South Central.

Phoebe and Peggy were among the handful of African American students at Westlake, and they did not make any close friends while they were there. "As twins, Peggy and I were pretty much our own contained unit anyway," Phoebe remembered. "I only went to another girl's house once during my time at Westlake, while not once did any of the other girls come to visit us." But academically, the twins were woefully behind. "At Washington, I was in precalc," Phoebe said. "At Westlake, I tested in at seventh-grade math." She was also deeply deficient in English, history, and Spanish. But she *loved* school. And at Westlake, studying wasn't frowned upon. Instead, it was fostered. Phoebe and Peggy dug in and made progress, while some of their less intellectually gifted classmates struggled. Phoebe also started gravitating toward science classes. She loved the observation and the experimentation, the innate symmetry of physical laws, and the never-ending quest for answers. The sisters graduated in 1986. Peggy took off for UC Davis to embark upon a career as a veterinarian, while Phoebe headed up Highway 101 to Santa Barbara.

She loved UCSB. "I made my best friends there," she added. Phoebe worked hard and got good grades, and even took ancient Greek—"So I could read the Bible." After becoming intrigued by the work of one of her professors on ape skeletons, she ended up majoring in anthropology. But she had no real idea of what she wanted to do with her life, and only a vague clue as to what graduate school actually entailed. She also chafed a little at the notion of spending the rest of her life on a college campus, being drawn more toward some form of applied science. Then she heard about *forensic* anthropology, specifically of using anthropological science to help solve crimes, and was immediately intrigued.

A-ha, she said to herself, *that's for me*.

Up until then, Phoebe had been throwing away all these envelopes from graduate schools that had been arriving in her UCSB mailbox, figuring that she didn't have a way to pay for any more education. But once she got bit by the forensic bug, she quickly changed her approach. "I took the last two envelopes that arrived, and saw that they each had forensic programs," she recalled. "So I applied to both of those schools. One was Washington State and the other was the University of Texas." She got into both. "But I didn't know anything about either school, so I started asking the graduate assistants at UCSB if they knew anything. One of them said, 'I heard the Texas program is pretty good.'" And that was that. She headed to Austin to get a master's degree.

Her two years at the University of Texas were a hodgepodge of ups and downs. She liked the laid-back college town and learned a great deal about her field. But she also concluded that one of her advisers was a two-bit tyrant. He had given her very specific instructions on how to write her thesis in a certain fashion. She did so, but when she turned in her draft, he announced, "This won't do," and declared it unacceptable. "I had a key to his office," Phoebe remembered. "So, I snuck in one day and looked at the theses of his previous students and saw how they'd done theirs. Then I went home and wrote mine the same way." But the adviser didn't like that either. "This looks," he said, "like it was written by *another person*." Only he wasn't finished. "He started insisting that I add more data," Phoebe recalled.

Then he started criticizing her for her weight.

It was one comment too many.

"I stood up and slammed my hands down hard on his desk," she remembered. "Then I told him that where I come from, people didn't put up with remarks like that." She was boiling mad and ready, if necessary, to fight him, right then and there in his campus office. "I thought I could take him. And I was ready to go," she said. "Well, he got scared and backed off."

A little over a year later, after she had completed her degree, Phoebe quit her job as a cashier at a local H-E-B grocery store and shipped her books and most of her belongings to some friends. Then, late one warm Austin afternoon, she boarded a Greyhound bus and settled in for a thirty-hour ride east along Interstate 10.

Gainesville, Florida, August 1995.

"Have you ever seen a dead body before?"

The interlocuter was William R. Maples, a skinny banker's son from Texas who now, at fifty-eight years of age, was arguably the world's most famous forensic anthropologist. Like Clyde Snow, whom he knew well, Maples could read human remains with astonishing insight and precision. From skeletons buried deep in the woods to bodies that had been tossed in rivers, burned in incinerators, or hidden in landfills, not only could he determine the time and nature of death and the age, weight, and gender of the victims, but his expert testimony had sent dozens of killers to a life behind bars or on a one-way trip to the gas chamber. The director of the C.A. Pound Human Identification Laboratory, one of the most renowned forensic labs in the world, Maples also served on the anthropology faculty at the University of Florida. Indeed, his expertise was so great, he had been called in to help solve some important historical mysteries as well. The same hands that were now gripping the steering wheel of the car headed out of Gainesville had traced their fingers along the rib bones of Francisco Pizarro, the Spanish conquistador, and cradled the skulls of the Russian royal family, sent to their deaths by Bolshevik revolvers in the blood-drenched summer of 1918.

"Freshly dead or embalmed?" came the reply.

"Either."

"Yes," Phoebe said. "An embalmed one."

Now twenty-seven years old, she was a brand-new PhD student under Dr. Maples's tutelage at the University of Florida. Together, the two of them—the esteemed white professor and the unknown and untested African American student—were driving out to view the body of a woman that was being held at the medical examiner's office in a nearby county. The local coroner had concluded that the woman, whose body had been found near a lake, had been murdered two weeks earlier. Maples was skeptical, and he had brought along his new student to see what she thought. It didn't take long. Phoebe could immediately tell, both by the condition of the woman's skin and by the larval stage of the maggots that had already begun to develop inside the corpse, that the woman had been dead for only three or four days. Phoebe had passed the test. But more than that, she and Maples discovered that they were made for each other.

Twenty-five years later, in September 2020, Phoebe and I are on a Zoom call together. She is back in Gainesville, where she is now the interim director of the C.A. Pound Human Identification Laboratory. Like her late mentor, William Maples, she juggles multiple responsibilities, including teaching at the university, instructing graduate students in proper lab procedures, and assisting sheriffs and police departments across the state of Florida in helping to identify murder victims whose remains have been discovered in their jurisdictions. Like most scientists, she is focused and dispassionate while working on a case. "My job," she will say, "is to let the bones speak." Nonetheless, she wrestles with the moral implications of her work, especially when dealing with the remains of victims of sadistic killers and sociopaths. "I'm a Christian, and I believe in Hell," she once told me. "And I think and hope that when I die, that I'm not going there. But Hell must be an awfully terrible place if even some of these sexual-torture murderers can keep from going there by confessing their sins and repenting."

But despite being both a highly respected scientist and one of only a precious handful of African Americans in the field, like many people across the pandemic-stricken country, she must also deal with more mundane issues, such as, on this mid-September day, the threat of spotty internet coverage. Moreover, the lights in the lab where she is Zooming from are permanently set on an automatic timer, and every few minutes they will go out. And when they do, Phoebe has to wave her arms about, like a wide-open basketball player looking for a pass from a point guard, so the motion detector will switch them back on.

The subject of our conversation is, of course, Tulsa.

Her relationship with the city is both long and deep. Not only was it her parents' hometown, but her family roots in Greenwood stretch back before the massacre. Phoebe is related to Ellis Walker Woods, the dynamic principal at Booker T. Washington High School whose beautiful home at 531 N. Detroit was looted and torched by whites during the massacre. She has visited the city numerous times over the years to visit with cousins and now-elderly aunts and uncles. Greenwood wasn't foreign territory to Phoebe. It was the old sod, where an aged aunt and uncle still lived. But it was also a place for which she harbored mixed emotions, a city where she felt that opportunities for African Americans were terribly constrained. "Had I been raised here," she told me more than once, "I don't know what I would have become."

Soon, however, she would have a chance to change her ancestral hometown forever.

For on September 14, 2020, we got the word. The second dig was a go.

We were going back to Tulsa.

THE DIRT WHISPERERS

The morning was cold and bleak, with a cutting wind blowing in from the north. Most of the scientists and the city crew had their hands jammed in their pockets and their hoodies pulled up under their hard hats. For even though the trees at the cemetery were still in their full summer glory, all green and lush, this would not be a typical Oklahoma fall day, with rising temperatures and plenty of sunshine. Nearby, on the Inner Dispersal Loop of the interstate, the late morning traffic whooshed by with a dry, rocket-like sound. It was time to begin our second dig.

With her floppy hat and insulated parka worn beneath her fluorescent green safety vest, and holding an official-looking aluminum notebook with her gloved hands, Phoebe Stubblefield looked like a field commander issuing orders to her troops, which, indeed, she was. And as the morning unfolded, the potter's field at Oaklawn Cemetery again stirred to life. Graduate students set up a sifting station where buckets of dirt would be passed through fine-mesh metal screens. A city worker was dispatched to Lowe's to pick up some last-minute supplies. Kary

Stackelbeck, meanwhile, marked off the locations of anomalies in the Original 18 Site with small yellow flags and numbered plastic cones. Later, she would use a can of orange spray to outline the areas that the city workmen were to excavate. A couple of camera crews and a handful of observers were lined up along the cemetery fence on the Eleventh Street side. Some gutted out the bitter weather on the sidewalk, while others had retreated to their cars, with the engines running and the heaters on.

Setting up took hours.

Finally, at exactly 2:11 p.m., Twinkie lowered the boom of the John Deere track hoe and scraped the first bucketload of grass and dirt off what is now called Unit 6. A rectangular area, perhaps five feet wide by eight feet long, it featured a particularly strong anomaly picked up by the ground-penetrating radar. There was hope that the anomaly, which showed up as a dark, blurry shape on the digital images, might represent metal casket hardware or perhaps a heavy belt buckle. Some had even speculated about guns being buried with the victims. Regardless, we would soon know something. For inch by inch, bucket by bucket, and minute by minute, the Unit 6 pit slowly deepened. It took more than an hour to go two feet.

By four o'clock, a discovery had been made.

It was not what anyone has been looking for. Instead it was the end of a rather flimsy and thoroughly rusted length of metal, perhaps two feet long. It was clear to me from the start what it was, namely part of a temporary grave marker, and my spirits immediately fell. For even though the identifying information on whose grave it was had long since eroded away, there were now some much bigger concerns. Was this rusty piece of metal what the ground-penetrating radar picked up on? Is *this* the anomaly? Moreover, what possible connection might there be between a temporary grave marker and the graves of massacre victims? This was not a good omen.

A half hour later came another find.

It was a piece of crockery.

Then, at four thirty, one of the city workers spied something whitish in color in the Unit 6 pit. Approximately three inches long and three-quarters of an inch wide, it was a piece of bone. Quickly, Phoebe, Kary, Angela Berg, Deb Green, and Jessica Cerezo-Román, a forensic anthropologist at the University of Oklahoma, gathered in the hole. Phoebe pulled out a well-worn hand trowel, as well as a probe that looked like a long wooden chopstick, and carefully exposed some of the soil where the object had been found. "Humerus?" Angela whispered. Jessica then produced a jeweler's loupe and studied its surface. Twenty-five minutes later, there was a verdict. The bone was nonhuman.

We were also now done for the day.

On the walk back to our cars, Phoebe and I discussed the ground-penetrating radar data and how unhelpful it had been. That night, at the hotel, sleep did not come easy. Anxious and unhappy, I was worried that we were on the verge of another failed dig. Instead of the remains of massacre victims, we were finding temporary grave markers and construction fill.

Day Two. October 20, 2020.

Another gray morning, though not as cold. There was little wind.

First thing, Lee Bement and Deb Green guided a white GMC pickup, with the Oklahoma Archeological Survey's coring rig mounted on the back, to a spot near the big oak tree that was located south and a little west of the headstones for Reuben Everett and Eddie Lockard. Carefully working their way west, toward the cemetery fence, they took a series of core samples. Meanwhile, at Unit 6, the blue plastic tarp was pulled off the hole, while Twinkie started up the track hoe and lowered the boom.

We hit something on the very first scoop. It was a mixture of wood and bone.

The wood appeared to have been the top of a casket, while the bones were small dark fragments, most the size of an acorn, and nearly the same color as the surrounding soil. I turned to Bob Pickering, the TU archaeologist, and quietly asked, "We found human bone?" He gave me a wry smile, nodded his head, and whispered in a mock-conspiratorial tone, "We call it 'material.'" Everyone on the site had been asked to keep their voices down, in order to keep rumors from flying on the other side of the fence.

As the day unfolded, the excavation of Unit 6 would now be done by hand. Kary took the lead here. Her fingers are slender and strong, like those of a concert pianist. Her attention to detail marks her as a formidable archaeologist. Under her direction, slowly but surely the outlines of a coffin emerged, while the dirt around the skeletal remains was carefully transferred into five-gallon blue plastic buckets. These were then walked over to the screening station that was manned by graduate students from both Oklahoma and Florida, who kept an eye out for anything of interest.

The bones themselves were extremely fragile. The rib cage of the individual buried in Unit 6 had collapsed, while other bones were to the point of crumbling if even barely touched. Preservation has not been good in this part of Oaklawn, though enough of the skull remained intact for Phoebe to determine that it belonged to a female. But the larger reality was that we'd discovered human remains in a part of the cemetery where no one was supposed to have been buried. Then there was a small metal plaque with the words AT REST inscribed upon it, probably a decorative element for an inexpensive coffin. Both Phoebe and I thought it likely that the unknown woman represented a single burial, one that was unrelated to the massacre.

Meanwhile, perhaps ten yards to the west, preparations were in high gear to begin a second excavation, this time near where the coring took place. To be known as Unit 12 & 13, it too was in an area where several anomalies had been detected. Once again, the track hoe was maneuvered in place, this time with David at the controls. And as he lifted out the first bucketful of earth, my emotions were pinballing between optimism and despair. While there was no question that African American massacre victims were buried in unmarked graves at Oaklawn, any confidence that I had once placed in ground-penetrating radar had long since vanished. It felt like we were shooting in the dark.

Only the feelings did not last for long.

And this was because professional archaeologists see things in dirt that the rest of us simply do not. They notice the subtlest gradations in soil color and texture, and they can spot the tiniest bits of foreign matter. Both scientists and craftspeople, they are dirt whisperers who can see and feels things that others miss. And by a little after three o'clock that afternoon, Lee and Deb had both climbed into the rapidly enlarging pit that was Unit 12 & 13, their gazes fixed downward. Lee then outlined something on the floor of the hole with his hands, and soon enough, I could see it as well. On the bottom of the pit, the outlines of two rectangular shapes could be faintly seen. Resting side by side, and at the same level, they were separated by only a couple of inches of dirt. I caught Lee's eye. "Coffins?" He nodded yes. Then he motioned for Tim to start up the track hoe once again, and to keep extending the hole to the west.

By a quarter after four, the outlines of three more coffins had been discovered.

Forty-five minutes later, when we quit for the day, the sun was shining.

Day Three. Wednesday, October 21, 11:08 A.M.

"I think we're done here."

The voice belongs to Lee Bement. All that morning, with David operating the track hoe, Unit 12 & 13 became a trench, approximately six feet deep and six feet wide, that stretched for at least thirty feet toward the iron fence along the western edge of Oaklawn. The outlines of twelve coffins, each laid side by side, had by now been discovered. Most appeared to be simple pine boxes, the cheapest kind of coffins. But there also may be others. For while we had established the east-west limits of this particular burial event, we didn't know if there might be more adjacent rows to the north and south. Moreover, it was possible that these twelve coffins were, in fact, stacked on others. And at the very western edge of the site, Lee had discovered steps that had been cut into the earth, presumably to make it easier to bring the coffins into the hole.

This wasn't just a burial pit.

It was a mass grave.

Three days later, both sites were filled back in.

At Unit 12 & 13, a long roll of breathable geotextile fabric was draped over the twelve coffins, followed by a layer of sand. Then, with either David or Twinkie at the controls of the track hoe, the dirt that had originally been removed was returned. "We've gone to Plan B," Phoebe had told me the day before. For as much as she and the other scientists had hoped to examine the remains in the coffins in situ, or right there in the actual trench, they now hesitated. The extremely fragile condition of the skeletal material of the lone burial in Unit 6 had convinced them that any analysis would need to take place in a secure, indoor, climate-controlled laboratory setting. "We're only going to have one shot at doing this," she added. "And we've got to do it right."

Much would have to be done before then.

In order for the remains to be removed from the trench, an exhumation order would have to be issued by a judge. The Public Oversight

Committee, meanwhile, would need to decide whether DNA should be extracted from the remains. Some daunting technical issues would also have to be solved, including how to physically remove the dirt-filled coffins from Unit 12 & 13 while doing as little harm as possible to the skeletal materials themselves. Moreover, once the actual exhumation occurred, the remains would need to be studied, and then reburied as quickly as possible. Despite all the challenges ahead, however, no one wanted to put on the brakes. Clyde Snow always said there are stories in bones that need to be told. And these stories needed to be heard. Before the week was up, plans were already afoot for a return to Oaklawn. If everything worked as planned, we'd be back by early summer.

Less than twenty-four hours after the final coffin was uncovered at Oaklawn, an email arrived in my in-box regarding a gentleman who was said to have knowledge concerning the burial of massacre victims at Newblock Park. His name was Hugh McKnight. Seventy-seven years old and long retired, he had spent most of his career working for the parks department for the City of Tulsa, eventually becoming a top administrator. I called him the next morning at his home in Amarillo, Texas.

This is what he had to say:

In 1970, he had just moved to Tulsa and taken a supervisory job with the department. His office was at Newblock Park, and one day an older employee named Buck Mosier pulled him aside. "There's something you ought to know about," Mosier told him. Then the older man showed him two places in the park where he said that riot victims had been buried.

There was no doubt in my mind that, at the very least, the story had potential and needed to be looked into further.

"If I were to send you either a map or an aerial photograph of Newblock," I asked McKnight over the phone, "do you think that you could mark these two locations that Mosier showed you?"

"I can do you better than that," McKnight replied. "I'll meet you in Tulsa and show you myself."

A date was quickly agreed upon, and two weeks later, I was headed back to Tulsa. In the meantime, I did some research on Buck Mosier, whom McKnight had described as a "real country kind of fellow." In a search on Ancestry.com, he turned up. Lloyd Columbus Mosier had been born in 1917 in Cowlington, Oklahoma, a scratch of a town in Le Flore County, not far from the Arkansas state line. In 1940, when he signed up for the draft, Mosier was living in Tulsa, where he worked for the parks department. He was still there in 1968, when he was listed in a city directory as a foreman. He certainly fit McKnight's description. And the fact that Mosier was working for the department only nineteen years after the massacre was encouraging. Since he was only four years old in 1921, it was clear that Mosier had been told by someone else about the burials. Still, despite it being a thirdhand account, the story had promise, and I was looking forward to meeting McKnight.

We met at Newblock at noon on Saturday, November 7. He'd driven in from Amarillo that morning. Dressed in khakis, a red plaid shirt, and cordovan penny loafers with white socks, he had a box of Marlboro Reds stuck in his shirt pocket and an olive-drab Chevy ball cap on his head. We went over his account together, bit by bit. No, he didn't know how Mosier knew where the bodies were buried. But he didn't have any reason to doubt him. As soon as he heard the story, McKnight took it up with his supervisor, who waved the news away and told him to forget about it. "There's no proof anyway," his boss added.

The two locations, which were only twenty yards or so apart, weren't anywhere we had looked before. Both were near the small creek, now banked in concrete, that gently coursed through the park. When I asked McKnight how he knew where the two locations were that Mosier had pointed out to him some fifty years earlier, he pointed to a huge cottonwood tree, one that was likely eighty or even a hundred years old or more. Both sites had some issues. One was on a narrow strip of grass between the left-field edge of the softball field and the parking lot. The other, located near the cottonwood, was on ground that looked to have been built up over the years. But both sites were clearly worth checking out.

"I just love Tulsa," he told me.

Before he got back into his truck and made the five-hour drive back to Amarillo, I asked McKnight a somewhat personal question. I'd figured out when he had been born and when he got done with college, and it seemed like he had been the perfect age to have been drafted and sent to Vietnam. "Well, I was," he told me. But when a family friend on the draft board in Amarillo tipped him off that he was about to get taken, he decided to join the Marines, figuring that they were the best trained and, as a result, would be the most likely to survive the war. So, on the appointed day, he showed up for his physical. "I was standing there, buck naked, and the doctor was looking me over," he recalled. Then the doctor went around behind him.

"When did you have polio?" the doctor asked.

"I never did."

"Like hell you didn't. Your spine is twisted every which way."

The discovery got him out of the Marine Corps and going to Vietnam. Later, McKnight told his mother about what had happened. "You know," she said, "the summer when you were about ten, you were really, really sick. And we never could figure out why."

For fifty long years, Tulsa's murderous spring lay hidden.

Buried beneath lies and obfuscation, hatred and heartbreak, shame and guilt, reminders of what happened were quietly swept away. Official records vanished from file folders or were sent up the line, never to be seen again. Photographs and newspaper articles disappeared, while those who dared to speak on what had happened faced threats and censure. In time, even the landscape of the massacre changed beyond recognition. Greenwood, of course, rebuilt itself. But the Drexel Building, the original offices of the *Tulsa Tribune,* and the 1921-era county courthouse all had fallen to the wrecking ball. And in textbooks and local histories, a fairy-tale version of the city's past arose, one in which the massacre either didn't happen or was of no importance. Rather than openly face up to the past, residents talked about the truth only in certain parts of town, and quietly when at all. "Tulsa lost its sense of honesty," was how John Hope Franklin once put it.

Finding it again has been no simple task.

Because history isn't just a chronicle of events. Rather, it is a mirror of both who we are and who we want to be. For us to learn from the past, we have to look at and wrestle with *all* of it—the sad and the ugly as well as the good and the great. And while we can't take credit for the accomplishments of previous generations, we can learn from their mistakes.

With each new documentary and each new television episode, each new headline and each new discovery, Tulsans of today have had to face up to a part of their past that earlier generations would not. They are not, however, by any means alone. For all across America, and, indeed, all across the world, we are living in the Age of Reevaluation. Long-standing institutions are coming under brand-new scrutiny, histories are being challenged and reexamined, statues are toppling. Moreover, those whose voices have long been kept from being heard are claiming their rightful places at the table, while others are waiting in the wings.

If what has happened in one Middle American city during the past century is any sort of a guide, there is a long road ahead of us. It won't be easy. But it will be necessary. And in some cases, the stories have been there all along.

EPILOGUE

"Oh, boy. Here comes the Grim Reaper."

The speaker is Tommy Matson, a former schoolmate, who can usually be found, seven mornings a week, sitting at the counter at Brookside By Day, a popular breakfast spot on the city's near south side. A clatter of dishes can be heard in the back, while two or three harried waitresses, all young white women in their twenties, dash back and forth with pots of coffee and platters heaped with omelets, home fries, bacon, and waffles for pairs of senior citizens, families with children, and an assortment of lawyerly types dressed for the day in suits and ties. Tommy has been a friend for years, and his smart remark is largely said in jest. But it also contains an edge of truth.

For many white Tulsans, learning the unvarnished reality about the massacre has been neither an easy nor a welcome process. Some have found it to be disturbing and distasteful, others have found it to be sinful and a source of shame. Some have pushed back against every revelation, while others want it to all simply go away. And the search for the graves has not only brought some of the emotion behind these positions into high relief, but it has also served as a proxy for the nation's deeper racial divide. "Why don't y'all look for mass graves of Native Americans?" someone named Frank Luna wrote on Twitter during the first dig at Oaklawn. "I'm sick of hearing Black Lives Matter all lives matter. One thing I learned in this country going up is they kept Black people alive for slaves but Native American they tried to wipe off the face of the earth. You need to look for mass graves of my ancestors the native America!"

Across town, in north Tulsa, the discovery of the mass grave elicited a range of responses. "I felt a sense of sadness and pain, thinking about these people and what had happened to them," said Bobby Eaton Jr., host of a radio talk show in Greenwood. "But," he added, "it's the discovery of a lifetime." Late on Thursday afternoon, October 22, one day after the last coffin was discovered, a group of African American ministers and community activists, under the auspices of the Greenwood Arts and Cultural Society, held a press conference just outside the Oaklawn Cemetery fence. "With the discovery of the bodies here, we want to make sure that justice is found," said a spokesman, as light traffic streamed by on Eleventh Street. "The men and women that are here that you see behind me are the reason that this earth was moved and why the truth has been found."

Not all of the truth about the massacre or its victims, of course, has been found. And even nearly a century later, there are still important and unresolved questions about what happened in Tulsa. But if there is one certainty, it is that the story of the massacre is not going to go away. Indeed, it's never been easier to learn about the events of 1921 than it is now.

Type "Tulsa race massacre" into Google and in less than one second, more than one and a half million results will be available. A few clicks later, you can access Wikipedia, Britannica, Vox, and Zinn Education Project web pages dedicated to the massacre, while the Library of Congress and the Chicago Public Library offer study guides. In a matter of minutes, you can find dozens of newspaper and magazine articles about the massacre, look at extensive photographs posted by the Tulsa Historical Society, the University of Tulsa, and the Greenwood Cultural Center, and watch or listen to stories about what happened in Tulsa in 1921 produced by National Public Radio, Fox News, NBC, ABC, CBS, Bloomberg, the History Channel, and Voice of America. The once secret tragedy is hidden no more.

On eBay one can purchase original 1921 newspapers with headlines about the massacre, autographs by riot survivor Olivia Hooker, and T-shirts emblazoned with BLACK WALL STREET—NEVER FORGET! At an online rare books auction in February 2020, a first edition of Mary E. Jones Parrish's *Events of the Tulsa Disaster* sold for $2,625. And, of course, television viewers across the globe can—and have—watched HBO's *Watchmen* series, which won no fewer than eleven Primetime Emmy Awards, including Best Limited Series, Best Lead Actress, and Best Supporting Actor, more than any other show produced that year. More documentaries, meanwhile, are in the works, as are books and articles. Never before has knowledge about the history of the massacre been so readily available.

Reckoning with that history, however, is a different matter.

Two decades ago, the State of Oklahoma walked away from the chance to pay reparations to one hundred or so survivors of the Tulsa race massacre, opting instead to present them with a gold-plated medal. Now, with the one-hundredth anniversary of the massacre, the question will again ring out. Only this time, Tulsans will no longer be alone. For as the role of slavery in the economic, political, and social life of the nation has come under increased scrutiny, including on Wall Street and Ivy League college campuses, a nationwide call for reparations is once again simmering just below the surface. It is not likely to soon disappear.

In the meantime, Tulsa is far from the only place in America where the victims of racial violence were buried in unmarked graves. In patches of woods and mountain hollers, on windy plains and in unmapped cemetery plots and prison grounds, victims of Jim Crow violence lie scattered across the land. Some, like Florence Fairchild's family, had been cut down by Night Riders. Others were lynched, shot, beaten to death. Murdered by the hundreds, they are a grim accounting of segregation's evil grip. Most lie in graves that will never be found, because the knowledge of where they were buried has been lost. But not for all. And in cities and towns across the country, there are those who know where the bodies are buried. It is time for them to speak. It is time for us to listen, to remember, and to honor those we lost.

Meanwhile, the true impact of the discovery at Oaklawn is yet to be known.

Too many questions need to be answered, and many more voices need to be heard. There is a chance, though, that it may one day be seen as a turning point, at least in Tulsa if nowhere else, where the lost and forgotten of 1921 were brought back into the national story. Plans are already underway for a memorial to honor the victims of the massacre, and if and when that is built, it will likely become a shrine of national interest and importance. For fifty years, the story of the massacre had been suppressed. Then, for fifty more, that story was brought to light. In the next fifty, we will learn what it means.

There will be plenty to do.

But before the last of October started to slip away, and other duties carried me away from Tulsa and back on the road for the long drive to Ann Arbor, there was one more place I needed to go.

Scott Blackburn picked up on the second ring. As always, he was cheerful and happy to help. We agreed to meet in a half hour in the parking lot behind the fire station at Newblock Park. He was already there when I pulled in, sitting in his F-150. A pack of American Spirit Originals lay on the dash, while a Travis Tritt song was playing on the radio. I hopped in and we started the short drive through the park, past the dirt bike track, and up on the levee to the edge of the Canes.

October is a glorious month in much of the country, and that is most certainly the case in Oklahoma. The sky is a purer and deeper blue than any Dutch master could ever hope to paint, while the leaves, for the most part, still hold their green. The days are often warm, but light blankets and quilts come out at night. But it's the light that is the most remarkable, soft yet strong. William Faulkner once talked about August days in Mississippi when there was a foretaste of autumn, when the light was "as though it came not from just today but from back in the old classic times." Riding in the truck with Scott Blackburn that morning felt like one of those days.

The river was bright and luminescent, with the morning sun glancing off the surface.

Born in the Rocky Mountains just outside Leadville, Colorado, where snow buttercups and marsh marigolds line its banks, its waters already had traveled more than a thousand miles before they got here. Countless generations of Osage and Kiowa hunted buffalo, elk, and deer along its banks. Spanish explorers and African slaves, under the command of Vázquez de Coronado, had been the first non-Indigenous people to set their eyes upon the river back in 1541, while a few miles downstream from where Scott Blackburn and I were riding in his truck, glass beads brought by French trappers had been coaxed out of its muddy banks by teams of archaeologists. Glistening in the morning sun, the outline of an ancient river crossing was visible still, as well as a shelf of limestone, often exposed during dry spells. Herds of buffalo had splashed across these same rocks, as had runaway slaves, Union and Confederate soldiers, and scores of homesteaders looking for a new life. The land on either side of the levee wasn't just a little-used public park surrounded by one of the oldest neighborhoods in town. It was a memory book of the past.

When we reached the end of the levee, Scott parked the truck and we got out and walked. The wind had picked up a little, rattling the dry outer leaves of the cane. We could smell campfire smoke, and as we entered the upper level of the homeless camp, the first of the jumble of tents came into view. Smoke's was there, covered in a newish-looking blue tarp, as were some of the regulars', and there were some new tents as well. There weren't, however, many people around. Most had already left for the winter.

Scott handed out some packets, while I offered bottles of water. Trash was once again scattered across the trough that we had surveyed back in March, and weeds had grown up along what the survey archaeologists thought might be a couple of individual graves closer to the river, probably of a more recent vintage. I shouldn't have been at all surprised that the site looked much the same as it had before, but it was still a relief that it was. Someday, I told myself, we'd be back. There was no question in my mind that Bob Patty had been right, that somewhere not far from where Scott and I stood, massacre victims had been buried in a trench. Whether it could be found was another question. But the search needed to go on.

Scott and I lingered for a few minutes and looked out across the river. Then we started back up the hill toward the truck.

"Oh, I forgot to tell you," he suddenly said. "I found out what happened to Angel."

"Really?"

"Her family had been really worried about her. Apparently, she had gone off of her meds, and they didn't know where to find her. Finally, one of her uncles came out, all the way from California. Somehow he found her and took her home."

I couldn't help but smile.

Angel had made it, I thought. She had made it to where she needed to be.

Perhaps, God willing, the rest of us can as well.

ACKNOWLEDGMENTS

If there was an irony to Mrs. Gillam's racist vitriol in the lamp shop on that spring morning in 1966, it was that my education on racial matters was soon to take a decidedly different turn. Before the summer was finished, my best friend, Mark Walker, had passed around a copy of *Manchild in the Promised Land* among our set of Little League teammates and fellow Boy Scouts. Not only were we mesmerized by Claude Brown's riveting story of growing up in Harlem and by its vivid descriptions of an American life far different from our own, but it was likely the first time that any of us had read anything written by a person of color. That fall, when most of us entered Orville Wright Junior High School as seventh graders, we still didn't have any Black classmates, despite the fact that the *Brown* decision had been issued a dozen years earlier. I did, however, have an African American shop class teacher, Robert Maxie, a man of towering patience who was tasked not only with teaching us how to use a drill press, but how to behave like human beings. The winds of change were blowing, however erratically, and when I first walked through the doors of Central High three years later, in the fall of 1969, I suddenly found myself going to school with scores of African American students. Through them, not only did my racial education truly begin, but the foundation for all my subsequent work on the massacre was assuredly laid.

In putting together this book, I have benefited from the advice, memories, and views of more people than I can thank. But there are some that need recognition, beginning with a number of my former Lee, Wright, and Central schoolmates, including Connie Cope, Cliff Cronk, Jim Edwards, Charlie Hill, Henry Johnson, Pam Johnson, Tommy Matson, Laura Misch, Susan Neal, Monte Northam, Cheryl Hamilton O'Meilia, Craig Ryan, Bruce Scott, Linda Scott, Peter Walter, Rick Westcott, Terry Westemeir, and the family of the late Mark Walker—Dick, Robin, and Mary Gaye. A special thanks goes out to Patty and Gary Himes, as well as to Fred and Randi Wightman, who not only offered wise counsel, helpful connections, and great meals, but a room of my own back home before the pandemic hit.

Many years ago, John Strawn, my thesis adviser at Reed College, impressed upon me the importance of establishing and maintaining good relationships with archivists. "It's because of the Effie Maes of the world," he declared, "that good history gets done." And while I don't know a single Effie Mae, anyone researching the history of the massacre, me included, is lucky to be able to work with Marc Carlson, the director of special collections at the McFarlin Library, University of Tulsa, and Luke Williams at the Tulsa Historical Society and Museum, both of whom are consummate professionals. Thanks as well to Hillary Pittman of the *Tulsa World* and to Chad Williams at the Oklahoma Historical Society, who graciously went out of their way to provide me with copies of decades-old articles from the *Oklahoma Eagle,* the *Tulsa World,* and the *Tulsa Tribune*. Special thanks are in order for Mechelle Brown and Frances Jordan-Rakestraw of the Greenwood Cultural Center, who have tirelessly kept the stories of Greenwood and of the massacre alive for decades, and to Mary Moore of the Tulsa City-County Library, who confirmed my memories of the Oklahoma Room.

In the ongoing search for the unmarked graves of massacre victims, I want to thank, first and foremost, the other members of the Physical Investigation Committee, which I have been honored to chair. They include: Phoebe Stubblefield of the C.A. Pound Human Identification Laboratory at the University of Florida; Kary Stackelbeck, state archaeologist of Oklahoma; Bob Brooks, former state archaeologist; Lesley Rankin-Hill, professor emerita at the University of Oklahoma; Scott Hammerstedt, Amanda Regnier, and Debra Green of the Oklahoma Archeological Survey; Angela Berg and Carlos Zambrano of the Office of the Chief Medical Examiner; and Alicia Odewale of the University of Tulsa. Hats off are also in order for excavation team members Leland Bement of the University of Oklahoma, Greg Maggard at the Oklahoma Department of Transportation, Heather Walsh at Florida Gulf Coast University, and Bob Pickering at the University of Tulsa. Members of the Public Oversight Committee have also played a vital role in the ongoing search, especially committee chair Brenda Alford, former chair Maxine Horner, and members Reverend Robert Turner, Kristi Williams, Michelle Place, Regina Goodwin, Chief Egunwale Amusan, Vanessa Hall-Harper, and Greg Robinson.

The search for the graves would not have been possible without the leadership and support of the City of Tulsa, especially that of Mayor G. T. Bynum, Deputy Mayor Amy Brown, and dozens of dedicated public servants, including Ashley Philippsen, Mark Hogan, Terry Ball, Michelle Brooks, Mark Weston, Nick Doctor, Tim McCorkell, and Joe Bryan. Special kudos are also in order for Betsy Warner and Kavin Ross. Betsy stayed true to her promise to carry on the research undertaken by her father, Dick, and made hugely important contributions to the search. During the long decades between the end of the first search and the beginning of the second, Kavin did more than anyone else to help keep the investigation alive. And once the search was restarted, along with the current effort to win reparations for massacre survivors, numerous Tulsans stepped up to offer help and valuable insights, including Terry Baccus, Scott Blackburn, Ken Busby, David Busch, Scott Chesney, Paul DeMuro, Fred Dorwart, Bobby Eaton Jr., Patricia and Amley Floyd, Reuben Gant, John Patrick Kinnear, Ken Levit, Mike McConnell, Hugh McKnight, Patrick McNicholas, Eddie Majors, Tim Mills, Bob Patty, Larry Phillips, Michelle Place, Noe Rodriguez, and Jimmie L. Scyffore Sr.

Fellow writers and historians, as well as journalists, researchers, photographers, filmmakers, and media professionals have also shaped this book. Thank you Maggie Astor, Marina Athayde Gonçalves, Bas Blokker, Jon Boorstin, DeNeen Brown, Kelly Kurt Brown, Adrian Brune, Michael Byhoff, Nia Clark, Crys Davis, Jonathan Delgadillo, John Donovan, Ben Fenwick, John Whittington Franklin, Megan Gannon, Caleb Gayle, Wade Goodwyn, Wayne Greene, Paul Hendrickson, Fred Hiebert, Karlos Hill, Nkem Ike, Kimberly Jackson, Tracy Jan, Hannibal Johnson, Melissa Kent, Ellen Knickmeyer, Salima Koroma, Randy Krehbiel, Rachel Levy-McLaughlin, Victor Luckerson, Tim Madigan, Kendrick Marshall, Annalisa Merelli, Steve Miller, Alexander Moore, Keiko Morris, Jess Olson, Nick Poppy, Joy Reid, Edwin Rios, Joe Rushmore, James Russell, Arnaud Sagnard, Mike Simons, Brent Staples, Laurie Thomas, Jenny Wagnon Courts, Eric Walker, and Marco Williams.

At CAA, hats off to my superb agents, David Larabell and Matthew Snyder.

It's been a complete joy to work again with John Parsley, editor extraordinaire—and editor in chief—at Dutton. Hearty thanks are in order as well for Christine Ball, Amanda Walker, Cassidy Sachs, Becky Odell, and Kaitlin Hall at Dutton, and Claire Leonard and Laura Corless at Penguin Random House.

My own family, Betsy, Johnny, and Will, graciously shouldered extra responsibilities while I retreated to the basement for ten months to write this book. Meanwhile, Cameron, our indomitable corgi, added something new to her bag of tricks. Appearing at the top of the stairs every day at exactly five P.M., she would remind me that it was time for her walk.

After this past year, we could all probably use one.

NOTES

Words don't always change, but their meanings can.

In 1921, the violence in Tulsa was also called a riot or race riot by both African American and white newspapers. "Tulsa Riot Was Deliberately Planned," *Norfolk Journal and Guide*, June 18, 1921. "Tulsans Suffering, Ask Relief: Riot Victims Face Winter Without Home, Food or Clothing; City Refuses to Help," *Chicago Defender*, November 2, 1921. "Tulsa Riot Based on Girl's Mistake," *New York Post*, June 8, 1921. "Tulsa Race Riot Jury Indicts Police Chief," *New York Times*, June 26, 1921.

The racial violence that had broken out in East St. Louis, Chicago, Washington, D.C., and other American cities and towns during the previous four years—acts that involved whites assaulting African Americans and invading Black neighborhoods—were then known as race riots. And for decades afterward, historians continued using the term to describe those World War I–era events. By the 1960s, however, the term *race riot* was being applied to a much different kind of event, namely the urban rebellions in Detroit, Los Angeles, and other cities. When three days of fistfights broke out between African American and white students at my high school during the 1969–70 school year, everyone called them a race riot, a term that was later applied to the violence that followed the Rodney King verdicts in Los Angeles in 1992. What happened in Tulsa in 1921 didn't change. What we call it has.

PROLOGUE

Interview with Robert Patty, Coweta and Tulsa, October 12, 2019. Telephone conversations and email correspondence with Rick Westcott and Pamela Johnson, former Tulsa police officers. Ronald L. Trekell, *History of the Tulsa Police Department, 1882–1990* (1989).

BOOK ONE

CHAPTER 1: 1921

The historical literature of the Tulsa race massacre continues to grow, and by the time this book is only a couple of years old, more books will either have made their way into print or will be written. That said, the most notable nonfiction works on the massacre thus far are as follows: Mary E. Jones Parrish, *Events of the Tulsa Disaster* (n.p.: 1922); Loren L. Gill, "The Tulsa Race Riot" (master's thesis, University of Tulsa, 1946); Rudia Halliburton, *The Tulsa Race War of 1921* (San Francisco: R & E Research Associates, 1975); Scott Ellsworth, *Death in a Promised Land: The Tulsa Race Riot of 1921* (Baton Rouge: Louisiana State University Press, 1982); Mabel B. Little, *Fire on Mount Zion: My Life and History as a Black Woman in America* (Langston, OK: Melvin B. Tolson Black Heritage Center, 1990); Robert N. Hower, *"Angels of Mercy": The American Red Cross and the 1921 Tulsa Race Riot* (Tulsa, OK: Homestead Press, 1993); Eddie Faye Gates, *They Came Searching: How Blacks Sought the Promised Land in Tulsa* (Austin, TX: Eakin Press,

1997) and *Riot on Greenwood: The Total Destruction of Black Wall Street* (Austin, TX: Sunbelt Eakin, 2003); Hannibal B. Johnson, *Black Wall Street: From Riot to Renaissance in Tulsa's Historic Greenwood District* (Fort Worth, TX: Eakin Press, 1998) and *Black Wall Street 100: An American City Grapples with Its Historical Racial Trauma* (Fort Worth, TX: Eakin Press, 2020); John Hope Franklin and Scott Ellsworth, eds., *The Tulsa Race Riot: A Scientific, Historical, and Legal Analysis* (2000), subsequently included in the *Final Report of Findings and Recommendations of the Oklahoma Commission to Study the Tulsa Race Riot of 1921* (2001); Tim Madigan, *The Burning: Massacre, Destruction, and the Tulsa Race Riot of 1921* (New York: St. Martin's Press, 2001); James S. Hirsch, *Riot and Remembrance: The Tulsa Race War and Its Legacy* (Boston: Houghton Mifflin, 2002); Alfred L. Brophy, *Reconstructing the Dreamland: The Tulsa Riot of 1921—Race, Reparations, and Reconciliation* (New York: Oxford University Press, 2003); Randy Krehbiel, *Tulsa 1921: Reporting a Massacre* (Norman: University of Oklahoma Press, 2019); and Karlos K. Hill, *The 1921 Tulsa Race Massacre: A Photographic History* (Norman: University of Oklahoma Press, 2021).

Chapter 2: After

On the duplicity of Tulsa's white leaders in responding to the destruction of the massacre, see: Ellsworth, *Death in a Promised Land,* chapter 4, "Law, Order, and the Politics of Relief." Mayor T. D. Evans even went so far as to endorse the looting and burning of Greenwood. "It is in the judgement of many wise heads in Tulsa, based upon a number of years, that this uprising was inevitable," he said. "If that be true and this judgement had to come upon us, then I say it was good generalship to let the destruction come to that section where the trouble was hatched up, put in motion and where it had its inception." Richard Lloyd Jones, the toxic-tongued editor of the *Tulsa Tribune*, needless to say, went even further. In a June 4, 1921, editorial titled "It Must Not Be Again," not only did he blame African Americans for causing the riot—"Well, the bad niggers started it," he announced—but his description of pre-massacre Greenwood, with its churches and missionary societies, school and hospital, and homes and businesses was a model of white racist propaganda. "It was a cesspool of iniquity and corruption," Jones fumed. "In this old 'Niggertown' were a lot of bad niggers and a bad nigger is about the lowest thing that walks on two feet. Give a bad nigger his booze and his dope and a gun and he thinks he can shoot up the world." On Richard Lloyd Jones's relationship with his cousin, the American architect Frank Lloyd Wright, see: Paul Hendrickson's brilliant *Plagued by Fire: The Dreams and Furies of Frank Lloyd Wright* (New York: Vintage, 2019).

Campbell Osborn, *Let Freedom Ring* (Inter-nation Co., 1954). Reverend Kerr quote: "Causes of Riots Discussed in Pulpits of Tulsa Sunday," unattributed June 6, 1921, article in the Tuskegee Institute News Clippings File, microfilm, series 1, "1921—Riots, Tulsa, Oklahoma," Reel 14, p. 754. Letter from Nancy Dodson, Tulsa, June 4, 2000, to John Hope Franklin, Durham, N.C. John Hope Franklin, "Foreword" in Ellsworth, *Death in a Promised Land*. "Destroy the Klan!" *Oklahoma Eagle,* June 8, 1946. On Maria Brown, see: "How an Act of Racial Violence Reverberates Across Generations," *CBS News*, June 7, 2020, https://www.cbsnews.com/news/tulsa-1921-how-an-act-of-racial-violence-reverberates-across-generations/.

CHAPTER 3: AWAKENINGS

The tremendous impact of World War II–era migrations and demographic shifts—as portrayed so vividly in Isabel Wilkerson's majestic *The Warmth of Other Suns*—on modern American life is only now being gauged. How many other Nancy Feldmans might there be scattered across the country, bringing new perspectives to their new hometowns? And in the case of Tulsa, how much longer might it have taken for the story of the massacre to emerge had she not moved there as a young bride in 1946?

On Nancy Goodman Feldman, see: Nancy Feldman, interview by John Erling, Voices of Oklahoma, November 20, 2012, https://www .voicesofoklahoma.com/wp-content/uploads/2014/02/Feldman_Tran script.pdf; "Oral History Interview with Nancy G. Feldman," by Juliana Nykolaiszyn, Oklahoma Women's Hall of Fame Oral History Project, March 19, 2008, https://dc.library.okstate.edu/digital/collection /Fame/id/741; and Tim Stanley, "Civic Activist Nancy Feldman Remembered for Devotion to Arts," *Tulsa World,* February 21, 2014. Interviews with Nancy Feldman by the author.

The role played by Don Ross both in helping to bring the story of the massacre to light and in shaping perceptions of Greenwood for people across the globe cannot be easily underestimated. Nor, for anyone who has ever met Don, is he easily forgotten. Brilliant, bombastic, a gifted orator, often loud, sometimes sullen, he could command any room that he entered. Once, at a birthday party for George Monroe, he showed up wearing a short-sleeved dress suit, complete with matching shorts, and with the sleeves on the jacket extending only to his elbows. Funny, insightful, and a world-class storyteller, he can also be a complete pain in the rear. Despite several entreaties through his son, Kavin, he refused to speak to me for this book. Carry on, Don. You changed your hometown, your state, and perhaps, one day, your country.

On Ross, see: "Oklahoma Black History Heroes: Don R. Ross," OKDems, https://okdemocrats.org/oklahoma-black-history-heroes-don-rross/; Gail Banzet-Ellis, "Q&A with Don Ross," *TulsaPeople,* September 21, 2018; "Don Ross," Uncrowned Community Builders, https://www .uncrownedcommunitybuilders.com/person/edit/37739; Ancestry.com searches for Israel Ross and Pearline Vann (Evette) Ross; columns by Don Ross appearing in the *Oklahoma Eagle*; and Hirsch, *Riot and Remembrance,* especially chapter 11, "Money, Negro."

Tim Stanley, "Martin Luther King Jr. Spoke in Tulsa Only Once. But 60 Years Later, His 'Inspiring and Electrifying' Presence Has Not Been Forgotten," *Tulsa World,* January 19, 2020. On CORE-led civil rights protests in Tulsa see, for example: "City Police Arrest 41 in Racial Tiff," *Tulsa World*, March 31, 1964; "Pleas of Innocent Entered for Participants of Sit-in," *Tulsa Tribune,* March 31, 1964; and "Police Book 54 After Sit-in Here," *Tulsa World,* April 2, 1964. I am indebted to James W. Russell, a former sit-in participant in Tulsa, and to Bobby Eaton Jr. for insights into the activities of the Tulsa CORE chapter. See also: "Front Line Soldiers: The Civil Rights Activists in Tulsa," KJRH, February 6, 2020, https://www.kjrh.com/news/local-news/front-line -solders-the-civil-rights-activists-in-tulsa.

Here are Don Ross's 1968 columns about the riot and the early history of Greenwood that ran in the *Oklahoma Eagle*: "Black Tulsa, Before and After Statehood," September 12; "'Little Africa,' the Negro Wall Street," September 19; "Tulsa, the City with a Questionable Personality," October 3; "Tulsa, the City with a Questionable Personality" (part two), December 5; "A History of North Tulsa," December 19; and "A History of North Tulsa" (part two), December 26.

On Don Ross's subsequent civil rights activities, see: "'Citizens for Progress' Formed by Tulsa Group," *Tulsa World,* March 30, 1967; "Negroes Lay Beliefs on Line at ORU Seminar," *Tulsa World,* December 12, 1967; and "Don Ross Resigns League Position," *Tulsa World,* November 16, 1972.

Interview with Ed Wheeler, Tulsa, February 27, 1998.

Ed Wheeler, "Profile of a Race Riot," *Oklahoma Impact,* June–July 1971.

CHAPTER 4: TWO SUMMERS

Susan Everly-Douze, "Lamp Shop Owner Illuminated Lives of Many Tulsans, Louise Gillam Retiring at 92," *Tulsa World*, October 4, 1992. "Louise Gillam Dead at 101," *Tulsa World*, August 22, 2001.

Robert Crisman and Ida Alice McClendon, "William H. McClendon: A Life," *Black Scholar* 26, no. 3–4 (1996): 119–20.

Polk-Hoffhine Directory Co., *Tulsa City Directory, 1921.*

Interview with Ruth Avery, Tulsa, February 20, 1998. "Ruth Sigler Avery," Prabook, https://prabook.com/web/ruth_sigler.avery/356596. "Ruth Avery-Parker, Race Riot Historian, Dies," *Tulsa World*, November 6, 2001. David Busch, a longtime family friend, helped decode the Avery-Busch-Ellsworth connection.

Interviews with W. D. Williams, Tulsa, July 1975 and June 7, 1978.

CHAPTER 5: DEATH IN A PROMISED LAND

Wesley C. Hogan and Paul Ortiz, eds., *People Power: History, Organizing, and Larry Goodwyn's Democratic Vision in the Twenty-first Century* (Gainesville: University Press of Florida, 2021).

Events of the Tulsa Disaster, Mary Parrish's slim but remarkable book on the massacre, is due to be republished by Trinity University Press in 2021.

"Mozella F. Jones, 79, Tulsa, Ok. Teacher, Dies," *Jet,* April 28, 1986.

John Hope Franklin and I ended up becoming good friends. One of America's greatest historians, he was also gracious and resolute, steadfast, funny, and down-to-earth. Yet despite all his honorary degrees—more than one hundred if I remember correctly—and his ability to command the attention of presidents, it was the respect that he was accorded by everyday African American citizens that was simply astonishing. They knew that the man who wrote *From Slavery to Freedom* had accomplished something significant, and they weren't at all reluctant to show their appreciation. Walking with John Hope Franklin down one city block in Manhattan would usually take two or three times as long as it should, as complete strangers would stop, introduce themselves, and thank him for his work.

One spring day in 1997, when I was visiting family in San Francisco, I picked up John Hope at the airport and drove him to the Sir Francis Drake Hotel, where the Organization of American Historians was holding its annual convention. The white desk clerk checked him in, then instructed the bell captain, an elderly African American gentleman, to take his suitcase and meet us upstairs. But when we got to the appointed floor, the bell captain looked at the room key and shook his head. "No, no. This won't do. Wait here for a minute." He then disappeared into the service elevator while John Hope and I stood looking at each other in the hallway, trying to puzzle out what was going on. The elderly gentleman reappeared a few minutes later and led John Hope to a different suite, this one even larger and more beautifully appointed. "Now this one," he explained, "has a view of Union Square. And the afternoon light is much nicer. You'll like this one better." Then, without waiting for a tip, the bell captain disappeared.

Pete Earley, "The Untold Story of One of America's Worst Race Riots," *Washington Post,* September 12, 1982. Pete Earley, "Tulsa Race Riot: Back in 1982, Young Author Told Me About What Happened That Day," http://www.peteearley.com/?s=Tulsa.

Tim Stanley, "Black History Month: Book: Death in a Promised Land, Scott Ellsworth," *Tulsa World,* February 21, 2020. Randy Krehbiel, "Author Works to Make Good Come Out of 1921 Race Riot," *Tulsa World,* June 4, 2010.

BOOK TWO

CHAPTER 6: WHERE ARE THE REST?

The literature on the bombing of the Murrah Federal Building in Oklahoma City is extensive. I am grateful to Ben Fenwick, an Oklahoma-based journalist who has covered the recent events in Tulsa for the *New York Times*, for fact-checking my brief account.

While Richard Hatcher has yet to find his biographer, an archival collection focusing on his time as mayor of Gary, Indiana, is located in the Calumet Regional Archives at Indiana University Northwest. Tom Coyne and Rick Callahan, "Richard Hatcher, Trailblazing Black Mayor Elected in 1960s, Dies at 86," *USA Today,* December 15, 2019.

During the fall of 2000, *Tulsa World* declared that Ross's achievements as a legislator had been "outstanding": "Don Ross," *Tulsa World,* October 16, 2000. Ross's fight to create the Greenwood Cultural Center was particularly impressive. Amy Latham, "RUINS to Renaissance: Greenwood Cultural Center Symbol of History, Hope," *Tulsa World,* October 15, 1995. See also: Steve Lewis, "Greenwood Story Needs to Be Told," Oklahoma Policy Institute, September 23, 2019, https://ok-policy.org/greenwood-story-needs-to-be-told-capitol-update/.

"Encyclopedia of Southern Jewish Communities—Tulsa, Oklahoma," created by the Goldring/Woldenberg Institute of Southern Jewish Life, is a concise yet superb historical and contemporary introduction to Jewish life and the Jewish community in Tulsa, https://www.isjl.org/oklahoma-tulsa-encyclopedia.html. "Enrolled Senate Resolution No. 98, Thanking Ken Levit for his Service as President of the University of Oklahoma—Tulsa," April 24, 2006, http://www.oklegislature.gov/cf_pdf/2005-06%20ENR/sres/sr98%20enr.pdf.

Jon Boorstin, the grandson of Sam Boorstin, a leading Jewish attorney in Tulsa, and the son of Daniel Boorstin, the Tulsa-bred historian, author, and former Librarian of Congress, is at work on a joint biography of his family and that of John Hope Franklin, one that will touch upon Jewish life in Tulsa during the early decades of the twentieth century.

Sam Howe Verhovek, "75 Years Later, Tulsa Confronts Its Race Riot," *New York Times,* May 31, 1996. Lois Romano, "The Fire That Seared into Tulsa's Memory: In the Ruins of a Riot, a City Learned Tolerance," *Washington Post,* May 30, 1996. Kelly Kurt, "Tulsans Recall Deadly Race Riot on 75th Anniversary," Associated Press., undated typescript.

Hirsch, *Riot and Remembrance,* 198.

No longer simply a genealogical platform, Ancestry.com has grown into an extremely powerful research tool for journalists, historians, criminologists, and a host of other researchers. Searches for basic biographical information that in earlier days might have necessitated visits to state capitals, university libraries, and the National Archives in Washington, D.C., can now sometimes be completed with a few keystrokes—and an Ancestry.com annual membership. In the case of George Monroe, a search taking less than a minute brings up his World War II–era draft card, which he signed in Tulsa on October 16, 1940; his entry in the 1940 US Federal Manuscript Census; his May 5, 1948, application for a marriage license; entries in Tulsa city directories and telephone books; and so on. In other cases, one can turn up baptismal records, family trees, immigration papers, photographs, death certificates, school yearbook photographs, Social Security applications, and voter registration records. And while there are many records that still require travel in order to access them, I have found the materials available on Ancestry.com to be an invaluable first step in sketching the outlines of individual lives, and I've used the website extensively in researching this and my previous two books.

Interview with George D. Monroe, Tulsa, July 11, 1998.

Michael Wilkerson and Dick Wilkerson, *Someone Cry for the Children: The Unsolved Girl Scout Murders of Oklahoma and the Case of Gene Leroy Hart* (New York: Dial Press, 1981). *Someone Cry for the Children: The Girl Scout Murders,* directed by Michael Wilkerson (Tulsa, OK: Barrister Productions, 1993).

On Clyde Snow, see: Christopher Joyce and Eric Stover, *Witnesses from the Grave: The Stories Bones Tell* (New York: Little, Brown, 1991); Robert D. McFadden, "Clyde Snow, Sleuth Who Read Bones from King Tut's to Kennedy's, Dies at 86," *New York Times,* May 16, 2014; Larry O'Dell, "Snow, Clyde," *Encyclopedia of Oklahoma History and Culture,* https://www.okhistory.org/publications/enc/entry.php?entry=SN001; Eyal Weizman and Clyde Snow, "Osteobiography: An Interview with Clyde Snow," *Cabinet,* Fall 2011; and Kenneth Anderson, *The Anfal Campaign in Iraqi Kurdistan: The Destruction of Koreme* (New York: Human Rights Watch, 1993). Snow was a marvelous mix of a worldly sophisticate and a down-home good old boy, one who was just as comfortable speaking on the phone with novelist Michael Ondaatje or testifying at The Hague as he was sitting in a run-down mom-and-pop restaurant on the edge of town.

In the 1960s, when Snow worked for the Federal Aviation Administration in Oklahoma City, he liked to have a cocktail after a long day at work in a cowboy bar located in the heart of the city's stockyards. Liquor by the drink was not then legal in Oklahoma, so bar owners got around that by declaring their establishments to be private clubs and charging customers a one-dollar lifetime membership fee. Regular customers still had to bring in their own bottles, however, which were stored in lockers behind the bar, and then were charged setup fees for individual drinks. Many of the regulars at this particular watering hole, however, complained that other cowboys were tapping into their bottles of Jim Beam and Jack Daniel's. But not Snow, whose bottles of dry vermouth and Tanqueray gin, which were used to make his martinis, lay unmolested. "They probably didn't know what to do with them," he said.

Lesley M. Rankin-Hill, *A Biohistory of 19th Century Afro-Americans: The Burial Remains of a Philadelphia Cemetery* (Santa Barbara, CA: Bergin & Garvey, 1997).

Chapter 7: The Lady with a Cane

Hower, *"Angels of Mercy."* Records of the American Red Cross regarding the Tulsa Race Riot. Petition for Naturalization for Maurice Willows, Scranton, Pennsylvania, October 1917, and Maurice Sheppard Willows Family Tree, available at Ancestry.com. A number of photographs of Red Cross post-riot relief activities in Greenwood can be viewed at the Tulsa Historical Society's online collection of massacre photographs: https://www.tulsahistory.org/exhibit/1921-tulsa-race-massacre/photos/. A statue of Willows holding up an African American child can be seen at John Hope Franklin Reconciliation Park at 290 N. Elgin in Tulsa.

"Richard S. Dick Warner," *Tulsa World,* September 23, 2009.

Walter White has been the subject of a number of biographies, as well as his own take, *A Man Called White* (New York: Viking, 1948). Kenneth Robert Janken's *White: The Biography of Walter White, Mr. NAACP* (New York: New Press, 2003) is a good place to begin. Walter White, "The Burning of Jim McIlherron," *The Crisis* 16, no. 1 (May 1918). On the Georgia lynchings, see: Walter White, "The Work of a Mob," *The Crisis* 16, no. 5 (September 1918).

Walter White, "The Eruption of Tulsa," *Nation,* June 29, 1921. Allen Satterlee, *Sweeping Through the Land: A History of the Salvation*

Army in the Southern United States (Atlanta: Georgia Salvation Army Supplies, 1989). Individual listings for Ole T. Johnson and Ruth Gibbs, *Tulsa City Directory, 1921.*

Newblock Park interviews: Ed Wheeler, Tulsa, February 27, 1998; Bruce Hartnitt, Tulsa, May 30, 1998; Joe Welch and Harvey Shell, Sand Springs, March 18, 1999; Frank Mason, Tulsa, March 26, 1998; and Bob Norris, Tulsa, March 25, 1998.

Interview with Richard Gary, Tulsa, March 16, 1999.

Historic Booker T. Washington Cemetery/Rolling Oaks Memorial Gardens interviews: Jeanne Goodwin, Tulsa, April 10, 1998; Larry Hutchings, Tulsa, April 10, 1998; Chris Brockman, Tulsa, April 14, 1998; Gladys J. Cummins, Tulsa, April 20, 1998; and John Irby, Tulsa, July 17, 1998.

Crown Hill Cemetery: interview with Mike McConnell, Tulsa, July 23, 2020.

Chapter 8: Tulsa Calling

"Kelly Kurt, a Newswoman for the Associated Press," *AP News,* May 25, 1999, https://apnews.com/article/7c712ab3481f8d6ffb2fb58008789ebe. Kelly Kurt, "Race Riot Remembered," *Oklahoman,* June 2, 1996. "Race Riot Investigated," *Guymon Daily Herald,* January 27, 1999. Kelly Kurt, "Tulsa Race Riot Commission Searching for Mass Graves," *Oklahoman,* January 30, 1999.

Julie Bryant, "Unmarked Graves May Hold Race Riot Victims," *Tulsa World,* January 29, 1999. Dick Warner and Scott Ellsworth, "Historical Information About the Tulsa Race Riot Received in Response to Newspaper Articles in the *Tulsa World* and the *Oklahoma Eagle,* January–February 1999," typescript dated March 24, 1999.

Interview with Clyde Eddy, Tulsa, March 17, 1999. 1920 and 1930 US Federal Manuscript Census entries for Clyde Joseph Eddy, Tulsa. In

1921, Clyde lived with his parents, William V. and Nellie Eddy, at 1008 S. Quaker Avenue. Clyde Eddy correspondence.

Draft card for Elwood Clinton Lett, 3830 Walnut, Kansas City, Missouri, October 16, 1940. Interview with Elwood Lett, Tulsa, May 28, 1998. Images of historic Santa Fe Railway Dining Car Service menus can be viewed online at http://www.texascompound.com/railroad -menus. For a route map and timetables for the Super Chief, go to https://www.santaferoute.com/2014/09/super-chief-route.html. Elwood Lett correspondence with the author.

Interview with Robert Fairchild, Tulsa, June 8, 1978. Florence Fairchild correspondence. Jewel Smitherman Rogers correspondence. Interview with Kinney Booker, Tulsa, May 30, 1998.

Jay Jay Wilson and Ron Wallace, *Black Wallstreet* (Long Island City, NY: Seaburn Publishing Group, 1992; rev. 2004).

David L. Maki and Geoffrey Jones, "Search for Graves from the Tulsa Race Riot Using Ground Penetrating Radar," Archaeo-Physics, Ltd., Minneapolis, 1998. Robert L. Brooks and Alan H. Witten, "The Investigation of Potential Mass Grave Locations for the Tulsa Race Riot," in Franklin and Ellsworth, *The Tulsa Race Riot*. Rik Espinosa, "Cemetery Probe Yields Some Results," *Tulsa World,* July 27, 1999.

Chapter 9: Reparations and Reprisals

"Tulsa Burning," *60 Minutes II,* CBS, November 9, 1999.

Melissa Nelson, "Burial Site May Hold Clues to Tulsa's 1921 Race Riot," *Oklahoman,* November 20, 1999. Randy Krehbiel, "Panel Recommends Race Riot Reparations: $33 Million Would Be Apportioned," *Tulsa World,* November 23, 1999.

Jim Yardley, "Panel Recommends Reparations in Long Ignored Tulsa Race Riot," *New York Times,* February 5, 2000. "After 78 Years, Race Riot Probed: As It Weighs Reparations, Tulsa Commission Hears the Grisly Details," *Chicago Tribune,* August 10, 1999. Claudia Kolker, "A City's Buried Shame: Tulsa's Long Cover-up of Horrific 1921 Race Riot Prompts a Search for a Mass Grave," *Los Angeles Times,* October 23, 1999. Warren Cohen, "Digging Up an Ugly Past: Tulsa Exhumes Race Riot," *U.S. News & World Report,* January 31, 2000.

Louis Gray, "Ross, Graves Battle over Rightness of Reparations," *Oklahoma Eagle,* February 10, 2000.

William M. O'Brien, "Tulsa Race War, 1921—Foreword," fax sent by Coni William, Tulsa Historical Society, to author, February 3, 1999. Interview with Bill O'Brien, Tulsa, March 2, 1998.

Of course, not all white Tulsans were ashamed of the massacre. When I was researching *Death in a Promised Land* in the late 1970s and early 1980s, the mother of one of my high school classmates, a white woman who had grown up on Tulsa's north side in the 1930s and 1940s, told me that she had a photograph of the riot. But she could never find it, and I soon forgot about it. But when I started coming back to town during the late 1990s for the riot commission, I dropped by her house one afternoon to say hello. "I found the picture!" she declared. The photograph, which showed huge clouds of black smoke rising hundreds of feet in the air over Greenwood, had the words RUNING THE NEGRO OUT OF TULSA. JUNE. TH. I. 1921 etched in white letters across it. But she hadn't just found the picture. She'd also had it framed and had hung it in her dining room.

And while it is unclear whether there was a connection to the massacre or not, in around 1965, an all-white Little League baseball team at Holmes Elementary School in Tulsa was called the Holmes Riots.

"Preliminary Report of the Oklahoma Legislative Commission to Study the Tulsa Race Riot of 1921," submitted by the Investigative Sub-Committee, February 4, 2000.

Kevin O'Connor, "What Lies Beneath," *This Land,* June 11, 2011, https://thislandpress.com/2011/06/11/what-lies-beneath/.

On the Tulsa Race Riot Commission shutting down the search for the graves, see: Randy Krehbiel, "Race Riot Commission Sets Goals," *Tulsa World,* June 30, 2000.

Hirsch, *Riot and Remembrance,* 328.

For a revealing window on the experiences of African American troops stationed in Great Britain prior to D-Day, see: Alan Rice, "Black Troops Were Welcome in Britain, but Jim Crow Wasn't: The Race Riot of One Night in June 1943," *The Conversation,* June 22, 2018, https://theconversation.com/black-troops-were-welcome-in-britain-but-jim-crow-wasnt-the-race-riot-of-one-night-in-june-1943-98120.

BOOK THREE

CHAPTER 10: THE STEPS TO NOWHERE

Both the story of Greenwood's rebuilding and revival and its decline through urban renewal and highway construction will be examined in Victor Luckerson's forthcoming book *Built from the Fire,* to be published in 2022 or 2023. In the meantime, helpful sources on the overall post-massacre history of Greenwood include: Hannibal Johnson, *Black Wall Street* and *Black Wall Street 100*; Hirsch, *Riot and Remembrance*; and Human Rights Watch, *The Case for Reparations in Tulsa, Oklahoma: A Human Rights Argument,* May 2020, https://www.hrw.org/sites/default/files/media_2020/11/tulsa-reparations0520_web.pdf; Tracy Jan, "The 'Whitewashing' of Black Wall Street," *Washington Post*, January 17, 2021; and Alex Albright, James Feigenbaum, and Nathan Nunn, "After the Burning: The Economic Effects of the Tulsa Race Massacre," scholar.harvard.edu, https://scholar.harvard.edu/files/nunn/files/tulsa.pdf.

Greenwood Cultural Center: https://greenwoodculturalcenter.com. John Hope Franklin Reconciliation Park: https://www.jhfcenter.org/reconciliation-park.

Charles J. Ogletree, *All Deliberate Speed* (New York: W. W. Norton, 2004). *Alexander III v. Oklahoma 100*, FindLaw, https://caselaw.findlaw.com/us-10th-circuit/1033795.html. Scott Gold, "Judge Weighs Suit on Tulsa's '21 Riot," *Los Angeles Times*, February 14, 2004. "Declaration of Dr. Scott Ellsworth," affidavit filed on behalf of the plaintiffs in *Alexander II v. Oklahoma*. Javier C. Hernandez, "Court Rejects Reparations Case," *Harvard Crimson*, May 23, 2005.

Bella Silviera, Izzy McKinnon, Jack Kelley, and Sofia Amster, "Tulsa 1921," National History Day Competition, Junior Division, Group Performance, 2020. Email correspondence with Jack Howley, Norton Middle School, Norton, Massachusetts.

Alicia Hall Moran, "Black Wall Street," http://www.aliciahallmoran.com/black-wall-street.html. Alvin Ailey American Dance Theater, "Greenwood," https://www.alvinailey.org/performances/repertory/greenwood. National Museum of African American History and Culture, https://nmaahc.si.edu/explore/collection/search?edan_q=%2A%3A%2A%2A&edan_local=1&edan_fq[]=place%3A%22Tulsa%22.

On Terence Crutcher, see: Derek Hawkins, "Black Man Shot by Tulsa Police Had Hands 'in the Air,' Says Pastor Who Reviewed Video of the Shooting," *Washington Post*, September 19, 2016; Arianna Pickard, "Church of Terence Crutcher's Family Determined to Keep 'Pressing On' Days After Fatal Officer-Involved Shooting," *Tulsa World*, September 19, 2016; "Officer Betty Shelby Says Race Was Not a Factor in Terence Crutcher Shooting," *60 Minutes*, CBS, March 30, 2017, https://www.cbsnews.com/news/officer-betty-shelby-says-race-was-not-a-factor-in-terence-crutcher-shooting/; Paighten Harkins, "Crutcher Family Stunned After Not Guilty Verdict in Betty Shelby Case," *Tulsa World*, May 17, 2017; Isaac Stanley-Becker, "She Fatally Shot an Unarmed Black Man. Now She's Teaching Other Police Officers How to 'Survive' Such Incidents," *Washington Post*, August 28, 2018; and Harrison Grimwood, "Crutcher Foundation Gives Back to Shelter:

'Terence Was Always Feeding the Homeless,'" *Tulsa World*, September 17, 2020.

CHAPTER 11: ROLEXES AND PICKUP TRUCKS

Helpful background sources on G. T. Bynum include: Jarrel Wade, "Odd Jobs, Family Ties and the 'Macho Man': How G. T. Bynum Became a Leader," *Tulsa World*, December 4, 2016; Michael Rothfeld, "School Board Candidate in Political Fray at 21," *Philadelphia Inquirer*, September 14, 1999; Barry Friedman, "Bynum Through the Storm," *Tulsa Voice*, July 2016; Mason Beecroft, "The Call to Serve," *Eastern Oklahoma Catholic*, January/February 2017; "Mayor G. T. Bynum Discusses Path to His 'Dream Job,'" *Collegian*, University of Tulsa, April 13, 2017; and "Happy Birthday, Mayor! See Photos of G. T. Bynum Through the Years," *Tulsa World*, August 28, 2017.

Bob Burke, "Bartlett, Dewey Follett," *Encyclopedia of Oklahoma History and Culture*, https://www.okhistory.org/publications/enc/entry.php?entry=BA029. On Dewey Jr., see: "Dewey F. Bartlett, Jr.," Keener Oil & Gas Company, http://www.keeneroil.com/about-personnel.php; and "Bartlett to Be Tulsa's Next Mayor," *Tulsa World*, February 23, 2019.

Interview with Robert Patty, Coweta and Tulsa, October 12, 2019. Interviews with former Tulsa police officers, 2019–2020.

CHAPTER 12: REMINDING A CITY OF HER SINS

On Reverend Robert Turner, see: "Reverend Dr. Robert Turner," Vernon AME Church, Tulsa, https://vernoname.com/about/reverend-turner/; "About," Robert Turner Ministries, http://robertturnerministries.net/about; Carol McPhail, "Mobile Minister, Community Leader Takes Pastorship in Tuscaloosa County," Alabama.com, January 13, 2019,

https://www.al.com/living/2014/12/mobile_minister_community_lead
.html; Kendrick Marshall, "Tulsan of the Year: The Rev. Robert Turner
Embraces His Role in Tulsa's Healing," *Tulsa World,* December 9, 2019;
Tim Landes, Kyra Bruce, and Morgan Phillips, "No Justice, No Peace—
Rev. Robert Turner," *TulsaPeople,* July 15, 2020; and Carla Hinton,
"Pastor Continues Call for Tulsa Race Massacre Reparations; Says
Historic Church Symbolizes a Way Forward," *Oklahoman,* August 2,
2020.

It is likely that no single event has spread awareness of the Tulsa race
massacre, both globally and among the under-twenty-five set, more
than HBO's *Watchmen* series. Clinton Matos, "Watchmen Pilot Causes
Surge in Google Searches for Tulsa Race Riot," Hypertext, October 24,
2019, https://www.htxt.co.za/2019/10/24/watchmen-pilot-causes-surge
-in-google-searches-for-tulsa-race-riot/; James Poniewozik, "Review:
'Watchmen' Is an Audacious Rorschach Test," *New York Times,* October 17, 2019. Official site: https://www.hbo.com/watchmen.

The revelation in December 2019 that data from the geophysical survey at Oaklawn had indicated the possibility of a mass grave made head-
lines across the country, and on a wide variety of news platforms. See, for
example: Jasmine Aguilera, "Archeologists Have Located a Possible Mass
Grave Associated with the 1921 Tulsa Race Riots. Here's What to Know,"
Time, December 17, 2019; Christopher Carbone, "Searching for Tulsa
Race Riot Graves, Archaeologists Find Possible New Evidence," *Fox
News,* December 18, 2019; Vanessa Romo, "New Research Identifies Possible Mass Graves from 1921 Tulsa Race Massacre," NPR, December 17,
2019; Claudia Harmata, "Experts Think They've Discovered Mass
Gravesite from 1921 Tulsa Race Massacre in Oklahoma," *People,* Decem-
ber 18, 2019; Anne Branigin, "Scientists Say They've Found Possible Evidence of Mass Graves from 1921 Tulsa Massacre," *The Root,* December
17, 2019; "Possible Mass Grave from 1921 Tulsa Race Massacre Found,"
Today show video, 0:29, December 18, 2019, https://www.today.com

/video/possible-mass-grave-from-1921-tulsa-race-massacre-found
-75274309709; Luke Darby, "Were Mass Graves from the Infamous Tulsa
Race Massacre Found?" *GQ*, December 17, 2019.

Scott W. Hammerstedt and Amanda L. Regnier, *Searching for
Graves from the 1921 Tulsa Race Massacre: Geophysical Survey of
Oaklawn Cemetery, the Canes, and Newblock Park*, Oklahoma Ar-
cheological Survey Research Series 5 (2019).

Nehemiah D. Frank, "Mass Grass Excavation Planned While Community Frustration Boils over Rolling Oaks," *Black Wall Street Times*,
March 3, 2020. "A Livid Rev. Robert Turner Expresses His Anger During Race Massacre Meeting," YouTube video, 3:19, posted by *Tulsa
World*, March 2, 2020, https://www.youtube.com/watch?v=Pl3wZ1n-
lxkg.

Tim Landes, "Scenes from Tulsa's We Can't Breathe Protest," *Tulsa-
People*, May 30, 2020, https://www.tulsapeople.com/the-voice/scenes
-from-tulsas-we-cant-breathe-protest/collection_78136dca-a2cb-11ea
-aaf7-2bbebe1126f7.html.

On the Trump presidential campaign rally in Tulsa, see: Ronn
Blitzer, "Dems Rip Trump for Planning Tulsa Rally on Juneteenth,"
Fox News, June 11, 2020, https://www.foxnews.com/politics/dems
-trump-tulsa-juneteenth; Burt Mummolo, "Protesters Weigh In on
Trump Rally Coming to Tulsa," KTUL News Channel 8, June 10, 2020,
https://ktul.com/news/local/protestors-weigh-in-on-visit-by-trump;
DeNeen L. Brown, "Trump Rally in Tulsa, Site of a Race Massacre, on
Juneteenth Was 'Almost Blasphemous,' Historian Says," *Washington
Post*, June 12, 2020; Suzanne Nuyen, "Trump Reschedules Tulsa Cam-
paign Rally 'Out of Respect' for Juneteenth," NPR, June 13, 2020; and
Corey Jones, "Tulsa Police Arrest Local Teacher in 'I Can't Breathe'
Shirt for Obstruction After Trump's Campaign Asked Officers to Re-
move Her," *Tulsa World*, June 21, 2020.

Kevin Canfield, "Black Lives Matter Message to Be Erased, Tulsa

Officials Say: 'There Is Just Not an Alternative,'" *Tulsa World,* July 29, 2020.

CHAPTER 13: BREAKING GROUND

Ben Fenwick, "The Massacre That Destroyed Tulsa's 'Black Wall Street,'" *New York Times,* July 14, 2020. "Search Continues for Remains from Tulsa Massacre; None Found," *U.S. News & World Report,* July 16, 2020. Dakin Andone, "Search for a Mass Grave from the 1921 Tulsa Race Massacre Ends Without Finding Human Remains," *CNN,* July 23, 2020, https://www.cnn.com/2020/07/23/us/tulsa-massacre -excavation-ends-trnd/index.html.

CHAPTER 14: BODIES OF EVIDENCE

DeNeen L. Brown, "White Anti-Mask Protesters Jeered a Black Pastor Demanding Tulsa Race Massacre Reparations," *Washington Post,* July 18, 2020. Stetson Payne, "Watch Now: Rev. Robert Turner Claims Video Shows Assault at Anti-Mask Protest, Plans to Pursue Charges," *Tulsa World,* July 15, 2020, https://tulsaworld.com/news/local/watch -now-rev-robert-turner-claims-video-shows-assault-at-anti-mask-protest -plans-to/article_ed63403c-3a18-5908-8284-0e821c43d176.html.

Randy Krehbiel, "'No Reconciliation Without Reparations' Says Race Massacre Panelist," *Tulsa World,* June 1, 2020. Ville de Chatou, "Hal Singer nous a quittés: 100 ans et 70 ans de carrière," Facebook, August 20, 2020, https://www.facebook.com/VilledeChatou/posts /10163073404238504. Kelsy Schlotthauer, "Hal Singer, Jazz Saxophonist and Tulsa Race Massacre Survivor, Dies at 100," *Tulsa World,* August 22, 2020. Natasha Ishak, "Community Restores the Childhood Home of 105-Year-Old Tulsa Race Massacre Survivor," All That's Interesting, March 9, 2020. Stetson Payne, "'Like a Queen': 105-Year-Old

Race Massacre Survivor's North Tulsa Home Gets Restored," *Tulsa World*, March 9, 2020.

On Damario Solomon-Simmons and the reparations lawsuit that he filed in 2020, see: Fred Jones, "Tulsan of the Year BTW Alumnus Demario Solomon Simmons," *Oklahoma Eagle*, January 6, 2017; Angela Startz, "A&S Faculty Help Shed Light on Dark Days in Tulsa" (unpublished paper, n.d.), https://www.cityoftulsa.org/media/10843/as-faculty-help-shed-light-on-dark-days-in-tulsa.pdf; "Crutcher Family Files Second Wrongful Death Lawsuit Against City of Tulsa," DSS, https://solomonsimmons.com/crutcher-family-files-second-wrongful-death-lawsuit-against-city-of-tulsa/; Lessie Bennington Randle et al. vs. City of Tulsa et al., CV-2020-1179 (Tulsa County District Court, September 1, 2020); and Tim Stanley, "Success of New Tulsa Race Massacre Reparations Lawsuit Hinges on State's Nuisance Law, Attorneys Say," *Tulsa World*, September 2, 2020. Jan Hoffman, "Johnson & Johnson Ordered to Pay $572 Million in Landmark Opioid Trial," *New York Times*, August 26, 2019.

Interview with Phoebe Stubblefield, Tulsa, July 18, 2020. Westlake School for Girls yearbooks, Los Angeles, 1985–1986. William R. Maples and Michael Browning, *Dead Men Do Tell Tales: The Strange and Fascinating Cases of a Forensic Anthropologist* (New York: Crown, 1994).

CHAPTER 15: THE DIRT WHISPERERS

Ben Fenwick, "Mass Grave Unearthed in Tulsa During Search for Massacre Victims," *New York Times*, October 21, 2020. DeNeen L. Brown, "Scientists Find Human Remains That Might Be from Tulsa's 1921 Race Massacre," *Washington Post*, October 20, 2020. Doha Madani, "Human Remains Found at Suspected 1921 Tulsa Race Massacre Mass Grave Site," *NBC News*, October 21, 2020, https://www.nbcnews

.com/news/nbcblk/human-remains-found-suspected-1921-tulsa-race-massacre-mass-grave-n1244189. "Human Remains Found at Site Linked to 1921 Tulsa Race Massacre on 'Black Wall Street,'" *CBS News,* October 21, 2020, https://www.cbsnews.com/news/human-remains -found-search-1921-tulsa-race-massacre-victims/. Jamiel Lynch and Nicole Chavez, "Investigators Find a Mass Grave While Searching for 1921 Tulsa Race Massacre Victims," *CNN,* October 21, 2020. Randy Krehbiel, "Archaeologists Uncover Additional Coffin As Researchers Close Excavation at Oaklawn Cemetery," *Tulsa World,* October 23, 2020.

Interview with Hugh McKnight, Tulsa, November 7, 2020. World War II Draft Card for Lloyd Columbus Mosier, Tulsa, October 16, 1940. *Tulsa City Directory, 1968.*

Epilogue

Telephone interview with Bobby Eaton Jr., Tulsa, December 11, 2020.

World Won Development, post-dig press conference, Facebook, October 22, 2020: https://www.facebook.com/watch/?v=38488600 9325533.

Mary E. Jones Parrish, *Events of the Tulsa Disaster* auction, Cowan's: https://www.cowanauctions.com/lot/scarce-events-of-the-tulsa -disaster-first-edition-1922-3998354. Nearly a century after Parrish wrote her book, her great-granddaughter published an account comparing the Tulsa massacre to the 2021 assault on the US Capitol building in Washington, D.C.: Anneliese M. Bruner, "My Grandmother Survived the Tulsa Massacre. 100 Years Later, I Watched a Mostly White Mob Attack My City," *The Lily,* January 9, 2021.

William Mills's *The Arkansas: An American River* (Fayetteville: University of Arkansas Press, 1988) is a magnificent volume, profusely illustrated with the author's photographs, about one of the nation's most remarkable waterways. Part history, part ecological essay, part celebration, and part lament, the book is dedicated to the author's wife, the late Beverly Jarrett, who, some forty years ago when she was an editor at the Louisiana State University Press, threw a lifeline to a twenty-six-year-old Tulsan who was trying to tell a long-buried story about his beautiful but broken hometown.

INDEX

A. H. (massacre survivor), 85

Abbot, H. O., 75

ABC News Nightline (TV show), 171

African American newspapers. *See Chicago Defender; Oklahoma Eagle; Oklahoma Sun; Tulsa Star*

African Ancestral Society, 251

African Burial Ground (New York City), 119

Aiyetoro, Adjoa, 250

Alexander v. Oklahoma, 191–193

Alford, Brenda, 46–47, 242

Alfred P. Murrah Federal Building bombing (1995), 101–103

Alvin Ailey American Dance Theater, 194

American Historical Association, 93

American Legion, machine gun of, 27–28

American Library Association, 175–176

American Red Cross, 122–125

America's Kids (Oklahoma City), 101

Anderson, Evelyn, 145

Anderson, W. L., 30

Angel (homeless woman), 3–5, 9–10, 224–225, 278–279

archaeologists. *See* burial ground search

Archaeo-Physics, 163

Arnley, Calvin, 122

Aronson, Diana, 153

Art's Chili Parlor, 187

Ashby, Guy, 35

Askew, Rilla, 194

Associated Press (AP), 149–151

The Atlantic (magazine), 229

Avery, Ruth, 78

Baccus, Terry, 243

Bakke, Allan, 91

Ballard, Currie, 176

Bardon, Dick, 23

Bartlett, Dewey, Jr., 204–206, 210

Bartlett, Dewey, Sr., 203–204

BBC, 179

Bell & Little Café, 89

Bella (student), 193–194

Belton, Roy, 19–20, 60

Bement, Lee, 242–243, 265, 268

Berg, Angela, 237, 239, 241, 265

Berry, Simon, Sr., 187

Berry's Beat Ballroom, 187

A Better Chance, 256

The Birth of a Nation (film), 26, 76

Blackburn, Bob, 150, 161, 168

Blackburn, Justin, 224
Blackburn, Scott, 224, 277–279
Black Lives Matter (BLM)
  burial ground search and effect of,
    230–231, 233–234
  Crutcher's death and, 195–199, 222,
    230, 251
*Black Wall Street Historic Picture Book
  and the Commission Report,* 195
Black Wall Street (Johnson), 194
"Black Wall Street" (musical
  composition), 194
Black Wallstreet (Wilson and Wallace),
    161–163
BOK Center, 4, 234
Booker, Kinney, 159, 167, 177–178
Booker T. Washington Cemetery.
  See Rolling Oaks Memorial Gardens
Booker T. Washington High School
  during massacre events, 22, 28, 31, 34
  Ross and, 53, 55, 59, 188
  Rowland and, 17
  Williams and, 78
  Woods and, 261
Bordens Cafeteria, 57–58
Boysie (enslaved person), 222
Brewster, Ken, 180–181
Britton, Jack, 136–138
Brooks, Bob, 119, 155, 163–165, 168, 174
Brooks, Garth, 136, 172
Brophy, Alfred, 174
Brown, Amy, 209, 210, 232
Brown, DeNeen, 223
Brown, Maria, 46
Brown, W. I., 33
Buck, Laurel G., 23
burial ground rumors and clues. *See also*
    burial ground search
  bodies dumped in local rivers and,
    126, 239
  Convention Hall and, 138–141
  death toll as mystery, 62, 111, 114–119,
    122–125, 150, 173–174
  mass graves suspected, 150–151
  Newblock Park and, 133–134, 135–138,
    269–271
  Oaklawn Cemetery and, 131–133
  Rolling Oaks Memorial Gardens

  (Booker T. Washington Cemetery)
    and, 141–147
  Warner on, 125–126, 130–133, 139–140,
    143–146
  White on, 127–128, 129–130, 133,
    165, 228
burial ground search
  BLM and effect on, 230–231, 233–234
  burial photos held by Tulsa Police
    (1973), 5–9, 211, 215–217, 223, 224,
    254, 278
  burials immediately following massacre,
    39, 78, 129–130, 228
  at The Canes, 223–226, 253–254
    (*See also* The Canes)
  COVID-19 and effect on, 230,
    235–236
  exhumation plans for, 118, 268–269
  forensic investigation (*See* Snow, Clyde;
    Stubblefield, Phoebe)
  ground-penetrating radar (GPR) used
    for, 146, 164, 168, 224, 227–229, 232,
    240, 253, 264–265, 267
  hidden information about massacre,
    44–45, 62, 84–88, 131–133
  at Oaklawn, 118, 168–169, 173,
    226–228, 229–230, 235–245, 254,
    265–269 (*See also* Oaklawn
    Cemetery)
  ongoing work of, 273–279
  Public Oversight Committee and,
    219–223, 229–233, 242, 268–269
  at Rolling Oaks, 232
  search for, 111, 114–119
  survey team and work for, 155–160,
    163–165
  tip hotline information about, 151–152,
    154–155, 172
  2019 search for, 209–217
Bynum, George Theron "G. T.," IV,
    201–203, 205–206, 210–211, 219, 221,
    223, 245, 254
Bynum, Suzie LaFortune, 201
Byrd, Donald, 194

C.A. Pound Human Identification
    Laboratory, 259, 260
Caine, Eric, 191

The Canes
    burial ground search in, 223–226,
        253–254
    modern-day homeless population at,
        3–5, 9–10, 216
Cannon's Dry Goods, 187
Caruthers, B. E., 89
Cash, Johnny, 116
Caver's French Dry Cleaners, 30, 186
CBS
    CBS This Morning, 229
    60 Minutes, 167–168, 197
Cerezo-Román, Jessica, 265
Chappelle, P. A., 30
Chicago Defender, 33
Chicago Police Department, 117
Chicago race riot (1919), 52
CIA, 212
Citizens for Progress, 58
Civil Rights Act (1964), 57–58
civil rights movement. See also King,
        Martin Luther, Jr.; NAACP;
        segregation and desegregation
    "colored" railroad cars and, 50–51
    Tulsa sit-ins (1964), 56–58
    Turner and, 222
Clark, Jim, 222
Clark, Vivian, 169
Cleaver, Barney, 21
CNN, 233
Coburn, Tom, 202
Cochran, Johnnie, Jr., 191
Community Relations Commission,
        57, 58
Congress of Racial Equality (CORE),
        56–58
Connie (salesclerk), 68–70
Connor, Bull, 222
Conrad, Fred, 159
Convention Hall
    burial ground rumors about, 138–141
    internment camp at, 35, 38
    tip hotline information about, 154
Coronado, Vázquez de, 277
Cotton, Wayburn J., 6–7, 215, 216
COVID-19 pandemic, 230, 235–236,
        247–248
Creek Freedmen, 220, 231–232, 243, 251

The Crisis (NAACP), 128
Cronk, Cliff, 71–72
Crosbie Heights, 8, 223. See also The Canes
Crown Hill cemetery, 147
Crutcher, Joey, 199
Crutcher, Terence, 195–199, 222, 230, 251
Crutcher, Tiffany, 196–199, 249

Daily Oklahoman, 150, 168
Daley, Charles W., 28
Dallas Morning News, 170
Dave (track hoe operator), 238, 267, 268
Death in a Promised Land (Ellsworth)
    publication of, 93–98, 192
    publicity about, 96, 97, 103, 105
    research for, 83–93, 111
The Diary of Anne Frank (Frank), 160
Discovery Channel, 116
Dixie Theater, 14, 16, 34, 38, 75
Dodson, Nancy, 45
Dreamland Burning (book), 194
Dreamland Theatre, 14, 16, 18–19, 34,
        81–82, 88, 147, 193–194
Drexel Building, 17–18, 60, 81, 194, 272.
        See also Rowland, Dick
Du Bois, W. E. B., 16
Duckery, Nathaniel, 89
Duke University, 83, 95

Earley, Pete, 96
Eaton, Bobby, Jr., 213–214, 274
Eaton, Joe, 56
Eddy, Clyde Joseph, 153–155, 163, 165,
        167–168, 228
Elks Club, 188
Ellsworth, Betsy, 178
Ellsworth, Scott
    Death in a Promised Land, 83–98, 103,
        105, 111, 192
    legal action by, 192
    Riot Commission work of, 161 (See also
        Oklahoma Commission to Study the
        Tulsa Race Riot of 1921)
    survey team and work of, 155–160,
        163–165
    Tulsa childhood of, 67–70
    The Tulsa Race Riot report role of,
        174–175

undergraduate/graduate research by, 72–82, 83, 91–92, 95

Warner's correspondence about Patty to, 8–9

Estill Springs (Tennessee), White on, 127–128

Events of the Tulsa Disaster (Parrish), 47, 60, 84, 85, 275

Everett, Reuben, 131, 132, 155, 226, 229, 254, 265

Fairchild, Florence, 158, 177–178, 276

Fairchild, Robert Lee, 51–53, 89, 108, 158, 177–178

Fallin, Mary, 208

Family Registration Project, 144–147

Faulkner, William, 277

Feldman, Nancy Goodman, 49–53, 55

Feldman, Raymond, 50

"Ferguson Effect," 199

Fields, Ernie, 187

Fifteen Fellows, 188

The Fifth Horseman (Avery), 78

First Baptist Church, 56, 85–86, 157, 189

First Presbyterian Church, 20, 43, 189

Floyd, Amecia, 177

Floyd, Amley, 112, 160, 177, 182

Floyd, George, 233

Floyd, Latrecia, 177

Floyd, Patricia, 112, 177

Ford, Beryl, 87–88, 97

forensic investigation. *See* burial ground search; Snow, Clyde; Stubblefield, Phoebe

442nd Infantry Regiment (World War II), 170–171

Fox News, 229

Frank, Anne, 160

Franklin, B. C., 38, 90, 147

Franklin, John Hope
    Ellsworth's book research and, 90–92, 95
    on hidden information about massacre, 45, 272
    John Hope Franklin Reconciliation Park, 190, 233
    media interviews of, 161
    parents of, 141
    on reparations, 108
    From Slavery to Freedom, 59, 90, 91
    The Tulsa Race Riot report, 174–175, 176, 177–178

Franklin, Wendell, 231

Freed, Abraham, 153

Friedman, Barry, 201

Friends of the Rudisill Library, 95–96

From Slavery to Freedom (Franklin), 59, 90, 91

Gary, Anna, 140

Gary, Hugh, 140

Gary, Richard, 140

Gary Post-Tribune, 104

Gates, Eddie Faye, 161, 168–170, 175

George Kaiser Family Foundation, 97

The George McKenna Story (TV movie), 254–255

George's Sandwich Shop, 112

George Washington High School (Los Angeles), 254–255

Getty, J. Paul, 125

Gibbs, Ruth, 39, 130

"The Gilcrease Story" (Wheeler), 61

Gill, Loren, 60, 77

Gillam, Louise, 67–70

Goble, Danney, 176

Goodman, Nancy (Feldman), 49–53, 55

Goodwin, Ed, Jr., 54

Goodwin, Edward L., Sr., 89

Goodwin, Regina, 219, 249

Goodwyn, Larry, 83, 93

Goodwyn, Wade, 107

Grand United Order of Odd Fellows, 131

Graves, Bill, 168, 171

Green, Deb, 242, 243, 265, 267

Greenwood (Tulsa neighborhood), 185–199. *See also* burial ground search; hidden information about massacre; legal actions; Tulsa massacre (May 31–June 1, 1921) events
    artistic expression about riot (1990s–present), 193–195
    as "Black Wall Street," 60, 150, 161–163, 188, 194–195

Greenwood (*Cont.*)
burials by African American
community, 143, 147
burial site excavation by, 230
Crutcher's death (2016) in, 195–199
drug problem of (post-massacre),
112, 113
Ellsworth's re-created map of, 74–76
Greenwood Arts and Cultural
Society, 274
Greenwood Cultural Center, 151–152,
190, 198–199, 263
John Hope Franklin Reconciliation
Park, 190, 233
lifestyle/businesses prior to Tulsa
massacre, 13–17, 38–39, 75–76
(*See also individual names of
businesses and churches*)
map re-creation of, 74–76, 80–82
1921 Black Wall Street Memorial,
107–108, 150, 171, 174, 190
1950s–1970s decline of, 188–190
1990s additions to, 190
at Public Oversight Committee hearing,
219–223
rebuilding by African Americans in, 42,
92, 112, 121–123, 147, 186–188
Steps to Nowhere, 185–186
Tulsa Police raids (1970s), 213–214
white Tulsa's promise for rebuilding/
land grab attempt, 41–42, 90, 147,
188–190
Griffith, D. W., 76
ground-penetrating radar (GPR), 146, 164,
168, 224, 227–229, 232, 240, 253,
264–265, 267. *See also* burial ground
search
Gumbel, Bryant, 102–103
Gutierrez, Maria Morales, 32

Hall-Harper, Vanessa, 219, 223
Hammerstedt, Scott, 219, 227–228, 253
Hantaman, Nathan, 106
Hart, Gene Leroy, 115–116
Hartnitt, Bruce, 135
Hartnitt, Wylie, 135
Harvey, Paul, 204
Hatcher, Richard, 103–104

HBO, 229, 275
Hickinbotham, Iris, 179–181
Hickinbotham, Susan, 179–181
hidden information about massacre,
41–47, 49–66, 67–82. *See also* news
media and publicity; Oklahoma
Commission to Study the Tulsa Race
Riot of 1921
by African American community, 45–47
Ellsworth's early research and, 71–82,
83, 91–92
Feldman's role in uncovering secrets,
49–53, 55
grand jury investigation of massacre,
41–42
by news media, 42–45, 70, 84–88
photos held by Tulsa Police (1973), 5–9,
211, 215–217, 223, 224, 254, 278
Ross's early role in uncovering secrets,
53–56, 57, 58–61, 64–66
Hirsch, James, 55, 108, 194
History of the Tulsa Police (Trekell), 209
Hoard, Mary, 75–76
Hodge, Victor, 89
Holocaust memorials, 146–147, 160
Holway, William, 24
homeless camp. *See* The Canes
Hooker, Olivia, 275
Hotel Small, 186–187
Howley, Mr. (teacher), 193–194
Hudson, Billy, 36, 146
HuffPost, 229
Hughs, J. P., 34
Hussein, Saddam, 117

infant mortality of African Americans, 221
Investigative Subcommittee (Riot
Commission), 173
Irby, John, 141–143
Izzy (student), 193–194

J. M. Davis Arms and Historical
Museum, 239
Jack (enslaved person), 222
Jackson, Doug, 209
Jackson, T. D., 30
Jack (student), 193–194
Japanese internment camps, 170–171

Jarrett, Beverly, 93, 95

Jim Crow. *See* segregation and desegregation

John Hope Franklin Reconciliation Park, 190, 233

John Melvin Alexander v. State of Oklahoma, 191–193

Johnson, Hannibal, 194

Johnson, Lyndon Baines, 57, 103

Johnson, O. T., 39, 129, 130

Johnson & Johnson, 252

Jolly Wives Club, 188

Jones, Jenkin Lloyd "Jenk," 85, 97–98

Jones, Mozella Denslow Franklin, 90–92, 95, 188

Jones, Waldo Emerson, Sr., 90–92

Keating, Frank, 109

Kennedy, Robert F., 60, 103

Kerr, Charles, 20, 43

King, Martin Luther, Jr., 56, 60, 103, 105

King, Rodney, 210

Kinlaw, Carrie, 35

Kinnear, John Patrick, 243

Kiowa (Native American tribe), 277

Krehbiel, Randy, 97, 169, 175, 239

Ku Klux Klan

    Black Wallstreet (Wilson and Wallace) on, 162

    Oklahoma political influence of, 203–204

    post-riot violence by, 158–159

    Tulsa activity of, 76, 106

Kurt, Kelly, 149–151

KVOO radio (Tulsa), 61

Ladies Auxiliary (Oklahoma State Medical, Dental, and Pharmaceutical Association), 188

LaFortune, Robert, 203

Landes, Jill, 167

Latimer, J. C., 35–36

Latimer's One-Stop Barbecue, 187

law enforcement. *See* Oklahoma National Guard; Tulsa Police Department

legal actions

    Alexander v. Oklahoma, 191–193

    grand jury investigation of massacre, 41–42

Oklahoma opioid lawsuit, 252

    reparations lawsuit filed in 2020, 250–253

Lett, Elwood, 146–147, 155–157, 163, 165, 177–178

Levit, Ken, 97, 105–107

life expectancy of African Americans, 221

Little, Mabel, 32–33, 42, 89, 96

Little, Pressly, 89

Littlejohn, Robert, 139

Litwack, Leon, 191–192

Lockard, Eddie, 131–132, 155, 226, 229, 254, 265

Lockard, Jane, 131

Lockard, Joe, 131

Lockard, Rina, 131

Los Angeles Times, 192

Lough, Lillian, 153

Louise Gillam Interior Lighting, 67–70

Louisiana State University (LSU) Press, 93, 95–98

Luna, Frank, 274

lynchings

    Alexander v. Oklahoma on, 191–192

    post-World War I rise of, 76

    Rowland's arrest and threats of, 17–23, 26, 39, 81

    tip hotline information about, 153

    White's research about, 127

Madansky, Harry, 106

Madansky, Max, 106

Madigan, Tim, 194

Maggard, Greg, 239, 241

Magic City (Rhodes), 194

Maids Domestic Club, 188

Maples, William R., 259–260

Matson, Tommy, 273

Maxey, E. W., 37

Maxie family, 147

May Brothers (store), 106

McClendon, William, 72–73

McCullough, Willard, 20–22, 39

McDaniel, Eunice, 152

McIlherron, Jim, 127–128

McKnight, Hugh, 269–271

McVeigh, Timothy, 102

Mengele, Josef, 116

Mental Health Association of Oklahoma, 4, 224
Metropolitan Baptist Church, 198
Midland Valley Railroad, 152
Milacek, Robert, 169, 171
Miller, George H., 23
Mills, Tim, 227, 228
Monroe, George, 107, 108, 112–115, 159–160, 167–168, 176–182, 195
Monroe, Martha, 113
Monroe, Olive, 113–114
Monroe, Osborne, 113–114
Moore, Roseatter, 36
Moran, Alicia Hall, 194
Moran, Jason, 194
Morrison, Arthur, 122
Mosier, Lloyd Columbus "Buck," 269–270
Mount Zion Baptist Church, 31, 33, 54, 189
MSNBC, 233
Muscogee (Creek) Nation, 131, 220, 230–232

NAACP (National Association for the Advancement of Colored People)
    The Crisis, 128
    Du Bois's visit to Tulsa, 16
    Greenwood chapter, 188
    Oklahoma sit-ins and (1956), 56
    White on burial of massacre victims, 127–128, 129–130, 133, 165, 228
"Nab Negro for Attacking Girl in Elevator" (Tulsa Tribune), 85
The Nation, 129
National Black Political Convention, 103
National Geographic (magazine), 239–240
National Guard. See Oklahoma National Guard
National History Day Massachusetts State Competition, 194
National Museum of African American History and Culture, 195
National Public Radio, 107, 229
Native Americans
    Creek Freedmen and, 220, 231–232, 243, 251
    Muscogee (Creek) Nation, 131, 220, 230–232

Osage and Kiowa, 277
    Trail of Tears and, 220, 230–232
NBC, 102–103, 107
Newblock Park
    burial ground rumors about, 133–134, 135–138, 269–271
    location of, 224, 277
    survey of, 164–165
    tip hotlines and, 152
Newkirk, Amos (A. S.), 38, 75
New Mexico Military Institute, 117
news media and publicity. See also individual names of news outlets
    ABC News Nightline, 171
    Associated Press story (1996), 149–151
    early national stories about Tulsa massacre, 96, 107–108
    on exploration and excavation of possible burial sites, 229, 239–240, 244, 274–275
    Floyd interviewed by, 113
    hidden information of media, 42–45, 70, 84–88
    Someone Cry for the Children (Discovery Channel), 116
    tips hotlines created as result of, 151–155
    Today (NBC) on Oklahoma City bombing (1995), 102–103
    on Trump rally in Tulsa, 233–234
    "Tulsa Burning" (60 Minutes), 167–168
New York Times
    on burial site exploration, 229, 239–240
    on COVID pandemic, 230
    handbill rumor in, 80–81
    Kinney profiled by, 159
    on Oklahoma opioid lawsuit, 252
    photo essay of massacre (2019), 215–217
    on reparations, 171
    stories about massacre (1990s), 107, 108
    on The Tulsa Race Riot report, 176
Nichols, Terry, 102
Nickles, Don, 202
Night and Fog (film), 160
Night (Wiesel), 160
1921 Black Wall Street Memorial, 107–108, 150, 171, 174, 190
Nixon, Richard, 60

Norris, Bob, 136
North Tulsa Historical Society, 144–147
Norton Middle School (Massachusetts),
    193–194

Oaklawn Cemetery
    burial ground rumors about, 131–133
    burial ground search in, 226–228,
        229–230
    excavation findings at, 235–245, 254,
        265–269, 276
    excavation plans for, 118, 168–169, 173
    Original 18 site, 226, 228, 254, 264
    Sexton's Site, 227–228, 229, 231,
        245, 254
    Site A and Trench B distinction, 241
    site identified by Eddy, 153–155, 163,
        165, 167–168
    survey of, 163–165
    tip hotline information about, 151–152,
        154–155, 172
Obama, Barack, 206
O'Brien, Bill, 172, 244
Odd Fellows, 131
O'Dell, Larry, 174
Ogletree, Charles, 191–193, 250–251, 253
Oklahoma City bombing (1995),
        101–103, 117
Oklahoma Commission to Study the
        Tulsa Race Riot of 1921 (Riot
        Commission)
    Black Wall Street Historic Picture Book
        and the Commission Report, 195
    burial ground research of, 114–119
    eight-point plan and public reaction,
        169–173
    formation of, 109
    Investigative Subcommittee, 173
    massacre terminology of, 210–211
    The Tulsa Race Riot (report), 174–176,
        177–178, 192
    work pace and tension between
        members of, 138, 161–163
Oklahoma Eagle
    Goodwin and, 219
    Greenwood businesses advertised
        in, 187
    hidden information of, 46

Monroe's advertisement in, 112,
        179, 181
    Ross and, 58–61, 92, 103
    tip hotlines and, 151–152
    white businesses advertised in, 188–189
Oklahoma Historical Society,
        110–111, 150
Oklahoma Impact (magazine), 64–66, 134
Oklahoma National Guard
    Alexander v. Oklahoma, 191–193
    hidden information about massacre, 45,
        66, 84–88
    martial law during massacre, 37–38, 39
    Oklahoma politics (modern-day)
        and, 208
    reparations lawsuit against, 250–253
    Wheeler's credentials and, 62, 65
Oklahoma (state). See also Oklahoma
        Commission to Study the Tulsa Race
        Riot of 1921; Tulsa (city)
    Alexander v. Oklahoma, 191–193
    Department of Transportation, 239
    hidden information about massacre,
        44–45, 62, 84–88, 91, 110–111
    Highway Patrol, 233
    Oklahoma State Bureau of Investigation
        (OSBI), 115–116
    opioid lawsuit, 252
    politics of, 201–208
    Public Oversight Committee and state
        legislature, 219
    Ross as state legislator, 103–105,
        107–111, 115, 175, 176, 190–191
        (See also Ross, Don)
    state archaeologists and excavation,
        219, 227, 235–245, 253–254, 265
        (See also Brooks, Bob; Stackelbeck,
        Kary)
    state medical examiner's office, 237,
        239, 241
Oklahoma State Medical, Dental, and
        Pharmaceutical Association, 188
Oklahoma Sun
    Greenwood readership prior to
        massacre, 16
    during massacre events, 25, 38
    opioid lawsuit, 252
Oral Roberts University, 58

Original 18 site (Oaklawn Cemetery), 226, 228, 254, 264
Osage (Native American tribe), 277
Osborn, Campbell, 43
Owens, Ray, 198

Page, Sarah
  conspiracy theory about, 173
  elevator incident, 18, 39, 41, 60, 77, 78, 81, 89
Parker, Harold, 35
Parks, Rosa, 56
Parrish, Florence Mary, 28–30, 85
Parrish, Mary
  during events of 1921, 25, 28–30, 36, 37
  Events of the Tulsa Disaster, 47, 60, 84, 85, 275
Patty, Bob, 211–213, 214–217, 223, 224, 254, 278
Patty, Robert, 8–9
Payne, Frank and Julia, 30
People (magazine), 229
Phelps, Ruth and Merrill, 38
Philadelphia Inquirer, 202
Phillips, Choc, 24
Pickering, Bob, 238, 266
Pigelle (bar), 213–214
Pitts family, 147
Portland Observer, 72
Potts, Ian, 179–180
Potts Photo Studios, 187
"Profile of a Race Riot" (Wheeler), 61–66, 77, 134
publicity about massacre. *See* hidden information about massacre; news media and publicity
Public Oversight Committee, 219–223, 230–233, 242, 268–269
pulseEKKO 1000, 163

Quigley, Cleo, 152–153

race relations. *See also* lynchings; reparations; segregation and desegregation
  anger of whites about burial ground excavation, 244
  The Birth of a Nation (film), 26, 76
  in Estill Springs (Tennessee), 127–128
  importance of honoring victims of racial violence, 276
  Investigative Subcommittee conspiracy theory and, 173
  Oaklawn excavation as first government search for victims, 236–237
  Oklahoma politics (modern-day) and, 208
  Tulsa City Hall clashes about reparations, 248
  in Tulsa (1960s), 56–58, 67–70
  white residents' accounts (1970s) of massacre, 85–86
Randle, Lessie, 249, 251
Rankin-Hill, Lesley, 119, 174, 219–220
Reagan, Ronald, 233
Reconstructing the Dreamland (book), 194
Reed College, 72–73, 76–82, 83, 91–92
Regnier, Amanda, 227–228, 253
reparations, 167–182
  Alexander v. Oklahoma, 191–193
  criticism of, 249–250
  Investigative Subcommittee and, 173
  lawsuit filed in 2020, 250–253
  for massacre survivors and younger generations, 248–249
  Monroe and, 159–160, 167, 176–177, 178–182
  Riot Commission eight-point plan and reaction, 169–173
  Ross on, 108–109, 176
  scholarship fund plans, 169, 171
  "Tulsa Burning" (*60 Minutes*) on, 167–168
  Tulsa City Hall demonstrations, 247–248
  The Tulsa Race Riot (report) and, 174–176
Rhodes, Jewell Parker, 194
Riot and Remembrance (Hirsch), 108–109, 194
Riot Commission. *See* Oklahoma Commission to Study the Tulsa Race Riot of 1921
Riverside Industries, 73–74

Robert E. Lee Elementary School, 69, 106
Robinson, Greg, 253
Rodriguez, Noe, 3–5, 9, 224
Rogers, Jewel Smitherman, 158–159,
    177–178
Rolling Oaks Memorial Gardens (Booker
    T. Washington Cemetery), 141–147,
    163–165, 232
Rosenbaum, Mike, 167
Ross, Don
    early life/career of, 53–56, 57, 188
    interviewed by national media, 168, 171
    Lett on, 157
    news interviews of, 161
    1921 Black Wall Street Memorial and,
        107–108, 150, 171, 174, 190
    at *Oklahoma Eagle*, 58–61, 92, 103
    Public Oversight Committee and, 219
    on reparations, 108–109, 176
    as state legislator, 103–105, 107–111,
        115, 175, 176, 190–191
    Wheeler's "Profile of a Race Riot" story
        and, 64–66, 134
Ross, Isreal, 53
Ross, Kavin, 240
Ross, Pearline, 53
Rountree, Billy, 58
Rowland, Damie, 17–18
Rowland, Dick
    arrest of and lynch threats to, 17–23, 26,
        39, 81–82
    conspiracy theory about, 173
    elevator incident, 18, 39, 41, 60, 77, 78,
        81, 89
    Fairchild and, 52
Rudisill Library, 95–96, 220
Rushmore, Joe, 215–216

Salvation Army (Tulsa), 39,
    129–130, 228
Sans Souci Club, 188
Santa Fe Railway, 156
Satterlee, Allen, 130
Savage, Susan, 172
Sawyer, Elizabeth, 15
Scarbough, Annie, 76
Scarbough, Arthur, 76
scholarship fund plans, 169, 171

secrets about massacre. *See* hidden
    information about massacre
segregation and desegregation
    African American businesses affected
        by, 162–163
    in cemeteries, 131
    "colored" restrooms of 1921, 17–18
    economic cost to Greenwood, 188–190
    of Tulsa schools, 69, 106 (*See also*
        Booker T. Washington High
        School)
September 11, 2001 attacks, 101
Sexton's Site (Oaklawn Cemetery),
    227–228, 229, 231, 245, 254
Sharpton, Al, Jr., 198
Shelby, Betty Jo, 197–199, 222, 230
Shelby, Richard, 222
Shoah (film), 160
Shusterman, Abraham, 107
Silver Shirts, 106
Silvey, Larry, 63–64
Simon, Bob, 167–168
Simons, Mike, 244
Sims, Veneice, 167
Singer, Hal, 249
Sixteenth Street Baptist Church
    (Birmingham), 222
60 Minutes (CBS), 167–168, 197
Smith, Alva, Jr., 152
Smitherman, A. J., 22, 26
Smitherman, John, 158–159
Smithsonian, 195
Smoke (homeless man), 225, 278
Snow, Clyde
    burial search information by, 130, 134,
        136, 269
    on death toll statistics, 173–174
    excavation plans and, 169
    forensic background of, 116–119
    Maples and, 259
    survey work of, 163
    testimony of, 151
Snow, Jerry, 117, 118
Sofia (student), 193–194
Solomon-Simmons, Damario, 250–253
Someone Cry for the Children (Discovery
    Channel), 116
St. Francis Hospital, 153

Stackelbeck, Kary, 210, 219, 229, 230,
    231–232, 239–240, 264–266
Stanley (Stanley-McCune) Funeral Home,
    131–133
Staples, Brent, 159, 176
Steps to Nowhere, 185–186
Stokenberry, Samuel, 75
Stradford, J. B., 186
Stubblefield, Peggy, 255–257
Stubblefield, Phoebe
    on the Canes as burial site, 224
    early burial ground exploration by,
        174, 220
    early life/career of, 255–260
    on excavation plans, 232
    forensic work at Oaklawn by, 235,
        239–240, 254, 260–261,
        263–266, 268
Styles, Virginia, 152

Tan's Place, 187
Tate Electric Company, 187
Temple Israel, 107
Thompson, Sarah Butler, 145
Time (magazine), 229
Today (NBC), 102–103, 107
"To Lynch Negro Tonight" (Tulsa
    Tribune), 81–82, 85
Trail of Tears, 220, 230–232
Travis, Dr. (dentist), 76
Trekell, Ron, 209
Trump, Donald, 206, 233–234
"Tulsa Burning" (60 Minutes), 167–168
Tulsa (city)
    African Americans and social indicators
        in (modern-day), 221
    Alexander v. Oklahoma, 191–193
    Chamber of Commerce, 63–64
    city directories of, 74–76, 140
    City Hall reparations demonstrations,
        247–248
    excavation funding by, 229
    grand jury investigation of massacre,
        41–42
    Jewish population of, 106–107
    Ku Klux Klan in, 76, 106
    manufacturing sector of (1970s), 73–74
    modern-day population (2019), 4

    politics of, 201–208
    reparations lawsuit against, 250–253
    Savage on reparations, 172–173
    Trump rally in, 233–234
    Tulsa City-County Library system,
        70–72, 74–76, 95–96, 97, 220
Tulsa County Board of
    Commissioners, 251
Tulsa County Court House
    African American veterans and white
        mob at Court House, 18–23, 81–82
    early gunfire at, 23–24, 26
    hidden information about massacre, 45,
        84–88, 91
    Rowland held at, 17–23
Tulsa County Historical Society, 87–88,
    144–147
Tulsa Democrat, 84–88
Tulsa Fire Museum, 239
Tulsa Historical Society, 125, 139,
    151–152, 172
Tulsa Magazine (Tulsa Chamber of
    Commerce), 63–64
Tulsa massacre (May 31–June 1, 1921)
    events, 13–39. See also hidden
        information about massacre; news
        media and publicity; Oklahoma
        Commission to Study the Tulsa Race
        Riot of 1921
    African American refugees of, 36, 38
    African American veterans and white
        mob at Court House, 18–23,
        81–82
    airplane bombs, 7, 30, 32–33
    anniversary (50th), 79
    anniversary (60th), 97–98
    anniversary (75th), 106, 108, 113, 150
    anniversary (100th), 223, 275–276
    burials immediately following, 39, 78,
        129–130, 228
    early written works about, 60–66
    Greenwood lifestyle prior to, 13–17,
        38–39
    gunfire, fires, and violence throughout
        Greenwood, 23–37, 113–115
    internment camps during, 33, 35–36,
        37–38, 130
    martial law declared during, 37–38, 39

1921 news accounts of massacre, 71–72, 81

1921 Tulsa Race Massacre Centennial Commission, 210–211

Oklahoma City bombing (1995) compared to, 101–103, 117

Oklahoma Commission to Study the Tulsa Race Riot of 1921, 109

photo postcards of, 43

race riot/massacre terminology, 123, 210

Rowland's arrest and lynch threats, 17–23, 26, 39, 81–82

white residents' accounts (1970s) of, 85–86

Tulsa Police Department

actions of, during massacre, 23, 28

African American arrests by (modern-day), 221

Alexander v. Oklahoma, 191–193

BLM and, 230–231

burial photos held by, 5–9, 84–88, 211, 215–217, 223, 224, 254, 278

Crutcher death and (2016), 195–199, 222, 230, 251

History of the Tulsa Police (Trekell), 209

Patty and, 211–213, 214–217, 223, 224

police officers interviewed (1970s), 86–88

Rowland's arrest by, 18–20

The Tulsa Race Riot (Riot Commission), 174–176, 177–178, 192

Tulsa's Black Wall Street (book), 194–195

Tulsa Star

Greenwood readership prior to massacre, 16

hidden information about massacre, 84–88

during massacre events, 21, 25, 38

Tulsa Tribune

Death in a Promised Land (Ellsworth) and, 96, 97

on death toll statistics, 123, 124

hidden information of, 43–45, 84–88

1921 accounts of massacre, 71–72, 81–82

original offices destroyed during massacre, 272

Tulsa World

on burial ground search, 151, 165, 210

Death in a Promised Land (Ellsworth) and, 96, 97

on death toll statistics, 123

hidden information of, 43, 84–88

June 1921 accounts of massacre, 71–72

at Oaklawn excavation, 239, 244

on Oklahoma opioid lawsuit, 252

on reparations, 169–170, 171, 253

Riot Commission coverage and, 150

on Rolling Oaks exploration, 232

tip hotlines and, 151–152

Turnbough, Tyler, 197

Turner, Robert, 221, 222–223, 232, 243–244, 247–248, 251, 253

Twinkie (track hoe operator), 238, 241, 243, 264–265, 268

University of California, 91

University of Oklahoma, 119, 230, 242–243, 244, 265

University of Oklahoma Press, 94

University of Tulsa (TU)

burial sites excavated by, 230, 238, 266

Ellsworth's research and, 84

Feldman at, 51–52

Gill's master thesis about massacre, 60, 77

Ross at, 55

Urban League, 58

USA Today, 229

US District Court, 191–193

US Supreme Court, 192–193

Vaden family, 147

Vernon AME Church, 187, 189, 190, 221, 222, 247, 251

Vessels, Billy Dale, 96

Vessels, Jane, 96

Vietnam War, 212

Vogue Art Club, 188

Wagoner County (Oklahoma) sheriff's office, 214–215

Walker, Mark, 71–72

Wallace, George, 222
Wallace, Ron, 161–163
Walsh-Haney, Heather, 238
Warner, Betsy, 125, 209, 211, 215,
    226–227, 228, 235
Warner, Dick
    on burial rumors and clues, 125–126,
        130–133, 139–140, 143–146
    daughter of, 209
    on photos held by Tulsa Police, 8–9
    survey of burial grounds by, 155,
        163, 165
    tip hotlines and, 151
Warner, Mary, 125, 144
Warner, Rick, 125
Washington, George, Jr., 136
Washington family, 147
Washington Post
    on Bartlett, Sr., 204
    first national story about Tulsa
        massacre, 96
    on massacre centennial, 223
    at Oaklawn excavation, 239–240
    stories about massacre (1990s),
        107, 108
Watchmen (HBO), 229, 275
Watteau, Carol, 153
Welch, Joe, 136
Wells, Dora, 15, 38
West, James, 28
Wheeler, Ed, 61–66, 77, 92, 134, 204, 224
Whitaker, Bill, 197

White, Walter, 127–128, 129–130, 133,
    165, 228
Whitlow, Henry, 54–55
Whitlow, Henry Clay, 89
Wiesel, Elie, 160
Wilbanks, Bill, 84–85
Wilkerson, Mike, 115–116
Williams, John, 147, 186
Williams, Kristi, 231–232
Williams, Leon, 30
Williams, Loula, 15, 147, 187
Williams, N. C., 89
Williams, Seymour, 89
Williams, W. D., 78–82, 85, 88–89, 95,
    123, 177–178
Williams Building, 14, 25, 147, 186
Williams Drug Company, 187
Willows, Maurice, 122–125
Wilson, Jay Jay, 161–163
Wilson, Lahoma, 153
Wilson, Luther, 94
Witten, Alan, 164
WKY radio (Oklahoma), 26
Woods, Ellis Walker, 261
Works Progress Administration (WPA),
    45, 85
World Trade Center (New York City), 101
World War II
    Holocaust memorials, 146–147, 160
    Japanese internment camps, 170–171

Zambrano, Carlos, 239, 241